# Dunstable in Detail

Nigel C. Benson

# DUNSTABLE IN DETAIL

---

An Illustrated
Guide to the Town
of
Dunstable

---

*written and illustrated*
*by*
Nigel C. Benson
B.Sc. (Hons), C.Ed., F.E.T.C.

*To Margaret*

First published November 1986
by The Book Castle
12 Church Street, Dunstable.



Typesetting by Turner Typesetting, Dunstable

Printed by White Crescent Press, Luton

ISBN 0 9509773 2 2

# CONTENTS

## The Cross Roads



## High Street North

### Northeast Quadrant



### Church Street

# AUTHOR'S FOREWORD

*'The dwarf sees farther than the giant,*
*when he has the giant's shoulder to mount on.'*

'The Friend' I.8 — Coleridge

A project such as this can never be really completed: however much work is done, there will always be more data to collect and analyse, new interpretations to consider, extra pieces to add, corrections and other improvements to be made. One could spend many years, indeed a whole lifetime, on this type of book, and still feel that it is unfinished! In addition, of course, there is the constantly changing environment which means that, whenever and whatever the publication, it can never be completely up to date. Consequently, at some stage a decision has to be made — in this case it was to set a deadline and then, whatever the problems, publication goes ahead. The product will therefore have inadequacies but at least it is available. It will also pave the way, depending on the response of others and personal circumstances, for a possible improved Second Edition at some future date. This is all part of the process and ritual of publication.

'Dunstable in Detail' (the title for which I thank Paul Bowes) is very much a case of having 'the giant's shoulder to mount on'! The majority of material in this volume is taken directly from other writers and researchers. This debt is partially acknowledged in the text and through the footnote references which link with the detailed Bibliography at the back. There are limited acknowledgements in the body of the text simply because the large number of names would have been clumsy and distracting in a book which is primarily intended for the general public. Lists of researchers' names and dates of publication are acceptable in academic works but most people are more interested in the content than the source of information.

Hence, a compromise has to be reached which, in this instance, favours the wider audience but still acknowledges others and allows for reference checking by more 'serious' readers. It is sincerely hoped this explanation is accepted in good faith, especially by those who may feel that they have been the victims of plagiarism. It was not the author's intention to step on anyone's toes in order to climb upon their shoulders!

'Giants' that have particularly, if often unwittingly, provided vital support include (in alphabetical order): Mr T.W. Bagshawe, Mr John Bailey, Mr L.R. Conisbee, Mr W.H. Derbyshire, Dr John G. Dony, Mr James Dyer, Mrs Vivienne Evans, Mr F.A. Fowler, Miss Joyce Godber, Mr Charles Lamborn, Mr John Lunn, Mr C. Les Matthews, Sir Nikolaus Pevsner, Miss L.M. Rowe, Mr Bruce Turvey, Mr Worthington G. Smith, Mr. W. Twaddle. (NB A further list of acknowledgements is given at the end of the book).

This book is therefore mainly a compilation of information, much of which has been previously published in many different places but never before in one volume. Some of the original sources are now difficult to obtain, being in old and out of print books. (e.g. Derbyshire 1882, Lamborn 1859), old magazines and newspapers, or distant museums and libraries. It is hoped that this new single source will be convenient but also satisfying and stimulating.

Despite extensive research and checking, there will no doubt be some (Bedfordshire) 'clangers'! Any written corrections or comments would therefore be welcomed at the Publisher's address and any improvements towards future editions will be fully acknowledged.

*Nigel C. Benson*
*Dunstable 1986*

# PUBLISHER'S FOREWORD

A bookseller inevitably feels a certain responsibility for the availability, or otherwise, of information about the town in which he carries out his trade. Dunstable, at the junction of two ancient 'roads', Watling Street and the Icknield Way, has a long, fluctuating and interesting history. Yet over a hundred years have elapsed since a full-length book devoted exclusively to the town was last published (i.e. since Derbyshire's book of 1882), and many new developments and discoveries have since taken place.

Clearly long overdue was an attempt to collate and supplement widely-scattered material, published and otherwise, into one convenient, readable volume. The circular-trail format will hopefully encourage exploration by visitors and residents alike, and is enlivened by many historical digressions at appropriate points.

Nigel Benson has fulfilled his brief better than I could have hoped. His attention to detail has been painstaking, his artistic outlook displayed admirably in the book's original drawings and other well-chosen illustrations.

The result is a book that provides a major contribution to the local literature, fascinating both for newcomers to the town and also those whose memories stretch back into previous generations.

I echo the author's thanks to all those who have helped him in this task, and hope that much pleasure given to many readers will be their reward.

*Paul Bowes*
*The Book Castle, Dunstable*

# PREFACE

## The Content of the Book

'Dunstable in Detail' is a collection of illustrations and descriptions of 100 features which can all be found within a half-mile radius from the centre of Dunstable.

The illustrations are accompanied by notes describing points of physical, historical or contemporary interest.

As well as the text on the 100 specific features, there are additional notes throughout the book on general topics which are important to this town e.g. local trades, traditions, influential families, etc.

## The Aims of the Book

In addition to being a straightforward, comprehensive and practical guide to the central part of Dunstable, it is intended that this book will be an interesting souvenir for visitors to the locality, as well as for residents. It can also provide a useful 'aide-memoire' for those who are either unable to move about the town freely or who live too far away to visit.

It is hoped that this book will partly satisfy and partly stimulate an interest in Dunstable, to the benefit of both individuals and the town as a whole.

There are many interesting facets of the town which are not generally recognised by people. All too often, travellers think of Dunstable as being just a place to pass through along the A5 or A505 (or pass by on the M1!), and many residents are also unaware of what is around them.

The main aim, therefore, is to help people perceive and appreciate Dunstable's interesting and unique features, and to promote the preservation of that which is of historical and cultural value.

### The Style and Design of the Book

Unfortunately, the works of local historians are often unnecessarily complex and poorly written, making them difficult to understand and frustrating to follow.

'Dunstable in Detail' has been written with an emphasis on simple English. Any ususual words that are used, such as architectural terms, are explained as necessary. This is to allow the guide to be understood by as many people as possible – including younger readers and foreign visitors.

This book has been designed with a simple and logical structure in the hope that people will find it enjoyable and easy to read, as well as interesting and informative. As a further aid to readers, high quality typesetting and a clear lay-out has been used.

### The Map

The map which accompanies the book has been designed so that features 01 to 50 are on the bottom half, while features 51 to 100 are on the top half. This arrangement should make reading the map much easier. In addition, certain groups of features can be seen on the map when it is folded up further. (Readers can find out more by experimenting with different foldings.)

### Further Information

For those who wish to read further, a list of publications is provided at the back in a detailed Bibliography which contains most of the sources of information used for this book.

Selected reading is recommended in the text at relevant places (e.g. Priory Church – works by F.A. Fowler and J. Lunn; Health Centre – book by M. Currie; Chews House – material by L.M. Rowe; Site of W.G. Smith's cottage – articles by J. Dyer).

# TIPS FOR TOURISTS

This book can be used as a guide for Dunstable tours.
4 types of tour are suggested:

### A) Short and Simple: The First 18 Features

For those people who don't have the time or inclination to see the whole town or seek out selected features, the first 18 places in the book can be seen: start at the Priory Church (01) and end at the Little Theatre (18) in High St. South. These features in themselves cover a great deal that is of importance and interest. (Distance 01 to 18 apprx. $\frac{1}{4}$ mile; Time apprx. $\frac{1}{2}$ to 1 hour.)

### B) Selection: 25 Selected ☆ Features

For those who would like to see a range of places, but who still have limited time, 25 features (each indicated by a ☆) have been selected as being of particular interest. This can be followed in the numerical sequence given (☆1, ☆2, ☆8, ☆11, ☆13, etc.) or on a more random basis. At least one hour should be allowed.

### C) Theme Trails

Several different specialist 'Theme Trails' can be followed using the symbols on the Map and the lists in the Appendix. Themes include: 'Coaching Inns', 'Churches and Chapels', 'The Straw Trade'.

### D) Complete: All 100 Features

To actually visit all 100 features at one time, it is advised that at least 2-3 hours is allowed to follow the sequence given. In addition to this, at least 20-30 minutes should be spent inside the Priory Church. Total distance apprx. 2 miles.

NB times are virtually impossible to give because of the huge range of individual abilities and interests, as well as external factors (weather, traffic, etc.). The distance covered may be of more use: the town centre is fairly compact, mostly within $\frac{1}{2}$ mile square, with no features more than about $\frac{3}{4}$ mile apart.

# INTRODUCTION TO DUNSTABLE

## Brief Description

### Size

Dunstable is a medium-sized town with about 35,000 inhabitants in approximately 12,000 homes. It is a residential and industrial area which is mainly confined within a two-mile radius from its central Cross Roads.

### Local Industry

Many people are employed in local factories and offices connected with the Motor Car Industry (Vauxhall, AC-Delco, Peugeot-Talbot, Renault, Ford, Network Rental, etc.)

Other major employers are: the Printing Industry (e.g. Ben Johnson, Waterlows), Education and Service Industries (Schools and Colleges, Hospitals, Welfare, etc.)

### Appearance

Much of the town is modern in appearance. However, parts of the 12th century Priory remain, (e.g. the Priory Church) and some of the High Street shops are developments of timber-framed buildings dating from the Middle Ages (e.g. in Middle Row, High Street South, West Street).

There are some interesting 18th century buildings (e.g. the Cart Almshouses, Chews House, Grove House, the Old Palace Lodge, the Ladies Lodge), and 19th century buildings (e.g. the old Grammar School, now Ashton Middle School).

Some of the modern buildings, especially from the 1970s, are notable for their interesting shapes, integration and good taste (e.g. the Ashton Square and the Eleanor Cross Shopping Precincts.

## Location of the Town

*Map of S.E. England*

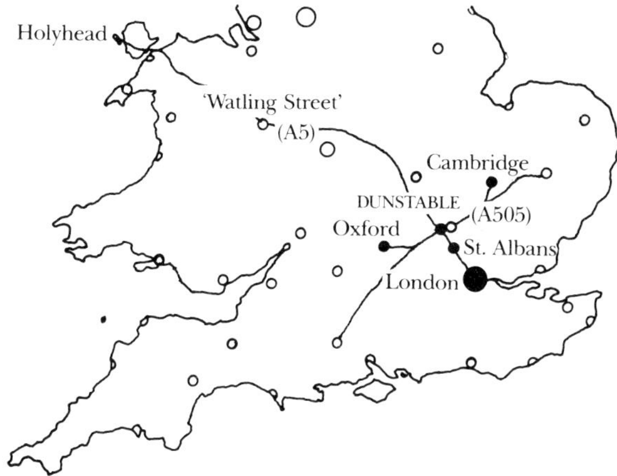


Dunstable is about 33 miles north of London and is half-way between Oxford and Cambridge (about 40 miles from each).

*Map of S. Beds*

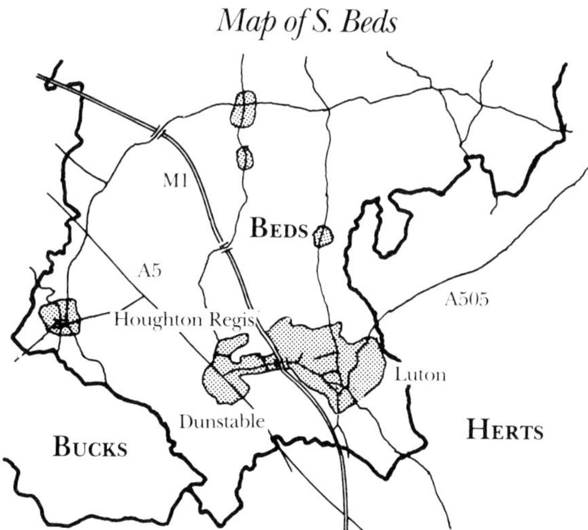


Dunstable is situated at the southern end of Bedfordshire and is surrounded by open country except to the east and north-east where Dunstable joins on to Luton and Houghton Regis.

*Map of Dunstable and The Downs*

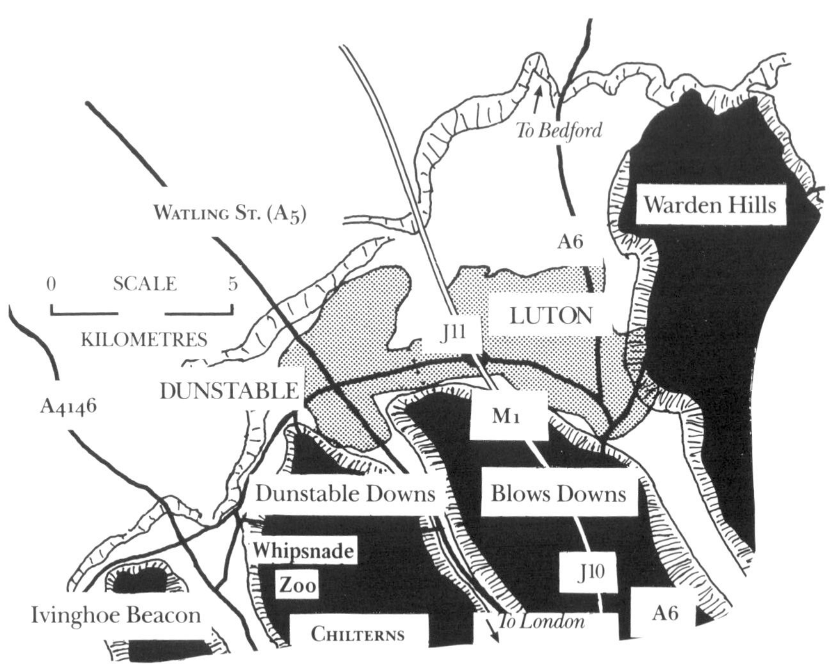


Dunstable is at the north-eastern tip of the Chiltern Hills: the southern part of the town sits in the chalk valley between Dunstable Downs (west) and Blows Downs (east) while the rest lies along the northern edge of these hills.

The town is therefore built around the central Cross Roads.

### The Cross Roads: An Important Location

The town's location has given it importance mainly because it is on the Cross Roads of the London – Holyhead (A5) and Cambridge – Oxford (A505) routes.

These two main roads have a long history since they are based on trading routes which existed long before the Romans arrived.

# A BRIEF HISTORY OF DUNSTABLE

## Ancient History

A few remains of ancient occupation have been found around Dunstable, especially on the nearby hills and in local villages, e.g. 'Stone Age' tools at Caddington, 'Bronze Age' huts at Puddle Hill. A large circular earth workcalled 'Maiden Bower', which dates from the Stone Age, exists about 2.5 miles from Dunstable near the Green Lanes.

## Romans

The Romans built 'Watling Street' (now the A5), the first proper South-North road, when they occupied Britain in the 2nd century A.D. This well-made road allowed their troops to move quickly and easily from London to the North. The East-West route was much less important but parts of it were developed by the Romans.

Some sort of small Roman fort was probably built near the Cross Roads, since it was about one and a half days march from London and therefore a useful place to rest, change horses, etc. This fort was known as 'Durocobrivis'. (There are no visible Roman remains today.)

The Roman fort to the south was 'Verulamium', now St. Albans, about half a day's march (13 miles) away.

## The Dark Ages

As with most parts of Britain, very little is known about the area after the Romans left. Once the Roman forts were abandoned, it is likely that many settlements near the main roads were also deserted since they were vulnerable, with no forces to control and protect people.

It is thought that a succession of small groups occupied the local hills and valleys, with various atttackers and invaders intruding from time to time.

For a long period, this area was probably the scene of many battles since it was the boundary between the invaders from the north and east and those from the south.

Saxon remains have been discovered in and near Dunstable e.g. the Saxon burial ground at Marina Drive.

## The Normans: The Founding of Dunstable c1100

The Normans invaded England in 1066 and in 1086 William the Conqueror ordered a survey, the 'Domesday Book', of his new territory. Nothing of note existed at Dunstable then but there was mention of settlements at Houghton Regis, Luton and at several local villages (including Caddington and Kensworth).

King Henry I, the son of William the Conqueror, built a Palace and started a priory near the Cross Roads during the early 12th century. The town was called 'Dunestaple' possibly because it was a market place marked by a post (staple) near the hill (dune). The area was probably covered with trees and bushes then, so the King would have wanted to make the roads safer for himself and other travellers by clearing parts of the woods, especially near crossroads. Old records suggest that the area around Dunstable was infested with thieves, one in particular being called 'Dun the Robber'. (There is a myth that Dunstable was named after this Dun). King Henry I built a palace at Dunstable so that he could come to stay here and keep an eye on the development of the huge Priory whilst being able to go out hunting on the local hills and woods. Before the Priory was completed, the Royal Palace and the new town of Dunstable were given to the Dunstable Priors. Dunstable was thereafter controlled by the Priory which took taxes from the parish, including the market-place.

## The Middle Ages (13th-15th c.)

The presence of the market led to the construction of permanent shops and buildings near the Cross Roads. These catered for visitors to the market and also travellers passing through Dunstable along the Watling Street. Places to eat and sleep were required so beer-houses, bakeries and inns were established.

## The End of the Priory (16th c.)

When King Henry VIII closed all the monasteries in 1540, the Dunstable Priory was 'Dissolved' and ownership of the town was tranferred to the King. Dunstable then went into a period of decline for about a hundred years, until the coaches came along.

### The Coaching Era (18th c.)

Coaches brought back prosperity to Dunstable since they brought many travellers, some of whom were very wealthy. Coaching Inns, such as the Saracen's Head and the Sugar Loaf (both still running today), prospered in the town. This development continued until the coaches suddenly decreased when the railways opened in 1842.

During the late 18th and early 19th centuries, Dunstablians benefited from a group of Charities and Trusts that were set up by some closely related people — members of the Marshe, Chew, Cart and Ashton families. Examples of their gifts, which can still be seen today, are: Chews House, the Cart Almshouses, and the Ashton Schools.

### The Straw Plait Industry (19th c.)

When the coaches no longer ran through the town, the inns and beerhouses lost much of their business and many closed down. By this time, however, the straw plait industry had started to expand rapidly so factories were set up in Dunstable — some of which were in old inns and beerhouses, a convenient re-use of these premises.

Dunstable became famous for its 'Dunstable Bonnet' and other items made from straw plait. At one time, almost every woman and girl was employed in the straw industry. This industry declined, however, when the Luton railway opened its direct line to London: the factories started to move to Luton in order to be nearer to the transport.

### The Motor Car Industry (20th c.)

The last hat factories closed in Dunstable during the 1920s and 1930s. Some engineering works had meanwhile started (e.g. Bagshawe's, which built conveyor belts) so with the demand for jobs in the 1930s several Car Factories were opened in and near the town, the most famous being Vauxhall's.

After the Second World War (1939-45), the steady increase in car sales and related products caused many people to come and live in Dunstable to work in the Car Industry. Today, the town still relies heavily on the Car Industry for jobs. However, there are now many small companies in the town which provide a wide variety of employment for the inhabitants.

## Summary

The area where Dunstable is today has been occupied, on and off, for several thousand years — since the Stone, Bronze and Iron Ages.

The main reason for this occupation is that this is the place where two ancient trading routes crossed: a North-South route and an East-West route (the Icknield Way).

The Romans built the Watling Street along the North-South trading route and built a fort called Durocobrivis on or near this spot.

The town of Dunstable was founded by King Henry I in the early 12th century when he cleared the area around the Cross Roads and built a Palace and a Priory (founded 1131).

The town developed around the Cross Roads and catered for travellers, especially during the coaching era in the 18th and early 19th centuries.

The main local industry in the late 19th century was Straw Plaiting and Hat Manufacturing.

In the 20th century, Dunstable developed and expanded as a result of the Motor Car Industry.

Today, there are many travellers through Dunstable and many visitors. The town is a good location from which other places of interest can be visited, being central for London, Cambridge and Oxford. A major local feature is the Whipsnade Zoo.

## A Town Tour

The Priory Church is Dunstable's most important building. There is no reason why a tour of Dunstable must begin here, of course, yet it is a logical starting point for both historical and practical reasons: the Priory Church is the town's oldest building, with many past associations, and it is conveniently situated in Church St. near to the Cross Roads.

# THE PRIORY CHURCH

*(Founded 1131)*

*The Priory Church (West Face)*

# THE PRIORY CHURCH

## The Priory Church

The Priory Church of St. Peter at Dunstable is a great historical monument which has played an important role in the history of the country, as well as the town. This Norman building is still awesome today even though it is, sadly, a mere remnant of the Priory's former glory.

## The West Face

The western front of the building is at first sight, as Pevsner said, 'both confusing and confused.'[i] The original symmetrical structure was destroyed very early in the church's life when, in 1222, two west towers (one on each corner) collapsed during a violent storm. The front was rebuilt without towers but the part to the right of the main entrance was not fully restored to the original design.

The SW corner now consists of a 15th century buttress connected by a piece of brickwork with a square Victorian angle-turret. It can be seen that there is less frontage to the right of the main door than there used to be. (The line of symmetry would have run through the middle of this door). The architecture to the left of the main door, on the other hand, is probably much nearer to the way it first looked, except that the tower on the NW corner (the left), with its higher stair-turret, was added in the 15th century.

Despite past architectural mishaps, however, and also because of them, the west end today is a unique and interesting face, with a certain enigmatic charm in its asymmetry — for those who are prepared to spend a few moments to contemplate and appreciate it.

Refs: i PEVSNER (1968) p.75

### The Divorce of King Henry VIII

The Dunstable Priory Church is probably most famous for being the place where the divorce between King Henry VIII and Queen Catherine of Aragon was decided upon and announced in 1533. The judgement was made by a court set up in the old Lady Chapel. After Archbishop Cranmer had announced the marriage null and void, a notice of divorcement was fixed to the church door. King Henry then split with Rome and became head of the Church of England in 1535.

### The Totternhoe Stone

The original Priory stone came from a local quarry at Totternhoe, about two miles north-west of Dunstable. In addition to being near, this building material was useful since it could be carved easily. However, the Totternhoe stone weathered badly so it had to be repaired and replaced frequently. In recent years, the new stone has come from Caen in Normandy, France, because it matches the original colour quite well – although it takes a few years to darken. (The Totternhoe quarry is no longer in operation).

## INTERIOR

### Entrance

Inside the smaller of the two front entrances, leaning against the wall, is a much older door which was in use when the church was attacked by Royalists during the Civil War in 1644. The large bullet-holes can still be clearly seen!

### Nave

Lining the spacious Nave of the church are the towering Norman pillars which were built between 1150 and 1200. These huge columns are linked by two sets of arches: at the top and at the height of the side aisles. This is the finest example of Norman architecture in Bedfordshire and one of the most unusual in the country.

### The Internal Layout

The plan of the Priory (below) shows the layout inside the present church and the extent of the original building.

*Plan of Priory Church*
*(showing extent of original building)*

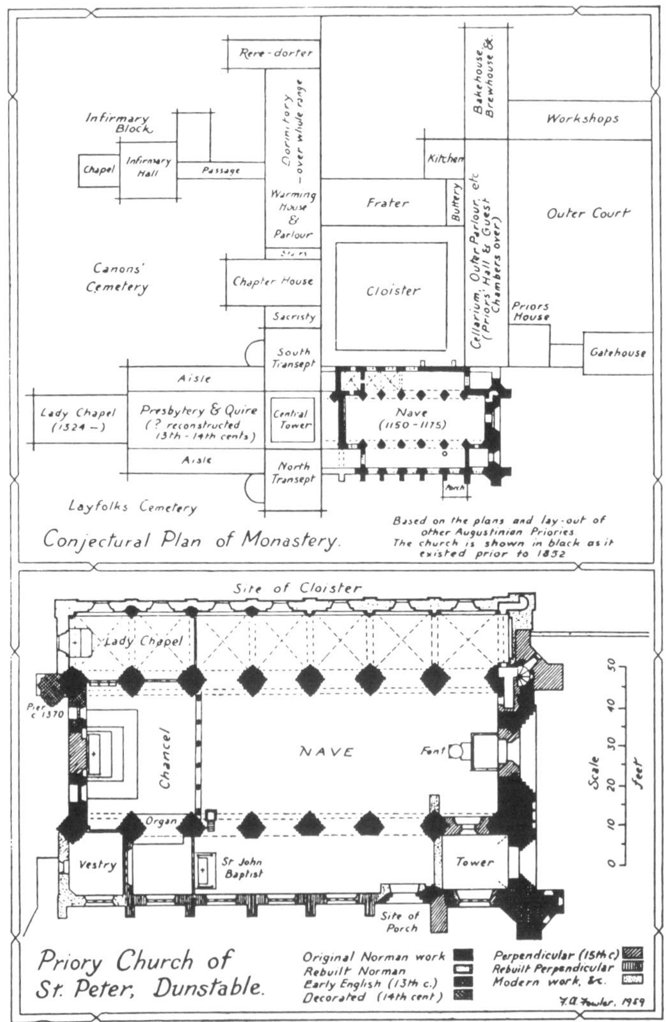

### The Roof

The wooden roof is a copy of the 15th century roof replaced in 1871, however, the figures of the twelve apostles are originals. On the north side can be seen a shield bearing the arms of Edmund, Lord Grey, of Flitton, Earl of Kent between 1465-1489. The Greys had been connected with the Priory for a long time and probably helped when the Nave was repaired in about 1475.

## EAST END

### The Wooden Screen

In front of the High Altar is the beautifully carved wooden Chancel Screen which is said to have been erected in about 1400, but it's unlikely to be that old. The Chancel Screen is particularly unusual since it has five open arches, whereas most screens are closed except for a central doorway.

### The East Wall

The wall behind the altar was once a stone partition, the old 'Rood Screen,' behind which was a very tall tower and, beyond that, the area where the original High Altar stood, the Presbytery. When this was a monastery, the church was more than twice the length it is today (see plan). On either side of the present High Altar can be seen blocked doorways which led to the original east end of the church. (NB These doors look small because the floor has been raised: it's not that the monks were all midgets!)

### 'The Marian Pillars'

The best piece of carving in the church is the set of ten wooden pillars over the Vestry door on the north side of the High Altar. These date from the period of Queen Mary (1553-1558) and may have been a gift from the Queen herself – hence their name – when she was trying to restore the Roman Catholic faith. The connection is especially strong, of course, because Mary was the daughter of Katherine of Aragon and King Henry VIII: as well as using the church for the divorce, Mary's father was responsible for closing down the Priory monastery.

## North Aisle

Originally, the people of Dunstable just had the north aisle to worship in: the rest of the Priory was for members of the Religious Order only. (It indicates how small the Dunstable population was in the 12th-14th centuries!) In the 15th century, however, the parishioners were allowed to use the main part of the church as well. The north aisle was built in the 19th century.

## St. John's Altar

The small chapel to St. John the Baptist, at the end of the north aisle, contains the only old side altar to survive. The actual altar itself only dates from 1925 but the original was consecrated in 1220 when it was established for the use of the people of Dunstable.

In 1442, a Fraternity of St. John the Baptist was founded to help support the Priory, using the chapel for prayer. A highly decorated velvet funeral 'pall' (cloth to cover the coffin) was donated to the Fraternity by Henry and Agnes Fayrey in about 1500. The Fayrey pall mysteriously disappeared after the Dissolution (presumably, to rescue it) and it wasn't returned until the end of the last century. For a few years it was hired at funerals to raise money for the church. Eventually, for safe-keeping, the valuable Fayrey Pall was given to the Victoria and Albert museum in London – where it can be seen today. The Fraternity itself was dissolved in 1547, but the illuminated Register Book still exists and that can be seen in the Luton Museum. A picture of the Fayrey Pall is on display in the aisle.

## The Chew and Cart Memorials

The most interesting 18th century memorials are in the north aisle, including those to William Chew (d. 1727) and Mrs. Jane Cart (d. 1736) who both set up some important charitable trusts in Dunstable, e.g. the Cart Almshouses (see 16). (NB The importance of the Chew and Cart families to Dunstable is dealt with later.)

### The Sanctus Bell

Hanging on the wall of the aisle is the 'Sanctus' (holy) bell which is thought to have been given by the townsfolk, during the Black Death, in 1349. In the 19th century it was used as a fire bell at the old Town Hall in High St. North. The bell is dedicated to St. Mary.

### The History Collection

Also in the north aisle is a small collection of drawings and writings, by the local historian Worthington George Smith, which were produced at the turn of the century. (NB A detailed account of the life of this man is given later – see 22.) Other items of historical interest are on display including two paintings on wooden boards (c. 1700) of Aaron and Moses.

### The Font

The large font was constructed in the middle of the 19th century as a replica of the original Norman tub-font. For many years the font stood at the West End until it was returned to its North Aisle position, in 1985, near the old parishioners entrance.

## THE WEST END

### The Bread Dole Shelves

The wooden shelves on the wall, which are now used as book shelves, were originally put up in the early 18th century to hold loaves of bread, under the instructions of Mrs Jane Cart who started a 'bread dole' (i.e. free bread) for poor people.

## SOUTH AISLE

### War Memorials

At the west end of the south aisle are two war memorials: one for the South Africa War (1899-1902) and one for the First World War. (The war memorial erected for the Second World War, used for Remembrance services, is in the Priory Meadow – see 4.)

### Flags

The three flags in the aisle are the Colours of the Dunstable British Legion which have been 'laid up' in the Priory since they are no longer paraded.

### Memorials

On the south wall of the aisle are several brass memorials which used to lie on the floor of the church, as well as a number of stone memorials. These are in remembrance of people who were wealthy and influential in Dunstable. The oldest brass is dated 1450 and shows the Pygott family. Some of the plaques mention London places since several families fled the city at the time of the Plague (1665) and the Fire (1666). In certain cases, the wealth that was brought by these men and women was of great benefit to the town.

### The Lady Chapel

At the east end of the aisle is the Lady Chapel, with its attractive 18th century wrought iron gates. It contains a velvet Pulpit Cloth mounted in a case on the wall which was another gift from Jane Cart, given in 1723.

Also in the Lady Chapel is the memorial to Mrs. Frances Ashton who was another Dunstable benefactress – particularly with regard to Schools (e.g. Ashton Middle – see 76; Ashton St. Peter's – see 96) and Almshouses (see 31 & 41).

### Further Information

For a full account of the church's rich and varied history, and a detailed description of the building, there are two inexpensive publications which can be obtained from inside the church: a 32 page booklet by Mr F.A. Fowler called, 'Dunstable Priory Church – A Brief History and Guide'; and a folded guide, cunningly designed to correspond with the internal lay-out of the building, by Mr John Lunn called, 'An Illustrated Guide to the Church'.

Refs: VCH (1904), FOWLER (1980), SMITH (1910)

# THE PRIORY MEADOW GATE

*(15th Century)*

*Priory Meadow Gate*

The Priory Gate stands next to the Priory Church and dates from about 1450. At the time of the monastery there was probably a Gatehouse on the west (right) side of the Gate and a Prior's House on the east (left) side. All that remains today is this 15th century carriage and pedestrian entrance which leads into the Priory Meadow, originally the outer court. On walking through the Gate one notices, almost immediately, the contrast between the noise and bustle of Church Street compared to the peace and tranquillity of the Priory Meadow itself.

Refs: FOWLER (1980)

# THE PRIORY MEADOW

## The Priory Buildings

After walking through the Priory Gate, the main part of the Priory Meadow can be seen on the left, (south) of the Church. At the time of the monastery virtually the whole of this meadow would have been covered in monastic buildings, including: the Cellarium (i.e. Outer Parlour, Prior's Hall and Guest Chambers), Workshops, Bakehouse, Brewhouse, Kitchens, Dormitories, Infirmary, Chapel, Chapter House, etc. These were probably arranged around cloisters and integrated with the main building which was, of course, much larger than the present Priory Church. NB There is a plan and a drawing in Fowler's booklet which depicts the possible layout (on p.2 & p.4).

## The Dissolution

After the monastery was dissolved in 1540, the great church and buildings were kept intact for a few years while a plan to create a 'see' (a place for a bishop or archbishop) at Dunstable was considered. The Priory Church would have become a Cathedral! But the scheme was abandoned and so much of the Church and all of the buildings (except the Priory House) were destroyed, the stone being taken by local people for use in other parts of the town. (It can still be seen in places e.g. in West Street – see 47.) A lot of rubble, however, remained on the site – this is why the Priory Meadow is both undulating and higher than the surrounding area.

## The Dunstable Pageant

On 4th June 1964, the Priory Meadow was the venue for the Dunstable Pageant which depicted 800 years of the town's history. The cast included over 1000 local performers! As well as being highly entertaining and educational this town event was socially valuable since it brought together many different Dunstablians for a common purpose.

Refs: FOWLER (1980); EVANS (1980) p.13.

# WAR MEMORIAL

The War Memorial, in memory of those who died during World War II, was unveiled on 13 May 1952 by the Mayor of Dunstable, Ald. T. Sandland. It is used as a focal point on Remembrance Day to remember those who have died in all wars.

## First World War (1914-18)

During the Great War, troops were billeted in the town and the Town hall was used as a Soldiers' Institute. In 1914, refugees began to arrive from Belgium. In 1915, the Dunstable Volunteer Training Corps was formed, street lighting was reduced and warning hooters were arranged in case of air raids. In 1917, the Dunstable Food Control Committee was appointed and, in 1918, a Food Ration Card system was enforced. After the war, several memorials were erected including those at: the Wesleyan Church, unveiled in 1921; Waterlow and Son Ltd. and the Priory Church, both unveiled in 1922. Also in 1922, the Dunstable Branch of the British Legion was founded and the United Services Club opened.

## Second World War (1939-45)

At the start of World War II, in September 1939, Dunstable received about 4,000 evacuees, mainly from London. In October 1940 a lone German air-raider machine-gunned the High Street. In July 1943 came the first news that some Dunstablians had become prisoners of war in Japan, after the fall of Singapore. In 1945 the V.E. Day Thanksgiving Service was held in Grove House Gardens in May, and the V.J. Day Thanksgiving Service was held there in August.

The first meeting to discuss a town War Memorial was held in December 1945. In January 1946, the Town Council acquired the Priory land and, in December, a War Memorial Fund was launched. The Priory Gardens were opened to the public in May 1947. In December 1950, Dunstable decided that the town's War Memorial should be an inscribed plaque in an alcove in the Priory Meadow and so this was built in 1952. The Remembrance Service is still held here annually.

*'When I am dead, think only this of me*
*that there's some corner of a foreign*
*field that is for ever England.'*

Rupert Brooke

Refs: TURVEY V.; DUNSTABLE DIR. (1951/2);

# PRIORY GARDENS

### The Gardens

Today, these beautiful gardens are carefully kept by the Council gardeners. There is a large willow tree and a sundial which can be seen alongside the simple network of paths between the flower beds. At the time of the Priory (i.e. 13th – 16th century) this area would have been part of a cobbled Great Courtyard, surrounded by barns, granaries, stables, cart sheds, etc.

### The Gate and House

On the far side of the gardens, to the west, is the Priory Gardens Gate which leads out into High St. South (the Watling Street, or A5). Next to the Gate can be seen the back of the large Priory House. This building was originally one of the Priory buildings, hence its name, and inside it are remains of an early stone vaulted hall. This internal stonework and the Priory Gate are the only surviving parts of the monastery outside the Church. (The Priory House and Priory Gardens Gate are covered in more detail in 11 and 12.)

# DUNSTABLE HEALTH CARE

The Health Centre is in the S.W. corner of Priory car park, cost about a quarter of a million pounds and was opened in July 1976. As well as containing a group of G.Ps, headed by the excellent Dr. Michael Day, there is a clinic for children and expectant mothers.

### The Kingsway Clinic

The Health Centre replaced the County Council Health Centre in Kingsway which had opened in October 1942. The old clinic was used a great deal, especially, for example, in January 1962 when hundreds of Dunstablians rushed there to have smallpox vaccinations following an outbreak in Britain. The Kingsway clinic eventually became too small for the ever increasing post-war population.

## HEALTH CARE IN DUNSTABLE

### St. Mary's Hospital

In about 1208 the Priory provided a 'spital', on the north corner of Half Moon Lane and High St. South. This early hospital, dedicated to St. Mary Magdalene, provided care for lepers and oher sick people away from the town centre. It apparently survived the Dissolution since it was called 'the Leper Hospital' in the 1624 Rent List. The hill where this stood, on London Road, is called 'Half Moon Hill' or 'Spital Hill'.

### The Pest House

A place for those suffering from highly contagious and deadly illnesses (e.g. smallpox, plague) was 'Coldharbour', later called the 'Pest House', on the east corner of West St. and Green Lanes. It was last used in c1784.

Today, the 'Luton and Dunstable Hospital' is the local General Hospital. (NB For a detailed account of local health care see Currie, 1982.)

### Dunstable: Health Resort

Dunstable always had a reputation for being a healthy place, mainly due to the fresh air on the Downs and the clean water from the wells. (The thick layer of chalk acted as a filter and purified the water.) Many people moved from London to Dunstable for health reasons, including W.G. Smith's and A. Bagshawe's families.

# CHURCH WALK

*Church Alley*

### Church Alley

Church Alley is part of Church Walk, a very old path, which may even date from the early years of the Priory in the 12th century. Today, Church Alley leads from the Priory Church car park, between two large buildings, into High St. South.

### North Side

The building on the right (north side) is the modern premises of 'Woolworth and Co.' All the buildings which used to be on the land to the right of Church Walk were burned down in 1841 when a huge fire destroyed 19 properties on the corner of High St. South and Church Street.

### South Side

The building on the left (south side) is called the 'Albion Buildings'. At the rear of this building, i.e. behind the wall on the left, was the Index printing business which became the present-day Ben Johnson (see 10).

### The Albion Buildings

The front of these 19th century premises is now occupied by the William Hill betting shop above which is the 'Planned Publicity Ltd' marketing company. Before this it was the 'International Stores' for many years.

In 1894 the 'International Tea Company's Stores Ltd.' was at '2 Albion Buildings', while '1 Albion Buildings' was then an ironmonger's shop of William Francis, immediately next to Church Alley. An old photograph of the Albion Buildings, taken about the turn of the century, shows that many of the ironmonger's wares were displayed on the pavement outside the shop and baskets were hung on a gas street lamp at the end of the Alley. A large sign above the shop advertised the range of items, including 'Furniture and Ironmongery'. There was also a horse and four-wheeled cart, to deliver goods, which was also tied to the conveniently placed lamp-post![i]

Ref: i BEDS. EDUCATION SERVICE '6 PHOTOS'

# THE MIDDLE ROW SHOPS

*Middle Row Shops*

The row of shops on the west side of High St. South, opposite Church Alley, is one side of the island of buildings known as Middle Row. (The other side is dealt with in 31.)

The oldest known part of Middle Row is the group of shops nos. 26 to 32, at the left (southern) end, with the lowest roofs. These premises were once the original main market hall during the middle ages.[i]

Ref: i BAILEY (1980) p. 98

### The Origins of Middle Row

This group of buildings started out, over 500 years ago, as a collection of market stalls which evolved into fixed counters, workshops, etc. Some of the timber inside the present buildings dates from the 15th century (recently discovered by John Bailey). The old age of the Middle Row structures is indicated on the outside by the interestingly distorted roofs. The fronts of most of these shops have changed frequently throughout the years, and they are still changing.

---

### THE BEER TRADE

*For several hundred years, Dunstable was known for its thriving beer trade. About a hundred years ago there were over 40 pubs in the town!*
*Middle Row used to have at least four pubs:*
*(1) 'The Britannia' — next to Middle Row Alley (on the north side) and which burned down at the end of the 19th century; the present site was Stotts furniture shop until 1985.*
*(2) 'The Rose and Crown' — where Keeps Corner (now 'Chiltern Sports') is at the north end of Middle Row. (NB There used to be two more buildings at the north end of middle row which were demolished to widen West St.)*
*(3&4) 'The Shoulder of Mutton' and the 'Swan With Two Necks' which were two pubs standing side-by-side immediately south of where Tilleys butchers now is. (NB The name of the 'Swan with two necks' derives from the 'Swan with two nicks,' referring to two nicks or marks on the bills of the Swans owned by the Victuallers.)*

*The last three pubs closed down during the first two decades of this century when there was a general decline of the beer trade in Dunstable.*

*Today, the only business in Middle Row associated with beer is the 'Brian the Brew' (Brian Freeman) shop which sells equipment and ingredients for home-made beer and wine. This modern trend (largely brought about by high pub prices), is, ironically, a return to a centuries old practice.*

---

# THE VICTORIA BUN HOUSE

*The Victoria Bun House*

The Greaves and Tompkins Estate Agents, between the Albion Buildings and 'Moore's' Clothes Shop, was until 1986 the quaint 'Victoria Bun House' which sold a wide variety of cakes, buns, etc. The sun-blind was raised and lowered daily, in order to protect the goods in the windows, and this helped to give the shop its charming traditional appearance.

## The Old Shop

The brick extension at the rear of the premises dated from the early 19th century (three bricks had '1825' and bricklayers initials on them). However, the original front section was very much older being based on a timber-framed shop which was at least 400 years old. At one time it may have been a beer-house called 'The Black Bull'.

## The Victoria Bun House

As the name implied, this shop was in existence as a bakery during the Reign of Queen Victoria. In 1869 George Strange was here as a 'confectioner' having previously been in Ashton Street in 1864. By 1876 Joseph Shepherd had taken over as 'cook and confectioner' and he remained until at least 1898.[i]

At the beginning of this century, the 'Victoria Bun House' was owned by Joseph Andrews who advertised as being a 'Wholesale and Retail Pastrycook, Confectioner and Caterer'. In 1903 he was awarded a Diploma of Merit at the Baker's and Confectioners' Exhibition, Agricultural Hall, London, for his speciality: Wedding Cakes. Other items sold by him included the mouthwatering selection of Raised Pork Pies ... Rich Madeira, Dundee, Mould, Dessert, and Luncheon Cakes ... Chocolates, Biscuits, Sweets ... Game Pies, Plum Puddings and Christmas Cakes![ii]

After Andrew had retired in about 1928, The Victoria Bun House was briefly owned by the Hobbly family who then sold it to Mr. E. Combes by 1933.

## The Two Bakeries

When the bakery changed hands in the early 1930s, a new law was enforced which made it illegal to bake underground so a new coal-fired bakery had to be built in the ground-floor extension behind the shop.

Refs: i KELLY, HARROD; ii SMITH (1904)

## The Old Bakery

The old underground bakery directly beneath the shop had a very old oven and an 'Improved Coal Oven Manufactured by Limbrey, Dunstable'. (Limbrey was an ironmonger who had a workshop in West St.) The old bakery was thereafter used only for storage but the ovens were still intact when the shop was sold in 1986. A curious feature of the underground bakery was a central support column, holding up the floor of the shop, which was actually an old ship's engraved mast!

The last bakers

In 1986 the premises were sold by the owner Mrs Bennett (the daughter of E. Combes) so the bakery was closed. The last bakers were Mr Ernest Richardson and his son Peter and daughter-in-law Maureen. Ernest had been baking at the shop since 1937 ('Coronation Year') and was 80 years old. (He said that it was too early to retire!) Consequently, these people were forced out of business, despite having many loyal customers, and the bakery finally closed after operating continuously for 100 years.

## Estate Agents

The new owners are an Estate Agents, Greaves and Tompkins. Jimmy Greaves is the famous ex-footballer who is now a witty T.V. commentator.

# MOORE'S CLOTHES SHOP

*Moore's*

'Moore's' is today owned by Mr. Frederick Moore and it is a comprehensive haberdashery as well as a high quality ladies' clothes shop. This business is numbered '21-23' High St. South because it now occupies what were once two separate shops: no. 23 was previously Boots Chemists and no. 21 was once occupied by James Tibbett, the well-known Dunstable printer.

## 18th Century

The Deeds of these premises date back to 1704 and parts of them are even older. During the eighteenth century, the buildings were 'modernised' in order to improve them and several alterations have taken place since then. (This is now a Listed building which limits any further changes.)

## 19th Century: James Tibbett

James Tibbett was a Dunstable printer who had eight children including three sons – James, Daniel and Thomas – who all became printers as well. In 1850 James Tibbett was at 11 High St. North (now no. 21) as a 'stationer, bookseller and toy dealer'. By 1853 he was advertised as a 'newsagents, printer, bookseller, stationer, and paper-hanger' and, in addition, the shop was described as a 'toy ware-house'. James Tibbett was a Methodist lay preacher who strongly supported the Temperance movement, so he also used his shop as the Bible Society Collecting Office.[i]

## Dunstable's First Newspapers

James Tibbett published the first newspapers in Dunstable: on 1st June 1855 he started 'The Dunstable Chronicle and Monthly Local Reporter', and on 5th June 1856 he brought out the weekly paper called 'The Dunstable Chronical and Advertiser'.[ii]

## Published Books

James Tibbett also published several books about Dunstable:

In 1853 he printed a group of peoms by George Derbyshire (a Parish Clerk) including *'Native Scenes',* about Dunstable's history, and *'The Graves of the Poor',* about Elkanah Settle.

In 1855 he printed a collection called *'Dunno's Originals',* a mixture of poetry, fact and fiction by Dunno, real name Mr. W. Nichols of 'Ikenild Row' (Sic) West St.

In 1859 Charles Lamborn's book on Dunstable called *'The Dunstaplelogia'* was published. (Charles Lamborn was the ex-Headmaster of the 'British School' in West St.)

In 1872 *'A History of Dunstable'* by W.H. Derbyshire (G. Derbyshire's son) was issued which was published again, in 1882, as a much larger Second Edition called, *'The History of Dunstable'.* (W.H. Derbyshire was Mayor in 1879-80). [iii]

Refs: i SLATER, CRAVEN; ii DBG 1965 p. 29; iii (ibid) p. 29

## James Tibbett and son

James Tibbett retired to a large house, 'Icknield Villa' at Icknield Street, in about 1869 and his son James Tibbett Junior (1841-1921) took over the High St. South business.[i]

## The Birth of the 'Dunstable Gazette'

Daniel Tibbett, another son of James Tibbett, set up his own business in 1864 as a 'printer, stationer, bookbinder, and newsagent' at 71 High St. North (now demolished, where Nicholas Way is). In 1865 Daniel Tibbett founded 'The Dunstable Borough Gazette' when he was just 26 years old, but he died in 1871 when only 33. James Tibbett Senior, although retired, ran the 'Gazette' until it was sold to Mr William Etchells in 1875. In July 1876, however, the newspaper was bought by Henry Ballans who moved it in June 1879 to the building on the corner of Albion Street (see 66), where the 'Gazette' stayed until August 1986. NB Tom Tibbett (1851-1941), meanwhile, had started the 'Enterprise Printing Works' in High St. North.[ii]

## 'The Dunstable Advertiser and Weekly Reporter'

James Tibbett Junior, who was running his father's old shop at 11 (now 21) High St. South, decided that he too would like to run a newspaper. So, on 2nd August 1884, he launched 'The Dunstable Advertiser and Weekly Reporter', using the Albion Press. This was, of course, a direct rival to the 'Gazette' and it continued until 23rd September 1905 when it became incorporated into the 'Luton Reporter'. (The 'Luton Reporter' closed in 1926.)[iii]

## The two shops: nos 11 & 12

In 1885, James Tibbett (Jnr) was at no. 11 (now 21), while no. 12 (now 23) was a 'glass and china warehouse' occupied by Mrs Jane Gadsden. By 1898, however, James Tibbett (Jnr) was at nos. 12 & 13, while no. 11 had Arthur Spendlove, a draper and dress-maker.[iv]

Refs: i DBG (1965) pp. 8-11; ii (ibid); iii (ibid); iv TRADE DIR.

By 1903 S.C. & R. Lester builders' ironmongers were at 11 High St. South but these had moved out by 1912, when the Tibbett family occupied both addresses: Ethel and Gordon Frank Tibbett were in 11 and Alfred James Tibbett was in 12.

### Moore's and Boots

In 1917 Charles F. Moore took over no. 11 (changed to 21 and 1921) in addition to his shop in High St. North. When Moore's first moved in, Tibbett's was still next door but, by 1924, 'Boots Cash Chemists Ltd.' had moved into no. 23. Moore's and Boots stood side-by-side for many years, until Boots moved out and Moore's took over no. 23. as well. Boots is now in the Quadrant.

In 1986, Moore's old crooked timber roof with its small tiles was torn off by violent winds, so it was replaced with a modern, straight tile roof.

### Index Printers

James Tibbett first started his printing business in 1840 and this was taken over by his son, James Tibbett Jnr., in about 1869. The printing was first carried out in the property that is now Moore's clothes shop, but by 1880 printing was being done at the rear of the old 'Victoria Bun House.' (Posters found stuck to the Bun House rafters, in 1986, were dated 1880 and 1903) Tibbett's printing works were called the 'Albion Press' and it ws run by J. Tibbett Jnr, until he died in 1921. James' son Alfred, and his son Cyril, then expanded the business. Index Publishers took over the Albion Press and built large works, during the 1930s, in Church Walk. These printing works (now demolished) extended behind the Albion Buildings and Moore's. Index specialised in the production of the railway and bus time tables and guides, including the world famous ABC guides. During the 1960s, Index moved to new and much larger premises on London Rd and the Church Walk buildings were pulled down to make way for the Priory Health Centre. In 1985 the Index company was taken over by Ben Johnson, an American firm, who now run the London Rd print works.[ii]

Refs: i TRADE DIR.; ii O.S. MAPS & TRADE DIR.

# ☆11☆ THE PRIORY HOUSE

*(18th C with 13th C chamber)*

*The Priory House*

The Priory House has attractive Early Georgian facades with arched windows. This is the site of the original Priory hospice or hospitium (i.e. a hostel, not a hospital) where travellers could stay, during the time of the monastery. Inside, on the ground floor, the medieval stone vaulting can still be seen.

## After The Priory

In 1545, just after the monastery was closed, Richard Greenaway was put in charge of the Priory buildings including this Prior's hostel. It was then bought and sold several times and owned by various families. One owner was Richard Denton, of the Lyon Inn, who bought the House in 1554 but sold it again soon afterwards. [i]

## 19th Century

In the 19th century, the Priory House was owned by the Munt family who built a hat factory next to it on the site of the present Priory Gate (see 12).

## 20th Century: Council Offices

In 1946, the Priory House was bought from the executors of the Munt family by the Council with the expectation that it would be used for meetings of local societies, and perhaps for a museum. Since 1956, the building has been occupied as offices for the Council's Public Health and Housing Departments. The Citizens' Advice Bureau is in the rear of Priory House. [ii]

Refs: i EVANS (1980) pp. 15-6; ii HAYWARD p .21

# PRIORY GARDENS GATE

*(Site of Munt and Brown's Hat Factory)*

*Priory House with Hat Factory (19th C.)*

### MUNT AND BROWN HAT FACTORY

Across the present entrance to the Priory Gardens, next to the Priory House, was the straw hat and bonnet factory of Munt and Brown. It was in existence from about 1839 until it was closed down and demolished about 1907. The gardens had a reputation for being well maintained but they were seldom seen by the townspeople until they were opened to the public after the last war. Munt and Brown's hat factory was one of several that existed in Dunstable. The straw hats were made from straw that had been carefully plaited.

### DUNSTABLE'S STRAW HAT TRADE

*Straw plaiting grew as a cottage industry, along with lace making, during the 16th century. In the 18th century, people began to move into the town from surrounding villages to work in small industries. By the 19th century, almost every woman and girl in Dunstable was employed either in straw plaiting or lace work, and the 'Dunstable Straw Bonnet' became well-known in London and in many other parts of the country. London manufacturers of straw goods began to open branches in Dunstable (e.g. Munt and Brown) when suitable straw became scarce. This happened mainly because the Italian 'Leghorn' straw, which was imported and used in London, ceased to be available towards the end of the Napoleonic wars. By 1869, there were at least five large factories and twelve small plaiting workshops in Dunstable plus some related businesses. The total workforce was then estimated to be 1,300. However, after the railway line was opened between Luton and London in 1858, the Dunstable straw hat trade began to decline as businesses gradually moved to be closer to Luton's main-line station. The last four hat factories closed down between 1925 and 1931, with Bennett's being the last one.*

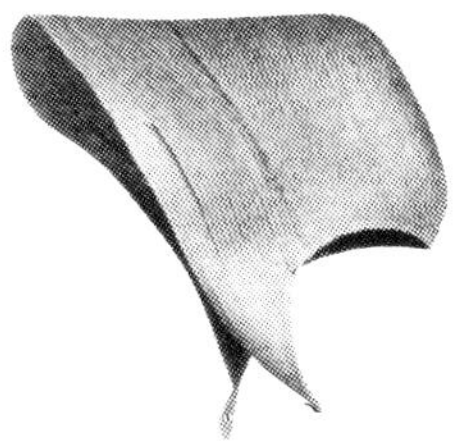

Further Reading: DONY (1942), FREEMAN (1953), EVANS (1985), DUNSTABLE GUIDE (1974), BUCK (1951, 1978)

# THE SARACEN'S HEAD P.H.

*(16th Century)*

*The Saracen's Head P.H.*

This is Dunstable's oldest surviving Inn: 16th century timber was recently discovered in the roof by John Bailey. One indication of the building's age is the fact that the pub floor is much lower than the road outside, with stone steps leading down from the front door. This difference in height exists because the A5 has been gradually built up to its present level and it causes real problems after a heavy rainfall – the pub soon begins to fill up with water!

### 16th Century

In the 16th century, Adam Hilton of the Saracen's Head was the 'Local Receiver' or 'Bailiff' (previously the Prior's bailiff) who collected the income from the local religious houses. At that time, there was another Inn next door to the Saracen's Head (to the south) called the 'Lower George'.[i]

### 17th and 18th Centuries

In the 17th century, from about 1645, the increasing road traffic along the Watling Street benefited the inn-keepers and the Saracen's Head extended to provide extra stabling and accommodation. In 1649 the Saracen's Head was mentioned in a Deed as belonging to Francis Dingley.

During the Civil War, the owner of the Saracen's Head was a Roundhead and he buried his gold and silver coins beneath the stables for safety. However, he died before he could reclaim them and they were not dug up until 1815 when the old inn was severely burned. The Saracen's Head, which had billeted some of the soldiers during the American War, was a blackened hulk after the fire. Consequently, it was rebuilt and the inn prospered throughout the rest of the coaching era, as it continues to do today.

### 20th Century

The Saracen's Head survived by adapting: at the beginning of this century the old coaching entrance and yard was converted into a garage for motor cars, and petrol pumps were placed in front of the pub.

In 1985 the interior of the pub was completely renovated and an extension was added at the rear. At the same time, the front of the building was redecorated to give it a more interesting appearance. The building has, however, retained its historical character.

Ref: i BHRS 63, 64;

*The Story of the Saracen's Head*

The inn sign of 'The Saracen's Head' was introduced into this country after the crusaders returned from the Holy Land. According to the legend, the name is a reminder of a rather gory incident which occurred while King Richard the First was overseas fighting the enemies of the Christian Crusaders, the Saracens. It seems that one day in 1191, while in between battles, Richard asked for roast pork for his meal. The royal chef, not daring to tell the King that pork was not available in the Holy Land, used his imagination and arranged for a Saracen prisoner to be killed, cooked and carved. After the meal, the leader complimented the cook and asked to see the head of the boar which had been so delicious, as was the custom. Unable to think of a way out of that, the trembling chef eventually presented the Saracen's Head itself. The King, however, laughed and announced that he and his folk would eat more! (Obviously, Richard the Lionheart had a strong stomach as well!)

NB The Saracen's Head provides lunch-time meals every day.

*The Saracen's Head Inn Sign*

Ref: WOODCOCK (1950)

## The Coaching Era (c. 1740-1840)

The first stage-coach to regularly pass through Dunstable was probably the one that was advertised on Monday 12th April 1742: it travelled from London to Birmingham and it took three days to cover the 116 miles. This coach was the only regular service for several years. However, other coaches then began to run and these increased in number until, at the peak of the coaching era, there were more than 80 passing through Dunstable every day!

The main coaching Inns were: The Saracen's Head, (High St. South), The Red Lion, The White Hart, and The Sugar Loaf, (High St. North, E. Side), and The Anchor, and the Crown (High St. North, W. Side).

Most of the town was involved with the travel business in one way or another – whether it be as smithies, saddlers, wheelwrights or grooms for the coaches, or as brewers, innkeepers, and bakers for the travellers.

There was a general air of excitement in the town, especially when some of the more famous passed through – people such as The Duke of York, The Duke of Gloucester, Henry Brahams (the musician), Daniel O'Connor (the Irish liberator) and Lord Byron, who all loved to take a turn in holding the reins whilst on a journey!

When the railways started, the number of coaches soon decreased: on 4 June 1836, 32 passed through the Puddle Hill toll-gate at the north end of Dunstable; 1837, 28 were running daily; and in 1838, 12 coaches ran in the first few months until, on the 4 June 1838, the last regular stage-coach passed through Dunstable.

This rapid decline and abrupt end to the coaching era was a direct result of the railways: the London to Leighton Buzzard line opened in 1838.

## The Chalk Cutting

The end of coaching didn't happen without a challenge. In 1837 the Chalk Hill cutting was made at a cost of £10,000, in order to save time wasted by going round the hill (The first coaches went over the top of the hill, but this required extra horses and was dangerous as well as expensive.) The cutting didn't keep the stage-coaches running but it did prove useful when the first motor vehicles arrived, and that was when Dunstable started to become busy once again!

## The Railway Era (c. 1840-1965)

Dunstable had two railway stations linked to two important railway lines:

The High St. North Station opened in 1848 connecting with the London and North Western Railway (L&NWR) line, linking Dunstable to London and Birmingham via Leighton Buzzard.

The Church Street Station opened in 1858 connecting with the Great Northern Railway (GNR) line, linking the first station (along a bridge across High St. North) to London and Welwyn via Luton.

In Dunstable, the railways destroyed first the coaching trade and then, more slowly, the straw hat trade. Many inns and public houses closed when the coaches stopped, and some became hat factories (e.g. the Old Crown). Some inns survived, however, partly by doing business with the railway companies. The Saracen's Head became an agent for the Midland railway; the Red Lion inn became an agent for the London and North Western railway (by 1864) and later the Great Northern railway (in 1877).

## End of the Line

The last passenger train left Dunstable in 1965 after the Government had decided to close nearly all the small branch lines in the country. The two Dunstable stations and High St. North railway bridge were demolished. Since then the Dunstable-Luton line has only been used by goods wagons to and from the cement works.

The passenger service along the foot of Blows Downs was a short and very pleasant journey from Dunstable into the centre of Luton. Many Dunstablians would like to see this service reopened: the roads become extremely congested at peak times and are hazardous (most drivers break the 30 mph speed limit on the Luton Road!), in addition to which car parking in Luton is now expensive.

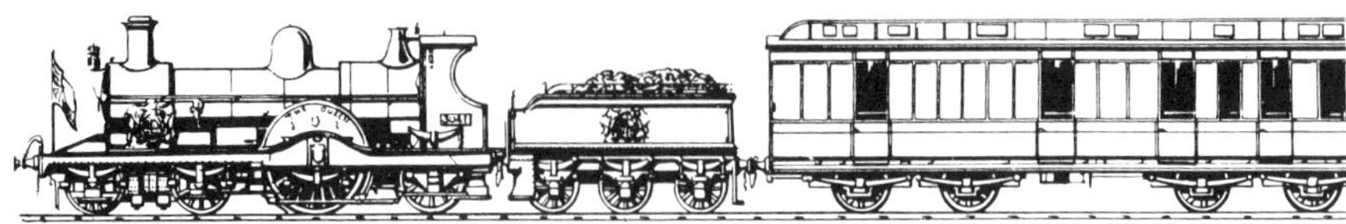

# THE GREY HOUSE

*(18th Century)*

*The Grey House*

This Georgian Town House, with its plain classical front, is a typical example of the standardised architecture that represented 'good taste' during the 18th century. It is perhaps surprising to learn that this was once an inn, called 'The Star', and later a hat factory. The building has been called 'The Grey House' for many years, probably simply because it has traditionally been painted a grey colour. After being a private residence, belonging to the Bagshawe family, it was turned into an hotel. Today it is a private club used by local businessmen.

## 18th Century: The Star Inn

The Grey House started as the Star Inn: the first known record of it is in 1764 when, according to the Dunstable Parish Register, 'Thomas Groom at ye Star' was buried.

A 1773 deed mentioned 'a farm house in Dunstable, formerly called Malting Farm, formerly in the occupation of Benjamin Johnson, now John Shilbourne, and now called the Starr Inn and Farm'.

The existing adjacent back buildings and the lane (Wood Lane) leading from the High Street to the garden of The Grey House fits in with the layout of a small farm. It was common at that time, and even quite recently, for inns, alehouses and beerhouses to be attached to small farms to help out with what could often be a precarious living. During the long opening hours, especially in slack periods, the wife might deal with a few customers while the husband could see to some poultry, cows, etc. or dig the kitchen garden. There was considerable competition in Dunstable for this type of business, which is perhaps why it did not last as an Inn.

Just before 1780 the Inn was converted into a private house and by 1830 the property was being used as 'three messuages or tenements'.

## 19th Century: Small Hat Factory

During the mid 19th century, at least part of the house was used as a straw hat and bonnet factory: a photograph of about 1870 shows some workers or 'hands' in front of the building.

The top floor (i.e. the second floor) would have been a large workroom where the women and girls worked. In the basement, the men would have stiffened the hats in baths of gelatine, dried them, and then softened them by steam and shaped them on wooden blocks on a blocking-machine.

In the backyard, near the rear door, was a well or tank (about six feet square and seven feet deep) containing soft water and connected to a hand pump in the scullery. The water was necessary to provide the steam in the basement.

Passers-by would probably have noticed the sickly smell, which usually emanated from these small hat factories, drifting up into the street via the basement window and steps.

The factory closed down, along with many others in Dunstable, sometime after Luton opened its railway line to London in 1858.

NB At the rear of The Grey House (reached via Wood Lane) can still be seen the elongated windows of the hat factory work-room.

### The Turn of the Century

In the late 19th century and early 20th century, the address and ownership of the house changed several times: in 1887 it was no. 30 High St. South, in 1897 it was no. 31, and in 1918 it was conveyed as no. 59 to Eric George Oakley — a brewer at the Benjamin Bennett's North Western Brewery in High St. North.

### 20th Century: Private Residence and Hotel

In 1923, Eric Oakley moved to Brewery House (next to the brewery) and the property was bought by Thomas Wyatt Bagshaw as no. 59 or 'The Grey House'. T.W. Bagshawe lived at The Grey House from January 1923 until April 1926, when Arthur Bagshawe died at The Grove House (see 79 and Bagshawe Family). The building was nearly destroyed in 1925 when the Luton Electricity Extension Order was approved for supply to the town and some houses changed from gas to electricity: a short circuit set a gas pipe on fire but, fortunately, there was little damage.

After 1926, The Grey House was occupied by Mrs Eliza Bagshawe, widow of Arthur Bagshawe, until the property was sold in 1950. In 1952 the premises opened as 'The Grey House Hotel' which lasted until it was recently converted into a private club.

Refs: BAGSHAWE (1967, 68)

# MONTPELIER CHAMBERS

## 61 High St. South

Montpelier House stands next to The Grey House, on the southward side. It was built just before 1870 and from about 1885 it was occupied by Augustus Morcom, a surgeon, who was also the medical officer of health for the borough, a borough magistrate, and town mayor (in 1890). Between about 1906 and 1908, the doctor's son, Alfred Farr Morcom, was his partner.

After the 1914-18 War, the practice was taken over by Harold Norman Little who kept stables at the back for hunting purposes.

Today the rear of the Chambers is used as a veterinary surgery by Molly Fardell B.V.S.C., M.R.C.V.S.

## 63 High St. South

The house between Montpelier Chambers and the Almshouses, no. 63 High St. South, is a late Georgian building of about 1785 with an elegant doorway. The Georgian style, however, was spoiled by the addition of Victorian bay windows.

The building was used for many years by Alexander Podd, an antique dealer who also had premises in Mayfair, London. Before that, it was occupied by Mrs Pocock who had previously lived for a while at The Grey House.

Today, no. 63 is occupied by SPS Printing Ltd., and is known as "SPS House".

Refs: BAGSHAWE (1967, 68)

# THE CART ALMSHOUSES

*(Built 1723)*

*The Cart Almshouses*

The Cart Almshouses, built in 1723, consist of a simple row of six two-storeyed terraced houses in blue and red brick. The Almshouses are built on a platform several feet above street level, with a single set of stone steps for access, which gives them a certain air of distinction.

## The Brickwork

Glazed bricks can be seen in the walls of the Almshouses. Such bricks were sometimes used on the visible sides of buildings because the glistening surface was considered to be more attractive than the dull appearance of ordinary bricks. These are hand-made bricks from local brickyards, e.g. at Caddington. The glazed effect was created on bricks that were very close to the kiln fire: the intense heat causing grains of sand to melt and later solidify as small pieces of glass. Other techniques were also used to deliberately achieve this effect.

Ref: COX (1979)

### The Founding of the Almshouses

The Almshouses are named after their founder, Jane Cart, who built them in 1723 for six elderly women of the town who did not have the means to run a home of their own. These women had to be either unmarried or widowed, and communicants of the Church of England for at least two years. A large plaque on the front of the building commemorates the donation, it reads:

> THESE ALMS HOUSES
> WERE ERECTED AND
> ENDOWED WITH LANDS
> FOR THE MAINTENANCE
> OF SIX POOR PERSONS
> OF THIS TOWN BY
> JANE CART
> WIDOW AND RELIC OF MR.
> JAMES CART
> CITIZEN OF LONDON
> AND DAUGHTER OF MR.
> THOMAS CHEW
> OF THIS TOWN AND
> ELIZABETH HIS WIFE IN
> THE YEAR OF OUR LORD 1723

### Jane Cart (1653-1736)

As the plaque says, Jane Cart was the daughter of Thomas Chew. He was a London haberdasher (a dealer in items for making clothing) who had connections with Dunstable through his wife's family. Jane had two brothers, Thomas and William Chew, and two sisters, Frances (who became Frances Ashton) and Elizabeth (who became Elizabeth Aynscombe).

Jane married James Cart who was a London merchant and, although they had nine children, she outlived her husband and all her sons and daughters. After Jane had become 'a widow and relic' she lived for a while next to her sister Frances, who was also a widow, in London. When Frances died in 1727 Jane was left alone.

By the time she was old, Jane owned much property, including the Sugar Loaf and other inns in Dunstable. When she died at the age of 83, Jane had no immediate family left alive and she left much of her estate to charities, including her own 'Cart Trust'.

### The Cart Trustees

When Jane Cart died in 1736, these Almshouses were left, along with land in Bedfordshire, to a group of Trustees so that her charity could continue. The Trustees met annually at the Sugar Loaf Inn (once Jane Cart's) in order to administrate her will. In addition to finding suitable women to place in the Almshouses, they had to find twenty poor clergymen and twenty poor widows, or unmarried daughters of clergymen, and pay them each ten pounds.

### The Almshouses

The six occupants of the Almshouses were each given money for food (2s. 6d.), for clothing (10s.) and for winter fuel (6s. 8d.). These allowances were gradually increased over the years so that by 1873 each of the almswomen was receiving an annual sum of five pounds and four shillings plus a gown, petticoat, two shifts, one pair of stockings and one pair of shoes, and two pounds fuel money. If one of the women died, then the Trustees would hold additional meetings so that no almshouse would remain empty for too long.

### Jane Cart's Bread

Jane Cart also provided an annual sum of five pounds four shillings with which the Priory Church had to provide bread for the poor of the parish. These loaves of bread were at first distributed after the Sunday afternoon service, at the Minister's discretion, from three shelves at the back of the Church. This custom continued into this century (as noted by W.G. Smith, 1904) and the shelves can still be seen in the Church.

NB There are two other sets of almshouses in Dunstable: the Ashton Almshouses (now called the Frances Ashton House in Bull Pond Lane – see 41) and the Ladies Lodge (in Church St. – see 99).

# CHEW FAMILY TREE

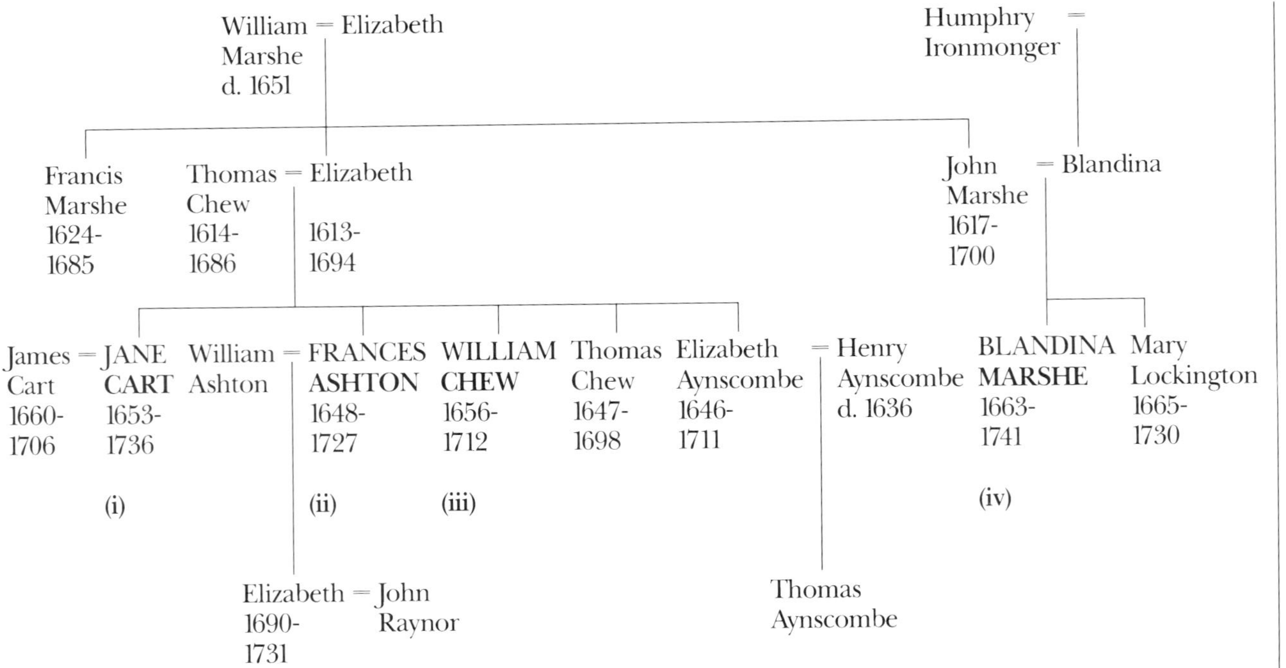

# NOTES ON FAMILY TREE

(i) **JANE CART** outlived her husband James and her nine children as well as her two brothers and two sisters. Consequently, when Jane Cart died in 1736, aged 83 years, much of her estate was left to charities in London and Dunstable. In 1723, Jane Cart built the Cart Almshouses in High St. South. She also provided free bread ('Cart's Bread Dole'), for poor church-goers, at the Priory Church.

(ii) **FRANCES ASHTON** died in 1727 and gave her money to a Charitable Trust. Her only daughter, Elizabeth, was left out of the will for marrying a man, John Raynor, of whom Frances Ashton did not approve. (Elizabeth died childless.) The money left by Frances Ashton was partly used to build and run the Ashton Primary School (now Ashton Lower School) opposite the Priory Church in Church Street. Her money was also used to build and run the Ashton Almshouses which used to be in West Street until they were demolished and new ones were built in Bullpond Lane. Later, some of the Ashton Trust's money was used to found the Dunstable Grammar School (now Ashton Middle School) in High St. North.

(iii) **WILLIAM CHEW** and his brother, Thomas Chew, lived in London and became distillers. William Chew died unmarried in 1712, aged 56, leaving his estate to his two sisters, Jane and Frances, and his nephew, Thomas Aynscombe. In 1715, these three built a school for boys, in memory of William, and named it 'Chews School' (now Chews House) in High St. South.

(iv) **BLANDINA MARSHE** and her sister, Mary Lockington, provided the 'Ladies Lodge' Almshouses, Church St., for 'six poor maiden gentlewomen' in 1734. Blandina never married.

Refs: L.M. ROWE (1972); J. LYNN (FAMILY TREE); HENRY (1981)

# CHEW'S HOUSE

*(Built 1715)*

*Chew's House*

This distinctive two-storey building was built as the Chew Grammar School in 1715 – hence the two sculptures of charity children, in blue coat uniforms, standing over the fine entrance. Like the Cart Almshouses next door, Chew's House is built well above street level, giving it a dominating appearance, with a set of stone steps for access. Above the high front is an interesting 'turret cupola' (a small tower with domed roof). The house is named after William Chew.

The plaque on the front of Chew's House reads:

> This School was erected
> and ENDOWED by
> MRS. FRANCES ASHTON
> MRS. JANE CART and
> MR. THOMAS AYNSCOMBE
> *Heirs at Law to* WM. CHEW esq
> *ANNO DOM 1715*

### WILLIAM CHEW

William Chew died in 1712 without a wife or children and without leaving a will. However, he had taken a great interest in the plight of poor boys and had for many years provided clothing for them. He'd also expressed the intention of establishing a free school in Dunstable. Consequently, when William Chew's estate (about 28,000 pounds) passed on to his two sisters and nephew — Frances Ashton, Jane Cart and Thomas Aynscombe — they arranged for a schoolhouse to be built in his name (See: The Chew Family Tree.)

### THE CHEW TRUST

The three founders set up a group of Trustees to run the school and issued a detailed set of Rules and Orders for the Trustees and School to follow. The first agreement, or 'Settlement', containing these instructions was in 1724, the second was in 1727. The Trustees, for example, were required to meet at certain times in specific places; to receive the rents from the Charity's tenants; to select the boys; to inspect and audit the accounts; to check the management and general running of the School, etc.

### THE SCHOOL RULES

The Founders were particularly concerned that the School should be closely connected with the Church of England: only certain people could be accepted as Trustees, Masters or Pupils. To be eligible as a pupil: a boy had to be over seven years old, born in wedlock, and able to read from the New Testament, plus his parents must have regularly attended services at their Parish Church for at least two years prior to application. Only one boy from a family could attend the school at any one time and each boy had to leave at the age of 14 years.

Refs: HENRY (1981); L.M. ROWE (1972); J. LUNN (in DBG 1965)

The school curriculum consisted of reading, spelling, writing and arithmetic. The hours were:
Summer: 7.00-11.00 a.m. & 1.00-5.00 p.m.
Winter: 8.00-11.00 a.m. & 1.00-4.00 p.m.
The Master was required to take the boys to Divine Service at the Priory Church every Sunday and holiday, for which a special pew was reserved.

At first, the boys were not expected to take time off for holidays, apart from two weeks at harvest time to help in the fields (the origin of school summer holidays). Later, in 1791, the Trustees allowed the boys to have four weeks at Harvest time and one week at Easter and Whitsun.

### The Ashton and Cart Wills

Both Frances Ashton and Jane Cart left provision in their wills (1727 & 1736) for ex-pupils to receive money for apprenticeships, including clothing, and even to set up in business. These grants were available for boys aged 14 years who had been at Chews School for three years or more.

### The School Expansion

During the second half of the 18th century, the Trustees found it difficult to pay the running costs but the School managed to survive, and even continued to supply free clothing until 1888.

After the 1870 Education Act, the Trustees drew up a new scheme for the School in 1880 which included plans to increase the size to 100 boys and to change the curriculum to that of a Grammar School, with an external examiner. Consequently, the land next to Chew's House was purchased and a new school building was begun in 1883. (This building is now The Little Theatre, see 18).

In 1888, however, the Ashton Grammar School opened in High St. North which also offered a number of free scholarships. The Chew's School Governors therefore decided to change their scheme and to make provision for educating girls. The Beds C.C. considered this move unnecessary, though, because Luton already had a new Girls Grammar School.

Refs: J. LUNN (in DBG 1965); L.M. ROWE (1972)

### The School's Closure

After many debates, in 1905 the Chew's School eventually closed completely and the governors decided, in 1910, that the Charity funds should be used for just local scholarships and apprenticeships, but still keeping to the Founders' wish that only Church of England members should benefit. Chew's Grants are still available under these terms.

### Chew's House Today

Chew's House is now used by several clubs and societies, e.g. the Dunstable Art Club. It is also used as a meeting place when Exchange Visits take place with people from Dunstable's 'Twin Towns' of Porz in Germany and Brive in France.

### The Exchange Visits

Since the 1950s, there have been annual exchange visits in which groups of young people from Dunstable go to a 'Twin Town' in another country for two weeks to stay in family homes and learn about their way of life. These host families then each send their son or daughter to stay in the home of their visitor's family in Dunstable. This simple swapping arrangement means that the cost is minimal since the organisation is provided for free by volunteers on the Youth Exchange committee. Any local youngster in South Beds between 14 and 18 years of age can take part.

Dunstable International Twinning Association (DITA), also arranges visits to and from the twin towns, especially for adults. DITA is mainly organised by the Dunstable Rep (see 18) and is supported by several organisations (e.g. the Tennis Club) which help with activities and trips (e.g. to London and Cambridge.).

Dunstable has two Twin Towns: Brive in France (Full name 'Brive-la-Gaillard'), and Porz in Germany. (NB Two roads in Dunstable are named after these towns: Brive Road on the Downside Estate, and Porz Avenue off Boscombe Road.)

It is appropriate that, at this point, another foreign town is mentioned – that of Dunstable in the USA.

# DUNSTABLE (USA)

Dunstable (USA) is in the state of Massachusetts and it is about 25 miles south of Manchester, 20 miles north-west of Bedford, and in the County of Middlesex!

## Early Dunstable (USA)

Dunstable (USA) is so named because, in the 17th century, a group of people left Dunstable (UK) and emigrated to America where they founded a settlement and named it after their home town.

Very little is known about the early settlers, but a man named Edward Tyng and his wife Mary are believed to have been among them. The date of emigration is also unknown, although it was probably during the troubled times of King Charles I (1625-49) or the time of the English Civil War (1650-59). Some believe that the first settlers arrived in 1630, but Dunstable (USA) today recognises 1673 as the year that it was founded.

## Today's Dunstable (USA)

Dunstable (USA) is on a Cross Roads but it is otherwise very different from Dunstable (UK): the population is only 1,895 (in 1986) and all properties have at least one acre of land. There are no shops in Dunstable (USA), nor are there any bars or hotels. The few public buildings include a white wooden church, a Town Hall, and a library.

The nearest town to Dunstable (USA) is Lowell, about 10 miles away, where the main industry is electronics (e.g. Wang are based there). Some people in Dunstable (USA) work in Lowell, commuting along Route 495, where they also get their local newspaper — the 'Lowell Sun'! Others work in Boston, about 55 miles to the south-west.

## Links with America

Dunstable (UK) has made contact with its American namesake on several occasions. In 1973 the Mayor of Dunstable, Ald. William Farbon, visited Dunstable (USA) and took gifts, including: a collection of Roman remains (pottery, coins, etc.) prepared by the Manshead Archaeological Society; a colour photograph album of Dunstable provided by Vauxhall; and a Downside School Scrapbook of interesting drawings, essays, etc. about Dunstable.

# THE LITTLE THEATRE

*(Built 1883)*

*Little Theatre*

This was originally built as an extension of Chew's School, in 1883, by the Trustees of the Chew's Funds. (The Chew's School was next door in Chew's House.) The building therefore had large windows to light up the school classrooms. After being used as a Public Library for almost 30 years, most of the windows were boarded up and the amateur theatre group moved in. The Foundation Stone can still be seen in the middle of the front section of the building.

## The Library

After Chew's School closed, this building was eventually taken over, on 24 October 1938, by the Dunstable Branch of the Bedfordshire County Library. (It states in the Deeds, written by the Chew's Trustees, that the premises should be used for educational purposes.)

Before moving into this building, the public library branch had been housed first in the old Town Hall (1925-27) and then in the Kingsbury Barn (1927-34) – now the Norman King P.H. – along with the Dunstable Museum (see 98). The town was also served by the County Library Van which made periodical calls in the Market Place.

The old school building was ideal for the library since it was detached with large windows in three of the four walls, which ensured plenty of natural light. The figured oak panelling and the polished oak furniture gave the rooms a certain dignity which suited the quiet mood of the library.

In its heyday, there were two main rooms well stocked with books: the Lending Library with a Children's Corner (nick-named "Lilliput Library" because of its miniature chairs and table for the little people), and the Reference Library with a good Local Collection. The place was a pleasure to work in (unlike today's library which can be impossible to study in!). The library was moved to new premises in the N.E. Quadrant in the 1960s.

## The Theatre

After the library moved out, the building was taken over by the Dunstable Repertory Company – the 'Rep'. This amateur theatre group had previously used the old Town Hall, until it was demolished. The large windows were then boarded up and the interior was converted into a small theatre – with stage, seating, dressings rooms, bar, etc.

It was officially opened in October 1968 as 'The Little Theatre' by the well-known actor Bernard Bresslaw. Since then, the Rep have staged many performances, averaging six plays per season.

## The First Recorded Play in England

It is fitting to orate here that Dunstable had the distinction of being the earliest recorded place where a play was performed in England!

This play was acted at Dunstable, very early in the 12th century, at a School in the newly founded town. (The exact location of this School is unknown but it is assumed to have been near to the Priory, which was still being built.) The performance was of the type known as a 'miracle play' and it was about the story of St. Katherine who was martyred on a wheel.

The reason that the play was recorded is in itself a drama because the costumes used by the actors were accidentally destroyed in a fire! These garments had been borrowed by the School Master who had organised the event, Geoffrey of Gorham, from St. Albans Abbey — where the details of this unfortunate incident were duly noted for posterity!

The play must have taken place before 1119 since, despite what happened, Geoffrey of Gorham later became Abbot of St. Albans from 1119 to 1146. In fact, Geoffrey would have been at St. Albans sooner if he'd arrived in time (from his native France) to accept an invitation from Abbott Richard to run a St. Albans School — it was because Geoffrey turned up late that he was temporarily posted to Dunstable in the first place!

Ref:VCH (1904); MANDER (1953) pp 81-3;

# SITE OF THE OLD WORKHOUSE

The old Dunstable Workshouse was on the site of the terraced row, north of the White Swan, between today's Kebab House and the Barber's Shop. It closed in 1836 and the paupers were sent to the Workhouse in Luton. After that the premises were sold and since then there have been a variety of shops and residences here.[i]

## The Poor and the Priory (12th-16th Cs)

Monasteries were reputed to care for the poor, so people came into the town from the 12th century onwards — hoping to be given food and clothing. The Priory, however, frequently had financial difficulties and often could not afford to be generous. Local businessmen sometimes came to the rescue, either by donating money and gifts to the Priory or by specifying how the poor should be helped and making provisions.

## The Poor and the Parish (16th-19th Cs)

When the monasteries were closed, in the 16th century, the parish churches continued to be an important source of help for the poor. Local parishioners were encouraged to place a few pence into the 'poor men's' box in their church. The government policy at this time was little more than to encourage this 'almsgiving' on Sundays. It was also official policy to discourage begging — by whipping if necessary. By the end of the 16th century, after official 'overseers' (collectors) had been appointed, it became law that each parish was responsible for all the sick and poor, both young and old. Locally, poor children had to make pillow-lace in order to raise money.[ii]

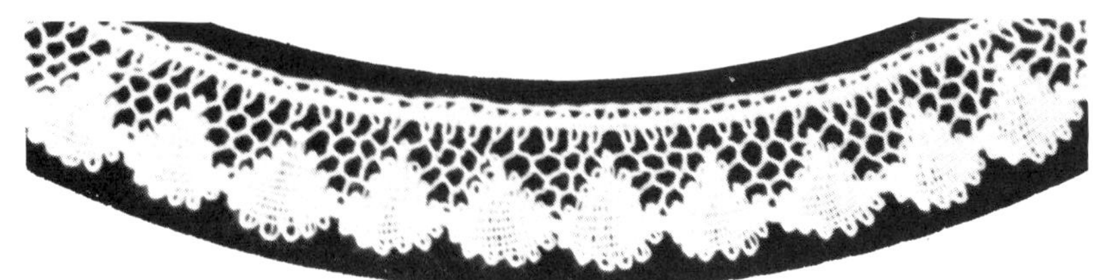

Refs: i SMITH (1904); ii GODBER (1969)

## The Poor and the Charities

In Dunstable, some poor people benefitted from wealthy families who were connected with the town, especially the Marshe, Chew, Cart and Ashton families. (See the Chew Family Tree, and 16 & 17).

## The Workhouse

By the early 19th century, almost every parish had a small workhouse for poor people. Unfortunately, nearly every workhouse was in a very bad condition and Dunstable's was no exception. Families were usually split up on admission, women and children were made to work hard, diseases were rampant, and many people died soon after they entered. Life was often deliberately made difficult in order to discourage wasters, since many people thought that the poor were simply lazy and so deserved harsh treatment (as some people still believe today!). The workhouse was therefore a last resort and only the really desperate would go there: destitute women with children, or the old or sick simply wanting a place to die.[i] W.G. Smith described the Dunstable Workhouse as being 'a comfortless and dilapidated structure of fourteen rooms'.[ii] Work was organised by the parish, e.g. digging in the chalk pits to make whiting.

## The Poor Law Act

The Poor Law Act of 1834 was an attempt at improving the workhouse system: the parishes were grouped together into 'unions' in the hope that these larger bodies would be more efficient by running much larger workhouses. But, as Dickens described in 'Oliver Twist', the conditions in the Victorian workhouses could still be very bad.

It was as a result of this Act that the Dunstable Workhouse was abolished in 1836. Under the new legislation, Dunstable was included in the Luton Union of Workhouses (despite attempting to become a separate Union), which is why the 42 paupers were transferred there.[iii]

Refs: i CURRIE (1982) pp. 36-7; ii SMITH (1904) p.185; iii GODBER (1969)

20

# THE WHITE SWAN

*(17th Century)*

*The White Swan*

## The White Swan

This attractive public house dates from at least the 17th century. It has undergone major internal alterations in recent years, mainly in the form of combining the separate ground-floor rooms into one large bar area (as is the current fashion). The pub has, however, managed to retain its traditional oak-beamed charm. It is affectionately known by some locals as 'The Dirty Duck'.

## Early History

The White Swan building existed in the 17th century and there is even evidence of 16th century timber framing inside. (A pub called 'The Falcon' was recorded in 1542 which may have been in the same place.)[i] In the 17th century, this inn was owned by the Fossey family. They were well known locally and had their own pew in the Priory Church. At that time, the inn was known as the 'Two Black Boys' but it was called 'The Swan' by the second half of the 18th century, (in 1780 George Fossey was recorded as being 'at the Swanne'). In the 19th century, the inn was taken over by another long-running family called the Gilberts (whose name could be traced back over three hundred years).[ii]

N.B. There is no known connection between the current name of the pub and the Swan Jewel found in the Old Friary Field (see 25).

*The White Swan Pub Sign*

Refs: i EVANS (1985) p. 93; ii WOODCOCK (1950)

# CHARLIE COLE'S BICYCLE SHOP

*Charlie Cole's Shop*

In March 1985 Charlie Cole's shop moved from 20 High St. North, where it had been for over 50 years, to the present premises. Before the bicycle shop moved in, this was 'Design 99', a shoe shop managed by Mrs Heather Benson (the author's mother). This row of shops was originally built in the 19th century but they have undergone many alterations since then. The Penny Farthing bicycle, which was a familiar landmark in High St. North, is now painted white above Charlie Cole's new shop.

### Charlie Cole

Charlie Cole was born in 1900 and had dedicated his life to racing and selling bicycles. His first shop was at 36 West St. In June 1970, aged 70, he won two classic races for Veteran Cyclists: a 30 mile race at the National Championships and a 25 mile time trial on the Isle of Man. In 1985, he celebrated 60 years in business and was still cycling at the age of 85!

# SITE OF WORTHINGTON G. SMITH'S COTTAGE

*(now The Priory Garage)*

Directly opposite Charlie Cole's Bicycle Shop is The Priory Service Station, at 142 High St. South. On this site stood 'Hawthorn Cottage' the home of Worthington G. Smith, the archaeologist, historian, biologist, illustrator and writer. The cottage was demolished in 1959 and this whole area, including the Brittany Court shops and flats, was redeveloped in the 1960s. NB. There is a 'Zebra' pedestrian crossing, on the busy High Street, a few yards to the north of Charlie Cole's and the Priory Garage.

## Worthington G. Smith

Worthington George Smith is known locally today as the author of the book 'Dunstable: Its History and Surroundings', published in 1904. In 1980 this fascinating book was issued again after being out of print for many years, thus making it available once more. Worthington G. Smith was one of the most talented personalities ever connected with Dunstable, although few people would know the full extent of his abilities and contributions. For these reasons, his biography (based on the research of James Dyer) is given here in some detail.

## Early Life

Worthington George Smith was born on 23 March 1835 at 19 Aske St., Shoreditch, London. His father, George Smith, came from Gaddesden Row (Herts.); his mother, Sarah Worthington, came from Lexton (Notts.). He grew up, an only child, in Shoreditch but visited his grandparents frequently at Gaddesden from where he learned about Dunstable's Priory Church and its antiquities.

## Apprenticeship

When he left St. John's Parochial School, W.G. Smith became an apprentice to Mr. A.E. Johnson, an architect of Buckingham Street, Strand, London. Later, when Mr. Johnson emigrated to Australia, he transferred to Sir Horace Jones. He studied the classical tradition of architecture which involved making many drawings of Greek and Roman sculpture in the British Museum.

### First Work

W.G. Smith's career began as a designer of ecclesiastical furniture for the Roman Catholic Church. His commissions included those of Cardinal Wiseman and Pope Pius IX. This work also brought him into contact wth the famous wood-engraver Orlando Jewitt from whom he learned much about architectural and archaeological drawing.

### Marriage

On the 24 April 1856, aged 21, Worthington Smith married Henrietta White of Dunstable. Over the next two years he won several prizes for architectural designs and he also produced many illustrations, including: Sir Gilbert Scott's restoration of Westminster Abbey, the new Law Courts, the restored interior of Cologne Cathedral, the interior of Worcester Cathedral, and many more. He also began to study fungi.

### Book Illustration and Writing

In 1858, W.G. Smith abandoned architecture in favour of book illustration using wood-engraving and lithography. His earlier meticulous studies of buildings gave way to botanical illustration. (He was later criticised for not changing his style: E.C. Large claimed that his drawing of a tomato 'looked exactly like an ornament off a wrought iron gate'!) In 1865, the Royal Horticultural Society awarded Worthington Smith the Banksian Gold Medal for his coloured plant drawings. In 1867, aged 32, Worthington published his first book, 'Mushrooms and Toadstools: How To Distinguish Poisonous Fungi'. In order to research this subject, he ate samples of each and noted the effects — the ones that made him most ill he labelled as very poisonous! (This technique is not recommended.)
The book was very popular and it soon reached a second edition. Other botanical books and more horticultural awards followed this. In 1869, Smith was making regular contributions to many publications, including: 'The Journal of Horticulture', 'The Gardeners Chronicle' and 'The Florist and Pomologist'. (Pomology is the study of fruit-growing.)

### Family

In May 1872, Henrietta bore her first child, George Berthold, but he died after less than a year. Later, though, three other children were born: Arthur, Edith and Edward. Arthur eventually became a pioneer of photo-micrography and a successful commercial photographer.

### The Potato Blight

In 1875, the Knightian Gold Medal was presented to W.G. Smith by the Royal Horticultural Society for his research into the potato fungus. This was particularly important then because potato crops were annually being ruined by an unknown infection. It was discovered soon after, in fact, that Smith's enthusiasm had led him to be too casual in his experiments and he had jumped to the wrong conclusion about the cause of the blight. A German professor, de Bary, discovered the real cause. However, Smith's 'cure' (i.e. burning the potato tops rather than letting them rot in the fields) was still effective, even if it was for the wrong reasons. He continued, therefore, to be hailed as the man who solved the potato blight mystery.

### Archaeology

Worthington's special interest in archaeology seems to have developed at the age of 43, in 1878, when he discovered Old Stone Age flint tools on Stoke Newington Common, London. In that year he presented a paper on his discoveries to the Anthropological Institute. Later he wrote several articles based on his research in the valleys of the Lea, Thames, Brent, Axe, and Ouse.

### The Move to Dunstable

During late 1884, Worthington developed heart trouble and was advised by his doctor to live in the country. Henrietta suggested her home town of Dunstable. By a curious twist of fate, on the first day that they went to look for a new home, Worthington found a Stone Age flint implement whilst walking down a road in Dunstable. (NB This is not meant to imply that the 19th century Dunstablians were still primitive!) Consequently, in 1885, when Worthington was 50, they came to live in Dunstable.

### Archaeology and Botany

Worthington continued to illustrate 'The Gardeners Chronicle' and other publications whilst developing his interest in archaeology. He illustrated Dr. Stevens' two volumes of 'British Fungi' and also the article on fungi in the Encyclopaedia Britannica (9th Edition) as well as the section on Bedfordshire in later editions.

### Worthington's Lectures

In 1887, two almost flattened burial mounds were dug into by a plough on the Downs, revealing the bones of two human skeletons. In December of that year, Smith gave a lecture on this in Dunstable which was enthusiastically received. He soon became well-known for his interesting style of presentation.

In 1888, Smith gave a lecture on 'Prehistoric Mill-Stones, The Mill-Stones of Ancient Dunstable and of The Bible'. During this many local querns or hand-mills were demonstrated (having been brought by horse and cart since they were heavy) and two ladies from the audience were invited to grind wheat in one. Later in the lecture, Smith cut a similarly prepared loaf, using a flint knife, and gave slices to the audience.

One of Worthingtons's strangest lectures was on 'The Music and Musical Instruments of the Barbarians' during which his younger son, Edward, and a Miss Marie Tacagni played music taken from performances by Australian Aborigines. The audience were asked to imagine that they were sitting on Dunstable Downs, listening to this, two thousand years ago!

### Local Archaeology

During these years, the tall figure of Smith could be seen on long walks around the local countryside. In particular, he kept a watchful eye on the brickpits at Gaddesden Row, Whipsnade, Caddington and Round Green, in the hope of finding prehistoric flint implements.

### The Caddington Neolithic Tools

In March 1890, aged 55, Smith's patient searching was rewarded by the discovery of many flint tools and chippings in a Caddington pit. About a ton of these were collected over the next few years and they were thought to be around 120,000 years old. (NB The best samples are now in the British Museum).

### Maiden Bower

In 1891, he discovered the series of ditches filled with bones to the north-west of Maiden Bower. These have since been interpreted as a causewayed camp of the New Stone Age, about 5,000 years old.

### Natural History Museum

In 1893, Smith wrote and illuminated the guidebook describing his oil-paintings of Sowerby's models of fungi, which are at the Natural History Museum in London.

### Man The Primaeval Savage

In 1894, Smith's most famous archaeological work, 'Man The Primaeval Savage', was published. It was mainly written on the train as he travelled daily between Dunstable and London. Later in the same year, Worthington and Henrietta left Dunstable for a short while to take a rest in Shrewsbury and the Welsh Marches. Here he spent much of his time sketching the countryside and discovering archaeological remains. This resulted in his five volume work, 'Sketches in Wales and the Borderland'. (Some rest!)

### Discovery of The Dunstable Charter

In 1899, Worthington Smith was asked by the town court to help out in a legal case between Major Brown and the local council, over drainage. This may sound like a mundane issue, but it actually led to a very important outcome. Smith was asked to find any ancient grant to the town which may have been recorded in an old charter. Immediately, he produced a copy of the Charter of Henry III taken from 'Monasticon Anglicanum'! This, however, was not acceptable as legal evidence, so he was asked to find the original.

After a fruitless search in the British Museum's Department of Manuscripts, he eventually found the Charter of Henry III at the Public Record Office. More important that this, though, he also came across the original Charter of Henry I, Son of William the Conqueror, which was granted 'to the Church of the Blessed Peter at Dunestapel'. This unexpected find was written in 1132 and, even today, is the most important document ever discovered on the history of Dunstable. (The drainage, however, still causes problems!)

### The Royal Pension

In 1902, aged 67 years, W.G. Smith was awarded a Civil List Pension by the Monarch of fifty-two pounds per year. This was granted on the advice of the Prime Minister in 'consideration of his services to archaeology and botanical illustration'. This money, along with that from his illustrations, provided a basic income. However, Smith was never a rich person: he never sold any of his antiques and he made it quite clear that he was not interested in making money.

### The First Freeman of The Borough

On Monday 9 November 1903, the citizens of Dunstable conferred the First Honorary Freedom of the Borough upon Worthington G. Smith. This was presented by the Mayor, Alderman C. Boskett, at the Town Hall.

### Dunstable: Its History and Surroundings

1904 was the year that the well-known guide book 'Dunstable: Its History and Surroundings' was published. It was an immediate success and many homes contained a copy (including that of the King!). By this time, Worthington G. Smith was well-known and his home often resembled a doctor's waiting room where people queued to have their 'finds' identified. On 24 April 1906, Worthington and Henrietta celebrated their 50th wedding anniversary. He was 71 then but was still working hard. That year he discovered two more Paleolithic sites: one at Gaddesden Row brick-pits, and the other at Round Green in Luton. He thought nothing of walking to both these in a single day – a round trip of about 20 miles!

### More Awards; More Illustrations

In 1907, he was awarded the Veitchian Gold Medal of the Royal Horticultural Society for his eminent services to horticulture. In the same year he finished what he considered to be his most important work, which had taken seventeen years to complete : 'Synopsis of British Basidiomycetes'. (NB Basidiomycetes are one of 4 classes of fungi which includes: mushrooms, puff-balls, stink-horns, etc.) This work was published by the Trustees of the British Museum and, unlike his other books, is a purely scientific work. In 1910, he prepared two large coloured sheets of Edible and Poisonous Fungi for the public gallery of the Natural History Museum. (It was fortunate that he survived the research!

### Other Interests

W.G. Smith had many other interests, too numerous to detail here, one of which was psychic research. He often carried this out with his friend the Rev. C. Drayton Thomas, such as when they investigated the supposedly haunted Half Moon House in High Street South.

### Last Works

Worthington's last main work was an article in the anthropological journal 'Man', in 1912, entitled 'Flint Flakes of the Tertiary and Secondary Age, with Reference to the Dunstable District'.

On 23 June 1917 Henrietta died, during a brief illness, after 61 years of marriage. Worthington continued his work for a short time but soon caught a bad chill while investigating the damage caused by a Zeppelin torpedo. He never recovered and died, at the age of 82 years, on Saturday 27 October 1917 – only four months after his wife.

Worthington G. Smith was a very popular but modest man. He requested that there should be no flowers or black-bordered stationery for his funeral. His cortege was followed by the Mayor and Corporation of Dunstable and many friends. Worthington was laid to rest beside his wife Henrietta and his first son, George, near the centre of the Dunstable Cemetery in West Street. (The tombstone can still be seen there).

## Postscript

Today, Worthington G. Smith generally has a high reputation among local historians, mainly because of his enthusiastic approach and the interest he created in the Dunstable district. By today's standards, Smith's work can be lacking in scientific discipline – sometimes being vague and inaccurate (e.g. in recording the location of finds) and rushing into wrong conclusions. His imagination was both a strength and a weakness: it helped him to put together, and to explain to others, the possibilities of history but the lack of distinction between supposition and evidence can limit the value of some of his writings. To be fair, Worthington Smith lived at a time when there was much sentimentality (e.g. the concept of 'primitive man' as a 'noble savage') and, of course, he didn't have the benefits of our technical achievements or our comprehension of scientific method. Assessment of W.G. Smith's contribution is therefore difficult to make but, whatever the reservations, he certainly helped to prepare the way for later writers and illustrators to extend and improve our knowledge and understanding.

Apart from the Honours awarded to Worthington G. Smith in his lifetime, Dunstable has not yet provided any tangible monument to the memory of this important man. Perhaps in the near future there will be some form of commemoration, as a statue or plaque or suitable dedication.

Refs: DYER (1978) pp. 141-179; DYER (1967) pp. 91-6; BAGSHAWE (1967) pp. 73-9.

# OLD CARPENTERS ARMS

The building with the Carpenters Arms on the front was recorded as being a public house during the 19th century and into the 1920s. By the Second World War, however, this had ceased to be a pub and it was converted into a private residence — as it is today.

## The Arms

This was probably not originally a pub in the usual sense but an example of a house owned by a tradesman who sometimes sold beer in addition to his main work. The owner, therefore, would have been a carpenter who also brewed beer. For this reason, the 'Carpenters Arms' shield, which can be seen on the front of the building, is a much later embellishment, i.e. this would have been a convenient sign which simply referred to a carpenter who sold beer, rather than a bona-fide member of the Trades Institution. Such origins are not uncommon, hence similar names such as 'The Blacksmiths Arms' which earlier this century was in West Street and owned by a blacksmith and whitesmith, named Costin, who was also a brewer. People would sit in the hallway of his house, with the door shut, and quietly sip their pints.

# PETROPOLIS HOUSE

*(Old Police Station, built 1930)*

*Petropolis House*

This grand looking red brick building, on the corner of Friars Walk, was purpose built in 1930 as a Police Station to replace the original Station in Icknield Street, off West Street (see 42). When the present Police Station (see 36) was built in West Street in the mid-1970s, these premises were bought by a Petrol company and converted into offices – hence the name.

## Petropolis House

Today, the Petropolis House contains the offices of the Motoring Centres division of Total Oil Great Britain Ltd., whose Registered Office is at 33 Cavendish Square, London W1.

## Dunstable's 2nd Police Station

The High Street South Police Station was opened in 1930 as a replacement for the Station in Icknield Street (see 42). In 1932, the Headquarters of the Luton Division of the County Police were transferred here from Luton. The first Police Inspector at High St. South was Insp. Albert H. Weedon who had joined the Force in February 1914. He moved from the old Icknield Street premises to live in the Inspector's accommodation, on the first floor of the Station. By 1933, Supt. Clark was also living in the Police House and Insp. James F. Whitehorn was running the Police Station. Insp. Weedon retired from the Force in 1939. By 1952, Chief Inspector J.H. Sandell and Insp. W. John were posted here.

## 'Gunstable'

In March 1968, the local people were invited to hand in any guns to this Police station. (There were still firearms around that had been obtained during the last World War and it became illegal to possess them without a proper certificate.) Everyone was assured that there would be 'no questions asked', so one person handed in a machine-gun![i]

## Friars Walk

The road next to Petropolis House is named Friars Walk, after the Friary which used to be in Friary Field on the right (north) side of it. This is not an old road, however, but a modern route developed in the mid 1930s. Until then there was an 18th century house on this site called 'Avon Lodge' which belonged to Richard Blackwell, a straw hat manufacturer who had workshops behind his home. The Blackwell family straw business in Dunstable dated from the late 1830s. Richard Blackwell retired in about 1900 and died during the First World War.

Refs: i TURVEY (1977) p. xi

# THE FRIARS

*The Friars*

## The Friars

The Friars is the building on the corner of Friars Walk and High St. South, at the southern end of The Square. It was named after the Friary which was in this area between the 13th and 16th centuries. The actual site of the main Friary buildings is now covered by the Thames Industrial Estate and the modern houses off Bullpond Lane. Since 1985, the Friars has been the home of the Dunstable Town Council who took it over from the 'Air Call' company (now based in Houghton Regis). Previously, this was the private residence of various wealthy local people.

## The Dunstable Borough Council (1864-1974)

Dunstable received its Borough status, by a Royal Charter issued from Queen Victoria, in December 1864 and elected 12 Councillors, 3 Aldermen and Mayor in March 1865 to form the first Borough Council. In October 1870 the Borough Council bought the Manor of Dunstable from Queen Victoria, the 'Lady of the Manor', for £750. This included the rights to collect Market Tolls, rents and other forms of income since the Council were then the 'Lords of the Manor'. If Dunstable hadn't been a Borough Council then it would probably have become part of Luton, which many Dunstablians didn't want. The group of businessmen who collected the petition (with over 500 signatures) and arranged for the Charter of Incorporation not only kept Dunstable separate from Luton but also helped the Borough financially through their astute dealings — especially, of course, by buying the rights of the Manor.

The Borough Council existed until 1975 when, due to Local Government reorganisation, Dunstable came under the control of South Beds District Council (SBDC). The tradition of Mayor was then continued by a group of 'Dunstable Charter Trustees'.

## The new Town Council (since 1985)

On 1st April 1985, however, Dunstable formed a Parish ('Town') Council in order to try to re-establish a Town identity while still being influenced by the District and County Councils on more general matters. The Mayor's role became official once again and the Town Council leased The Friars to house the Committee Room, for Council meetings, and the Mayor's Chamber, plus offices for the Town Clerk and clerical support.

In the Mayor's Room there are many items of interest including Worthington G. Smith's drawings (e.g. 'The Market Place' 1885) and transcripts (e.g. the Charters given to Dunstable by Henry I and Henry III), and there are also old photographs (e.g. by Chas Smy). In the large Committee Room, where Council and Committee meetings take place, there is a permanent exhibition of the 'Dunstable in Detail' line drawings.

The SBDC is still responsible for maintaining most of the town's services and amenities (including housing, roads, waste-disposal) so the new town Council is able to concentrate on improving Dunstable for inhabitants and visitors (e.g. by organising cultural and recreational activities). A particular interest is the promotion of tourism in Dunstable for which a special Working Party was established in 1986.

## The Friars

Nothing is known about the early life of The Friars but it was probably built on the site of an older house (Totternhoe stone is in the basement). The name of The Friars only dates from the beginning of this century: in the last century it was called 'Queensborough House' after a local family of that name. The modern name derives from the nearby site of the Friary.

### The Friary

The Friars who settled on this site in 1259 were Dominicans. They were actively supported by King Henry III (who reigned 1216-72) and his wife, Queen Eleanor, but the members of the Priory bitterly resented their arrival into Dunstable. There were quarrels and even fights between the two groups. On one occasion, the Prior and a Canon broke into the Friary buildings, with several townsmen, and assaulted and wounded three Friars – one was thrown into the pond and another two were put in prison!

The main reason why the Priory occupants didn't like the Friars was because they were receiving gifts from some of the local people. Previously, of course, the Priory had received all the 'Gifts to God' and so they felt that they were losing out. Some townspeople, however, preferred the Friars because they didn't own much – only their own house – and they didn't try to interfere with the running of the town. The Friars were poor, whereas the Canons were comfortable, so the Friars tended to receive more sympathy and help.

### The Dissolution

After struggling for many years, the Friary was eventually closed down in 1538 at the beginning of the Dissolution, when all religious houses were closed by Henry VIII. It is not known what happened to the Friars after that except that they did not receive a pension, whereas those in the Priory did. The Friary was pulled down and used as building material elsewhere, as happened with most of the Priory buildings. (It was probably originally constructed in wood and then later rebuilt in Totternhoe stone). There was apparently a 'Great Orchard' near the Friary which gradually disappeared until only the Friary Field remained. The Friary Field survived for about four centuries – until the recent housing estate was built on it.

### The Friary Field

The Manshead Archaeological Society excavated the Friary Field during the 1960s and 1970s, just before the houses were erected. There were many interesting finds including a well preserved medieval 'Beehive' oven.

### The Swan Jewel

The most famous discovery was made on 16 July 1965 by Maxene Miller, of the Manshead Archaeological Society, who found a medieval Swan brooch made of solid gold covered in white enamel feathers with black enamel eyes and feet. The Swan Jewel is quite small, about 1″ long and 1.5″ high, with a pin and catch on the back so that it could be worn as a brooch. There is also a gold chain attached to a coronet around the Swan's neck, with a gold ring on the other end, which was probably intended as a 'safety chain' in case the catch failed. The Jewel was dated as early 15th century and is very valuable so it is kept in the British Museum, London. It may have been a prize given to a knight during one of the many tournaments which are known to have taken place in Dunstable during the 14th and 15th centuries. There are no records of such a Jewel, however, so its existence in Dunstable is a matter for conjecture: it may have been lost by a knight or nobleman or it may have been left with the Friars for safe-keeping.

NB The story of this find, and the theories about it, is told by Vivienne Evans in the booklet 'The Dunstable Swan Jewel'.

The Friary grounds probably extended right up to the present Square, but the site could not be excavated fully because there were already buildings lining the Square, including the modern three-storey 'Thames House'.

In 1985, while alterations were being made to the ground floor of Thames House (to install the '7-11' take-away food shop), human bones were discovered. They may have been in a burial ground connected with the Friary.

Refs: VCH (1904) pp 395-6; EVANS (1982)

# THE SQUARE

*(site of old Market)*

The Dunstable Square is the piece of land lying along the west side of High St. South, from Friars Walk to the Middle Row. It is shaped, therefore, not like a square but like a triangle with two very long sides. The Square is now only used as a parking space for coaches, taxis and Police cars. For centuries, though, this was a Market Place, a site for Fairs, and a place for Public Meetings.

## THE DUNSTABLE MARKET

### Market Place

In the 13th century, Dunstable market was held in the area of the Square and Middle Row and it was strictly controlled by the Priory, since the Prior was responsible to the King for managing the town.

### The Market Rules

In 1221 a set of rules, 'The Customal', was published by the Priory stating how the market should operate. This was one of the earliest sets of Bye-Laws in England and it included the following:

– no dung heaps near the street or market place
– no pig-sties near the doors of houses
– no slaughterhouse waste in the streets
– all stalls to be cleared away each evening
– no trading to be carried out on the way to market (so the Priory got its commission)
– prices of bread and ale are strictly controlled
– no bulk buying of goods in order to change the retail price set by the Priory.

### Trading

Weekly markets were held on Wednesdays and Saturdays (as today) and the main trading was in wool, corn and hides. The Priory, for example, is recorded as selling some of its produce, including fleeces at 6d each, in 1225-50. The other traders in Dunstable included: blacksmiths, carters, butchers, fishmongers and bakers, plus at least one candlemaker, carpenter, tiler, brewer, poulterer, fruiterer and spicer. There were also many travellers passing through and staying at the various inns and hostelries.

### 16th-17th Centuries

By the 16th century, Dunstable was about the same size as in the 13th century but it was a market town with more emphasis on agriculture. It was also much more dependent on travellers. There were at least ten Inns, three beerhouses and a cookhouse. However, after the Priory closed in 1540, Dunstable declined in importance. During this recessive period, the cottage industries of lace-making and straw-plaiting began to develop.

### 18th Century

During the 18th century, the market was still important but other trades developed outside of the market place, especially those connected with Coaching. Due to its position on the Coaching routes, Dunstable became a town full of inns and stables catering for many travellers.

### 19th Century

By the 19th century, straw-plaiting had become the main industry and many items, e.g. hats and boxes, were bought and sold at Dunstable. The focal point of the market shifted to High St. North where a special plait market was held, with a plait hall inside the Town Hall. (The first part of High St. North became known as 'Market Place'.) When the railways opened in the mid-19th century the coaching stopped and the straw manufacturers started to move to Luton. The Square continued, however, as an agricultural market place.

### 20th Century

In the 20th century Dunstable became increasingly industrialised but the market continued, with livestock still being bought and sold on The Square and market stalls in High St. North.

### The End of an Era

The Cattle Market on the Square closed down on 3rd August 1955, when it moved to Tavistock Street for a short time before finally closing in Dunstable altogether. The Cattle Pens were still visible on The Square in the 1960s but there is nothing to be seen there now. The market stalls have all been moved to the new Market site in the Queensway car park (see 82). The closing of the Cattle Market in 1955 marked the final transition of Dunstable from a market town to an industrial town.

## FAIRS

### Early Fairs

From the 13th century, there were several fairs held in Dunstable, including five main annual fairs:

— Ash Wednesday
— May Fair
— 12th August
— 12th November
— The 'Statute Fair'

The first four were for the sale of cattle, sheep, goats, swine, horses, asses, mules, fruit, vegetables, and other merchandise. It is not known what the origins of the Ash Wednesday and November Fairs were but the May Fair was started by King John (1199-1216) in 1203: he provided a grant and instructed that the fair should be set up on the 10th May and removed on the 12th May. The August Fair was authorised by King Henry I (1100-35) for the feast of St. Peter. All four fairs continued until the first part of this century (the May Fair until 1914).

### The Statute Fair

The fifth fair was the autumn 'Statute Fair' which was for the purpose of hiring servants and labourers in husbandry (animal farming). This fair still continues today in the form of a 'fun fair' known as the 'Statty Fair'. However, it is no longer held on The Square: it was moved in the 1960s because it was holding up the traffic in High St. South. The Statty is now held in the Queensway Car Park.

### Public Meetings

The Square was used as a place for Public Meetings until quite recently. Among the last were two political gatherings: on 2 October 1959 the Prime Minister, the R. Hon. Harold Macmillan, gave his election speech and told everyone, 'You've never had it so good!'; and on 7 October 1964 the Prime Minister, Sir Alec Douglas-Home, also gave an election speech. (It's hard to imagine the Prime Minister giving a speech on Dunstable Square today!)

Refs: VCH 1:371-7; VCH 3:364-7; TURVEY (1977) p.75; EVANS (1980)

# HAT FACTORY MANAGER'S HOUSE

*(18th century)*

*No. 52 High St. South*

The notable late 18th century doorway on The Square, opposite the Priory Gate, was once part of the Manager's house attached to the Stuart, Sons, and Co. straw hat factory. The business did not close down until 1924, making it one of the last hat factories in Dunstable (the last one closing in 1931). In 1926, alterations were made to the building and it was converted from a hat factory into business premises. Today it is one of the offices of W.H. French & Co., Certified Accountants, who are also in Cardiff Rd., Luton.

### The H-Shaped Tree

There is an unusual 'H-shaped tree' (actually two trees joined in the middle) which can be seen through the wide right-hand entrance.

# METHODIST CHURCH

*(Built 1909)*

The present chapel was built in 1909 by Withers and Meredith after the previous two were destroyed by fires. It is constructed in a free Gothic style of brickwork with a tall N.W. steeple. The church was founded by a group of Wesleyan Methodists in 1831.[i]

## The First Wesleyan Followers

John Wesley (1703-91) apparently visited the town in 1758, when according to his Journal, 'the rain continued all the way to Dunstable'. It is not clear whether he preached here but he certainly did at Luton and Sundon, and his followers were very influential in the town. In 1812 one follower, a carpenter named John Darley, opened his shop in Church St. so that people could gather together to sing, pray and read the 'Word of God'. This group then moved to John Fossey's confectionery shop in High St. South. (It was at Fossey's shop that the great 1841 fire started which destroyed 19 buildings on the corner of High St. South and Church St!) The Methodists then used the old Quaker Meeting House in West St. for 10 years.[ii]

## The First Chapel

In 1831 the land on The Square was acquired, where the present chapel is. This land was next to a farm ('Snoxell's Farm') which was then owned by Mr. Goode who was a farmer and a mail contractor. Later, some of the farm buildings and a rick-yard (an enclosure for stacks of hay or corn) were bought from him. The first chapel was built during the 1830s. In 1844 a fire started in the adjoining farm and the Chapel was destroyed. It's not known whether the church was insured, but Mr. Good's property was insured with the Phoenix for £2,000.[iii]

## The Second Chapel

In 1845 the second Chapel was built which was then enlarged, in 1853, by adding an extra wing to accommodate 500 worshippers. By this time, Dunstable had become a separate circuit with two Ministers and 24 local preachers.[iv]

Refs: i PEVSNER (1968) p. 78; ii BROADFOOT, in DBG (1965); iii (ibid); iv (ibid)

*The Methodist Church*

### The School

The extension at the rear housed the Wesleyan Day School which was not, however, denominational or sectarian in its curriculum. There were two departments: the Mixed School run by Mr. R. Parker Graham, and the Infant Department run by Miss M. Anderson. About 450 pupils were attending this school at the turn of the century.[i] (NB In the 1850s a Methodist Mission Chapel was built near the Dunstable North Railway Station. This building eventually became the Waterlow Road Chapel in 1905.) In 1908, the second Chapel on The Square was destroyed by fire.

### The Third Chapel

On 31st May 1909, the Foundation Stone of the present Wesleyan Methodist Chapel was laid and the Church opened later the same year. Today, in addition to being used for worship, the premises are regularly used by many voluntary groups, clubs and societies. The main hall in the rear has a stage and functions such as barn dances and the amateur 'Square Theatre Group' productions are held here.

### Methodist Car Park: Site of Snoxell's Farm

The Car Park next to the Methodist Chapel is the site of Snoxell's Farm which was sold (including 150 acres of land) by auction on 28th June 1893 after the death of the owner, Alfred Oliver (who also owned Kingsbury House and farm). Today, by walking a few yards into the car park, some interesting old buildings can still be seen behind the premises which face the Square. NB The 'Methodist Car Park' is named simply because it is beside the Church – it is actually a Public Car Park. (In fact, all parking in Dunstable is free!)

### Taylor's Lane

The Car Park is possibly the site of 'Taylor's Lane' mentioned in 1542, including property owned by: William Bennett (a barn), Thomas Kyrke, fletcher, i.e. arrow-maker (a garden), William Molte (a garden), Henry Plowright (a garden), and the widow of Robert Milkoo (tenement with garden). Until the 1970s, part of a lane corresponding to this survived off the east side of Bullpond Lane.[ii]

Refs: i SMITH (1904) p. 18; ii BHRS 63,64

# ASHTON SQUARE

*(Site of Chapel Walk & Ashton Street)*

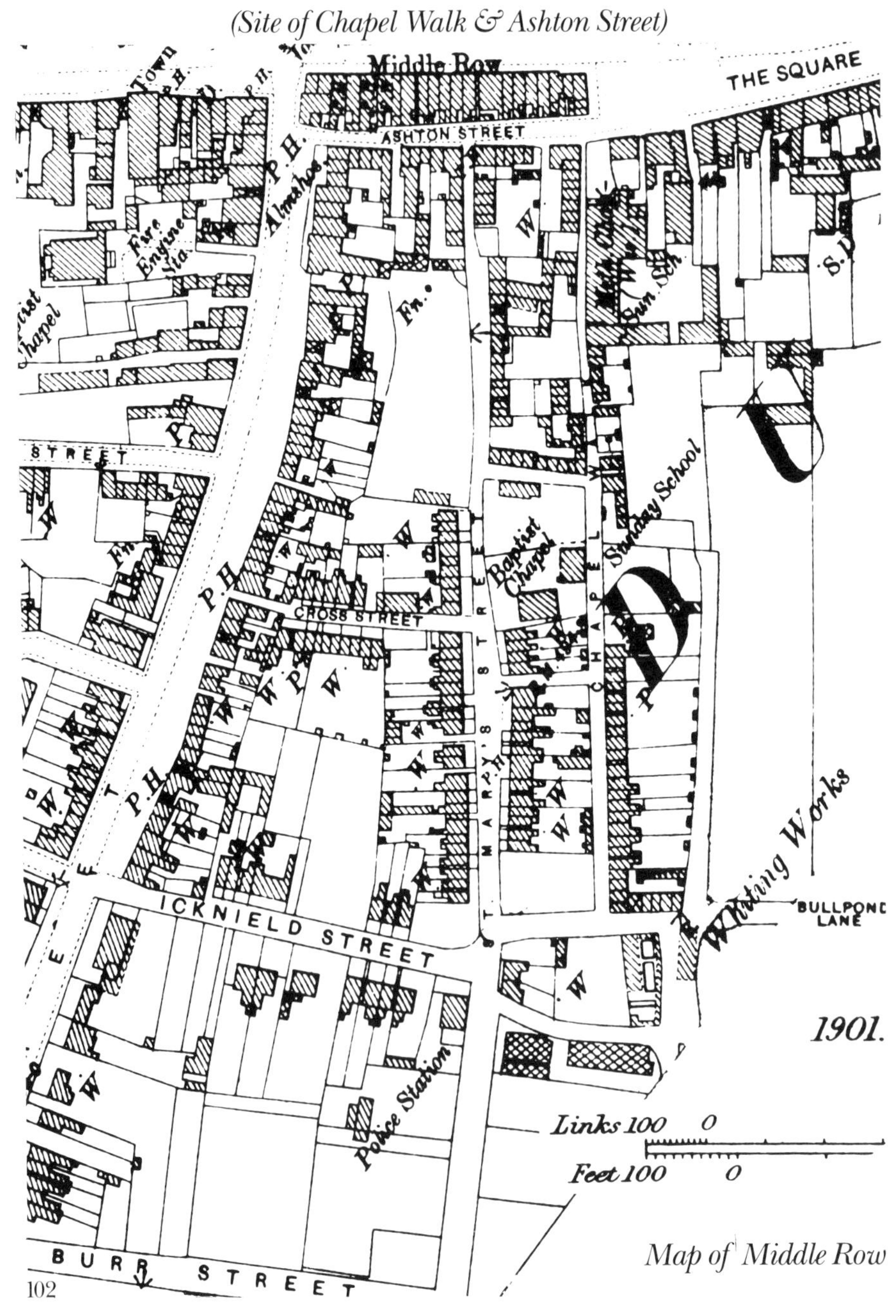


Map of Middle Row

## Ashton Square

Ashton Square is the focus of a modern pedestrian thoroughfare which was developed in the mid-1970s. There are two branches: one running alongside the Methodist Church and another alongside Middle Row.

The path that is next to the Methodist Church used to be called Chapel Walk; the path that is next to Middle Row is the site of a road called Ashton St. There also used to be a road called St. Mary's Street which led westwards from Ashton St., parallel to Chapel Walk.

## Chapel Walk

In the 16th century, this was the site of 'Havewyke Lane' and by the 19th century it was 'Hollowicke Lane'. The name changed to Chapel Lane, and then Chapel Walk, because it led to the Old Baptist Chapel which was first constructed in the 18th century (see 37). Since the 19th century, the path has also led past the Methodist Chapel.

## Ashton Street

This street was named after Frances Ashton whose Alms Houses were at the end, on the corner, in West St. (see 33). Previously it was 'Back Street', because it was behind Middle Row.

## St. Mary's Street

The site of St. Mary's Street is now covered by the new shopping complex. (It was where the coffee bar in Martins Newsagents is now). In the 16th century this was called Pothyn Lane.

In the 19th century the Eight Bells P.H. was on the corner of St. Mary's Street and Ashton St. (at no. 10 Ashton St.) which was demolished in 1958. The name was given to a new pub in Westfield Rd. in July 1958.

Refs: BHRS 63,64

# MIDDLE ROW ALLEY

*Middle Row Alley*

### Middle Row Alley

This old passage through the heart of Middle Row connects Ashton Square with High St. South. It can be thought of as being part of a path which continues eastwards, over the High Street, down Church Walk to the Priory Church. This path also once led westwards, before the modern shops were built, along St. Marys Street to Icknield Street.

Looking down the alley from Ashton Square: on the left (north) side was the Britannia P.H. which was burned at the end of the last century. The building which replaced it was for 50 years (1935-85) occupied by Stott's furniture shop. Stott's is now in Bullpond Lane, a short walk across Chapel Car Park, at the converted warehouse called 'The Friary Furniture Gallery'. On the right (south) side of the alley is Geoff Souster's Menswear Shop. Until recently, this was Buckles' Menswear which was a family business that had been trading in Dunstable since 1923. (Inside are old timber beams).

### W.G. Smith's Illustration

The illustration of Middle Alley corresponds with the same view drawn in 1887 by Worthington G. Smith. In his picture there is a rain-water tank perched on the left wall and two signs: one advertising 'Porter' (a dark-brown bitter beer) which was served at the 'Britannia', and a Notice from the Town Clerk.

NB W.G. Smith illustrated four Dunstable Alleys: Church Alley, Little Alley, and two Middle Row Alleys. The other Middle Row Alley has since been totally changed into the wide passage which leads through Middle Row to the Pedestrian Crossing in High St. South, opposite Gibbs and Dandy's.[i]

## MIDDLE ROW BUILDINGS

### 12th-13th Centuries

The Middle Row was originally part of the market place in Dunstable. By the end of the 12th century there was a collection of workshops and market stalls here.

Refs: i SMITH (1904)

## The First Buildings

During the 13th century, some of the workshops were made more permanent by constructing them in wooden lath and plaster. There were probably goldsmiths and blacksmiths here, also traders with portable barrows. Some records suggest that the Town Prison once stood in Middle Row, where no. 18 is now, being pulled down and rebuilt in 1295. (It was probably the only stone building here at that time.)[i]

## 14th-16th Centuries

During this period the market slowly grew larger: the area became a collection of shops, houses and enclosed paddocks known as 'Middle Rents'. It mainly consisted of two rows of timber-framed buildings, two or three storeys high, built back-to-back.[ii]

## 17th-19th Centuries

Middle Rents catered for visitors to the market and travellers through the town. In the last century, there were at least five pubs and up to six butchers at any one time, with the 'Rose and Crown' (run by James Gilbert) as both! The publicans often had other trades in addition to their pub work, e.g. at the 'Shoulder of Mutton' was Thomas Botterill, a boot and shoe maker; at the 'Swan with Two Necks' was Mary Higgs, a bricklayer![iii]

## 20th Century

During this century the shops on the High St. side have generally survived (with modifications) while the shops on the Ashton Square side tended to close down and become the backs of shops. By the early 1970s Ashton St. was just a rough road between an unsightly Middle Row and a large area of devastated land, which only had the old Methodist Hall and a toilet block left on it. After the Ashton Square development, however, the shops improved their backs and added rear entrances (as they originally had), making this an attractive and interesting shopping area. A good example is Tilley's — the old butcher's with the delicatessen rear!

Refs: i DERBYSHIRE (1882) pp. 80-1; ii BAILEY (1979); iii TRADE DIRECTORIES

# THE SITE OF THE ASHTON ALMSHOUSES

*(The Corner of Ashton Square and West St.)*

## The Ashton Almshouses

In 1715 Frances Ashton had six almshouses built on the corner of Ashton St. (now Ashton Square) and West St. — where the new shops are now. These almshouses were intended, according to Francis Ashton's instructions, for six poor women who were attending church every Sunday and who had been communicants in the Church of England for at least two years (i.e. similar terms to those in Jane Cart's Almshouse instructions — see 16).

## The 'Blues'

Frances Ashton organised a group of Trustees to maintain this Almshouse Charity after her death (in 1727). At first the Trustees paid each almswoman £6 a year to buy 'a gown and petticoat, all of the same colour' and firewood and other necessities. These women, therefore, were dressed in Blue clothes which made them easily recognisable in the town. The Cart Almshouse women were all dressed in Green. According to Lamborn, the groups were known as the 'Blues' and the 'Greens'![i]

## Suitability

The Trustees were responsible for choosing suitable occupants for the Almshouses and they also had the power to remove a woman if she became unsuitable, e.g. through continually failing to attend church!

## The Founding of Ashton School

The Ashton Almshouses Charity eventually had far-reaching effects for Dunstable. Some of the Charity's land was sold in 1858 for over £6000 — far more than that required to maintain the Almshouses. After discussions with the Master of the Rolls and local people it was decided that the extra money should not be given to the almswomen but used to build a Church of England school. As a result, in 1861, plans were drawn up for an elementary school and, in 1864, the Ashton School in Church St. was completed (see. 96).[ii]

Refs: i LAMBORN (1859) p. 137; ii DERBYSHIRE (1882) pp. 176-180 & LUNN in DBG (1965) p.27

### The Founding of Ashton Grammar School

In 1868 the Trustees of the Almshouse Charity sold more land, to the Midland Railway Company, for £14,500 and so they were again faced with the problem of how to allocate the extra money (which soon increased to £17,000). They decided not to spend more on the existing Elementary School since this would lose them the government grant which maintained the school. So the Trustees decided to establish another educational institution – a Grammar School for the sons of professional and other middle-class men in the town.[i]

### Problems

However, there were legal problems in trying to alter the terms of Frances Ashton's will a second time, and also problems in trying to keep the money and prevent it from being taken by the government's Endowed Schools Commission. The Trustees were afraid that the money would be used in ways of which Mrs Ashton would not have approved or that it might be used to build a school in Luton![ii]

### More Problems

While various plans were being drawn up, to further complicate matters, the Endowed Schools Commission was replaced by another government body called the Charity Commission. Further discussions took place and then a four-day public meeting was held in the Town Hall with one of the Charity Commissioners.

### The Final Foundation

Eventually, after a total of seventeen years, a scheme was agreed which received the official approval of Queen Victoria on 12 August 1885. This scheme established the Ashton Schools and Almshouse Foundation: the Almshouses and the Ashton Elementary School continued much as they did before but the Ashton Grammar School was established as a new day and boarding school for boys. Only one member of the Trustees, Thomson Hankey, was still alive at the end of all these negotiations, so he laid the foundation stone of the new Grammar School in 1887, in High St. North (see 76.)[iii]

Refs: i LUNN in DBG (1965) p. 27; ii (ibid); iii (ibid)

### The End of the Old Almshouses

The Ashton Almshouses were extensively repaired in about 1850. However, in time they became irreparable and so, after World War II, the buildings were pulled down – despite some opposition from those who thought the almshouses were of historical and architectural importance. The money received from the sale of the land was spent on building a new set of Ashton Almshouses, known as Frances Ashton House, in Bullpond Lane (see 41).

### The Old Stocks and Whipping Post

In front of the old Ashton Almshouses used to be some stocks and a whipping post. They were sited near to the Cross Roads so that many passers-by would see offenders being punished. They were also near to the market place, where many of the thieves and other trouble-makers would have committed their crimes. Punishment was often carried out on a market day to give maximum humiliation to the criminals and also a warning to those attending the market. (One wonders what the old ladies in the Ashton Almshouses thought about the whipping post and stocks being right in front of their windows!)

*Ashton Almshouses with Stocks and Whipping Post, drawn by Thomas Fisher c. 1815.*

# SITE OF 16TH CENTURY SHOP

*(Now Modern Shops)*

In the 1970s, before the modern shops were built, several very interesting old buildings were pulled down. Among these were no. 7 (Ellis's barber shop) and no. 9 West St. which had stood immediately next door to the Ashton Almshouses, where the Dunstable Motor Centre shop is today.

## The Original Shop

In the 19th century, Ellis's shop was a public house called the Old Vine. However, the timber frame dated from the early 16th century, as discovered by John Bailey. No. 7 was originally a shop which was built onto no. 9 and it had a jettied chamber above a narrow frontage, with a hall at the rear. This hall was the full double storey height of the building and it was windowless, acting as a smoke bay. The shop had large unglazed windows at the front which were secured at night by shutters. The shutters probably hinged down to serve as external counters outside the shop during the day. When Ellis's was pulled down, it wasn't obvious from the outside that it was a Tudor style building since several fronts had been layered onto the premises over the years. Fortunately, the shop was not destroyed but taken down carefully for reconstruction at the Chiltern Open Air Museum.

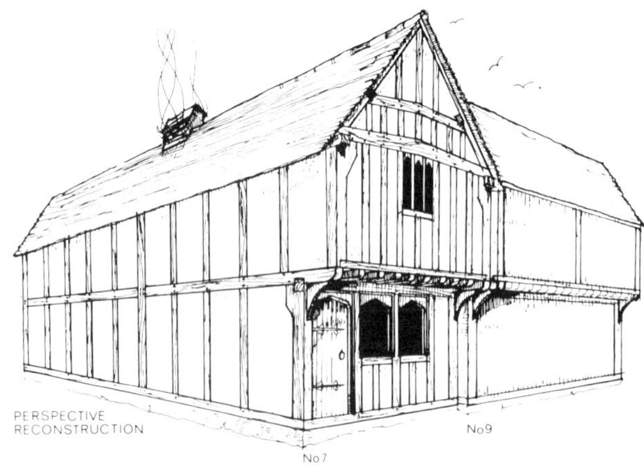


*7 & 9 West St., illustrated by John Bailey*

*Refs: BAILEY (1979) p. 22; BAILEY (1980) pp. 91-8*

# SOUTH BEDS SHOWCASE

### Site of Quaker Meeting House
### (and Darby Butchers/Benning Solicitors)

On land now opposite the West St. Baptist Church used to stand the Quaker Meeting House. The site was later occupied by Joseph Darby, a butcher, next to the Solicitor C.S. Benning. Today the land is mainly occupied by modern buildings, including the 'Payless' D.I.Y. shop and the South Beds Showcase, which occasionally has interesting displays.

### The Quaker Baker

A Quaker group formed at Dunstable in about 1654, when Quaker Richard Hubberthorne stayed at the home of baker Edward Chester, next to the 'Nags Head' in High St. North. This Quaker baker met with people from Sewell, including members of the Newman, How and King families.

### The Beckerings Park Meeting

In 1655 an historic meeting was held at Beckerings Park, Ridgmont, by George Fox, the founder of the Society of Friends. Shortly after, the Quakers organised themselves into regional groups and the Dunstable Quakers started to meet with their South Beds Friends at Sewell.

### The Quaker Beliefs

The Quakers soon made many enemies through their actions which included refusing to attend church or pay tithes. When taken to court, they also refused to take an oath on the Bible! They believed that, since God is in everyone, there should be much more equality and a rejection of the strong hierarchical and doctrinal ideas of the established Church.

### The Quaker Persecutions

When Charles II was restored to the throne in 1660, the Quakers were persecuted: 18 local people were arrested and jailed, including Edward Chester, Henry How and Henry Newman Snr. In 1668 the Archdeacon excommunicated Edward Chester, Thomas Halsey (maltster), Thomas Colard, and William Fossey (of the Swan/Red Lion) and Daniel Fossey (grocer).

Refs: WAGON (1954) pp. 267-71; GODBER (1969) pp. 236-8; EVANS (1985) pp. 79-81;

Despite all this, in 1669 there were still over 40 attenders at Sewell Meetings.

### The Sewell and Dunstable Meetings

In 1678 local Quakers leased some land at Sewell for use as a burial ground and a place to erect a Meeting House. In Dunstable the baker's shop was still used for meetings and it became an information centre, with Edward Chester as local representative.[i]

### The Dunstable Meeting House

In 1712, the Society of Friends built a Meeting House in West St. with a burial ground behind it.[ii] The Quakers continued to meet at Sewell, Markyate, and Dunstable throughout the rest of the 18th and early 19th centuries until they moved to Luton. The Dunstable Meeting House closed c. 1797[iii] and was later used by the Wesleyan Methodists for 10 years (1821-31), before they erected their own meeting house where the present Methodist Church is.[iv] In 1831 an infant school was temporarily opened in the Meeting House by Mr Pargetten. By the 19th century the Quakers were not only generally accepted but were often respected as honest, reliable businesspersons, e.g. it was a Quaker who ran the main local bank! (See 57)

### Darby the Butcher

The Quaker property in West St. was taken over in the 1840s by Joseph Darby (1819-79) who soon put it to a very different use — erecting a house, a butcher's shop and a slaughterhouse on the site. Lamborn wrote in 1859, 'No vestige of the old building remains, and the graveyard is desecrated by the tramp of cattle, and the blood of slaughtered animals destined to become the food of man'![v]

### C.S. Benning

From 1850, between Darby's property and the timber framed buildings (later 7 & 9), was the Solicitor's firm of Charles Stockdale Benning (later no. 11).[vi]

This firm stayed here until the 1970s when the redevelopment took place and it moved (as Benning, Hoare and Drew) across the road to its present location at no. 22 (see 47).

Refs: i GODBER (1975) p. 29; ii (ibid) p. 47; iii (ibid) p. 74; iv LAMBORN (1859) p. 164; v (ibid) p. 106; vi (CRO) DDBH 313

# SITE OF THE COMMERCIAL HOTEL

## The Commercial Hotel

The Commercial Hotel was on the site now occupied by the wallpaper and paint shop 'Decor-8' (previously Ripolin). Its full name was 'The Dunstable Temperance and Commercial Hotel' but it was usually simply called 'Marchant's' — after the name of the owners. Marchant's was a rival to the other main Temperance Hotel in Dunstable — Baker's Temperance and Commercial Hotel at no. 67 High St. North. Being Temperance, of course, meant that these Hotels did not sell alcohol or allow it to be consumed on the premises. They catered, therefore, for the travellers who were 'abstainers' or non-drinkers. In the latter part of the 19th century a strong Temperance Movement developed, mainly as a reaction against the severe alcoholism that was prevalent in society at that time. (Before the stricter licensing laws were enforced, people could be served drinks at 6.00 a.m.)

## The Marchant Family

At the beginning of this century, the proprietor of the West St. Temperance Hotel was John Albert Marchant who was apparently a quiet unassuming man with three talented sons: the eldest son became the first cinema owner in the town; the second a successful chemist who took over the pharmaceutical business of Joseph Flemons (at no. 73 High St. North — see 60) which had been established in 1881; the third son was a pianist who helped his eldest brother by providing background music for the films — his Sousa marches were known to excite the audiences.[i]

## Marchant's Hotel

Marchant's Hotel was advertised as having a 'Large Hall for Banquets, Dinners, Dances, Evening Parties, etc.' It also boasted a bathroom and 'perfect sanitation'. Small political meetings were often held there.[ii] The Temperance Hotel was demolished in the late 1950s.

Refs: i BAGSHAWE (1967) pp. 226-7; ii (ibid); iii TURVEY (1977) p. 25

# ST MARY'S GATE

*Site of Ewe and Lamb P.H.*

## St. Mary's Gate

St. Mary's Gate is a modern road, dating from the mid 1970s, on the site of a previous road called 'Cross Street' which connected West St. with St. Mary's Street. Today, St. Mary's Gate connects West St. to the 'Chapel Car Park' where the Old Baptist Church is situated.

## Origin of Name

'St. Mary's Gate' is the entrance to an area which used to be known as 'St. Mary's'. In the 17th century, when the Old Baptist Chapel was built, the field that it stood in was called 'St. Mary's Overs.' According to local tradition, there was a church called 'St. Mary's' in the vicinity of this Baptist Chapel.[i] NB The modern 'St. Mary's' with which it is not to be confused, is the Roman Catholic Church on the other side of West St.

## The Ewe and Lamb

The east corner of West St. and St. Mary's Gate is currently an unsurfaced car park. On this corner used to stand the Ewe and Lamb P.H. which closed down on 19 August 1961. The name was transferred to new premises which opened in Luton Road on 22 August, 1961.[ii]

The Ewe and Lamb probably took its name from the Sheep Fair which, during the 19th century, was held in West St. in the widest part of the road, east of Icknield Street.[iii] Sheep drovers used to drive their flocks of sheep from the Dunstable Downs along West St. to the railway station in Church St. These flocks could be as many as five hundred strong and folks would carry out pints from the Ewe and Lamb for the thirsty shepherds.[iv]

Refs: i LAMBORN (1859) ii TURVEY (1977) pp.20-1; iii LAMBORN (1859) p. 144; iv WOODCOCK (1950)

# POLICE STATION

*The Dunstable Police Station*

This station was purpose built in the mid-1970s to house the South Beds Police Force Headquarters. It replaced the Police Station in High St. South which is now Petropolis House (see 24). This is therefore Dunstable's third Police Station — the first being in Icknield St. (see 42).

In the last century, a public house called 'The Elephant and Castle' was recorded in 1839 on the site now occupied by the western part of the Police Station.[i]

Refs: i (CRO) DDBH 458

# OLD BAPTIST CHAPEL

*(Built 1849)*

*The Old Baptist Chapel*
*Illustrated by Percy Baker*[i]

The Baptist Chapel which can be seen today dates from 1849, however, it stands on the site of a much older Chapel and is surrounded by an old burial ground. The oldest date on the stones is 1740. This Chapel belongs to the 'Particular' or 'Strict' Baptists, as distinct from the West Street Baptist Chapel which was built by 'General' Baptists.[ii]

Refs: i BAKER (1975); ii BROADFOOT in DBG 1965 p. 19

## The First Baptists

In 1673 some of the followers of John Bunyan (who, in that year, wrote the first part of 'Pilgrim's Progress' in Bedford Jail) moved from Bedford to Kensworth, a village S.W. of Dunstable. There they formed a Baptist church with over 300 members scattered throughout more than 30 towns and villages, including: St. Albans, Shenley, Welwyn, Luton, Stony Stratford, Leighton Buzzard, Berkhamsted, and Hemel Hempstead. The largest group, with about 33 members, was in Dunstable and the first recorded meeting was held here in 1696.[i]

## The First Dunstable Chapel

In 1708 a piece of ground was bought and a Meeting House was built on it. The building was near the present Chapel and was described as being in 'Hallifax's Yard in West Street' and 'in part of a field called St. Mary Overs'. In 1807 the building was enlarged to twice its original size, with a double roof.[ii] NB The entrance to Hallifax Yard is opposite Matthew St., next to the 'Yum Yum' Shop.

## The present Old Baptist Chapel

The first chapel (called 'Eben-ezer' from 1818)[iii] suffered severely in a violent storm in 1849 so it was demolished and replaced in the same year by the present Chapel, which holds 400 people. Connected to the Chapel was a small 'Sabbath School'.[iv]

NB the 'Old Baptist Chapel' is therefore actually slightly newer than the West Street (General) Baptist Chapel, which was rebuilt in 1847. The term 'Old' doesn't refer to the building but to the age of the religious group: the 'General' Baptists were a later offshoot from the earlier 'Particular' Baptists.

Refs: i BAKER (1975) p. 3; ii LAMBORN (1859) p. 106; iii BAKER., (1975) p. 9; iv LAMBORN (1859) p. 107

# CHAPEL CAR PARK

*(Sites of The Foresters' Arms and The Queen's Head)*

This is a public car park, although it is sometimes known locally as 'Sainsbury's Car Park' because it extends to the front of the Sainsbury Supermarket and was developed by the company along with the Ashton Square shopping precinct. On this area used to be St. Mary's Street and Chapel Walk (partly a footpath and partly a road). These were both lined with many buildings, including 'Prosperous Row' (which didn't live up to its name!) Two of the buildings which stood here were The Foresters' Arms and The Queen's Head public houses, which are still remembered with affection by some local people.

## The Foresters' Arms

The Foresters' Arms was a very small pub in Chapel Walk and it was reputed to be very old although it may have only dated from the 18th century. It was previously called the 'Cock', which might have been a reference to the beer barrels which stood nearby at a brewery (in the area then known as Great Butts and Little Butts): each barrel had a tap or 'cock'.[i] From the 1830s to the 1880s it was run by Charles and Elizabeth Field who were also Whiting Manufacturers. From the end of the last century to about 1935 it was run by George Hall, followed by Sam Bodsworth, another long serving landlord. The pub was closed down on 10 March 1973.[ii]

## The Queen's Head

The Queen's Head was at 69 St. Mary's Street until it closed down on 24 September 1975. It was also a small pub, although slightly larger than The Foresters' Arms, and it probably dated from the mid-19th century – as indicated by the reference to Queen Victoria in the pub's sign. In 1871 it was known as the Queen's Head Inn, with James Collins in charge. Unlike the Foresters, the Queen's Head had many different landlords, including Henry Thompson in 1876 (an architect) and Vincent Phillips in 1894 (a coal merchant).[iii]

Refs: i WOODCOCK (1950); ii TRADE DIR.; iii (ibid)

# SALVATION ARMY CITADEL

*Bullpond Lane*

The hall used by the Salvation Army was built in the 1930s. The Salvation Army has, however, been active in Dunstable since the beginning of this century. They had close links with the Methodist Church – Col. Mary Booth, the grand-daughter of William Booth (founder of the Army) visited the Methodist Church on the Square in October 1944.

## Bullpond Lane

Bullpond Lane is one of the oldest lanes in Dunstable. The road once contained a pond and it used to lead through fields to Stipers Hill, where there was a bull ring. The cruel practice of slowly killing bulls used to be carried out there for 'sport' and for 'better meat' (sic).

## Harrison Carter

It was at the southern end of Bullpond Lane that the Engineering company J. Harrison Carter Ltd was founded in 1894. This firm specialised in agricultural machinery and, after being taken over by Johansson in the 1930s, it continued here until the 1950s (the building is no longer standing.) Harrison Carter's was very important when it started because it was the first major Engineering firm in Dunstable. This meant new opportunities and work for local people, many of whom had been made unemployed by the decline of the straw-plait industry. It also led the way for later industrial companies.

NB Harrison Carter, which came from Birmingham, should not be confused with the Frederick Carter scrap metal business on the Luton Road.

# BENNETT'S REC.

The Bennett Memorial Recreation Ground in Bullpond Lane was opened to the public in 1920. Known locally as 'Bennett's Rec.', the eight acres of land is almost entirely grassed (except the tennis courts) and it includes football and cricket pitches, also swings and slide, etc. for children. The Pavilion was opened in April 1960.

## The Butts

W.G. Smith's map of 1903 shows that the area of Bennett's Rec. was 'Butts Close' on the edge of 'Open and Common Fields'. Lamborn in 1859 referred to 'the Butts', which is only a corruption of the word 'bolt-ground', in allusion to those feats of archery, so often performed within its area, and which was thought so important as to be the subject of several statutes in the reign of Henry VIII.[i] Lamborn also described the Butts as 'that neglected piece of ground so long the eyesore of Dunstable, was at this time enjoying its high tide of popularity, and it is much to be regretted that ever it was appropriated to any other purpose than that of a public pleasure ground, being so conveniently situated'.[ii] Lamborn would, therefore, presumably have been pleased with today's use of this land.

## The Bennett Family

The area including Bennett's Rec. was owned by the Dunstable family of Bennett which gave some of their property to the council. This family also owned Bennett's Brewery (the site now occupied by the Chiltern P.H., etc.) and Bennett's hat factory in High St. North (now the 'Town Hall Chambers' building). The brewery continued until about 1940 and the hat factory closed in 1931, being the last hat factory in Dunstable.

Benjamin Bennett the brewer served on several committees and was, at various times: Ald. on the Beds.C.C.; Gov. of Ashton Grammar School; Chairman of Dunstable Gas and Water Co.; Pres. of the Dunstable Cricket, Hockey, Unionist and Chess Clubs; and Vice-Pres. of Dunstable Horticultural Society. By the beginning of this century he was a Kensworth landowner living in Kensworth House.

Refs: i LAMBORN (1859) p. 79; ii (ibid) p.79

# FRANCES ASHTON HOUSE

*(The New Ashton Almshouses – Built 1969)*

*The Modern Ashton Almshouses*

These new almshouses were built to replace those pulled down in West St. (see 33) and they are known collectively as 'Frances Ashton House'. The original almshouses were built in 1715 and they were maintained by a group of Trustees, as determined by Frances Ashton's will after her death in 1727. When the West St. land was sold to a property developer the money was used to build the present Ashton Almshouses.

The new buildings were officially opened on 30 October 1969. After a short service of dedication, performed by the Bishop of Bedford, the Mayor of Dunstable presented each tenant with a key to her new centrally heated home.

NB The homes for old people in the adjacent 'Swan Court' were erected by the Council.

# THE FIRST DUNSTABLE POLICE STATION

*(now private residence)*

*The Original Police Station*

The building which contained the first Dunstable Police Station is on the corner of Icknield St. and Burr St. at the end of Bullpond Lane. The house is now a private residence but the words 'Police Station' can still be seen on the front of the building.

## The First Police Force

In 1865, the new Borough Council (formed in 1864) fulfilled its duty to provide a Police Force and a Police Station: a Superintendent and a Constable were recruited and a station was built 'at the upper end of South Place'.[i] The site was given by Edward Burr and the building was completed in 1867.[ii]

Refs: i DERBYSHIRE (1882) p. 126; ii (ibid) p. 126

## 'Super' George

When the Police Station opened in 1867, Superintendent George, in the absence of any Council staff other than a part-time Town Clerk, also held several other titles: Inspector of Nuisances, Collector of Market Tolls, Town Hall Manager, Mace Bearer, Inspector of Weights and Measures, Inspector of Lodging Houses, Officer for Issuing Petroleum Licences, and Relieving Officer for Vagrants. He was also the town's 'Factotum', i.e. the man responsible for enforcing each new Act of Parliament as it came along! In 1890 the newly-formed County Council took over the running of the Dunstable Police Force.[i] After several years of complaints that the Station was inadequate, a new Station was eventually built in the 1930s in High St. South (see 24).

## The Coal-Hole Cover in Burr Street

Beside the Old Police Station, in Burr St., is an interesting circular coal-hole cover set in the pavement. Below the cover was a chute down which coal was sent into the basement of the Old Police Station.

*Coal-Hole Cover, Burr St.*

## Icknield Street

Previously called Icknield Road, this was one of the first 19th century residential streets. James Tibbett lived in Icknield Villa, and on the corner of West St. is the old rectory building, once lived in by the Whinnett family, which was named 'Evansville'.

Refs: i HAYWARD (1973) p. 22

# THE VICTORIA P.H.

The small red brick public house stands in the area of West St. still lined with trees. It was built during the reign of Queen Victoria so it is appropriately named, as is the road opposite — Victoria Street.

Queen Victoria visited Dunstable, with her husband Albert, in 1841 when she visited an exhibition of local lace and straw-plait work at The Sugar Loaf Hotel (see 63). (This was the last visit to the town by a monarch.) Queen Victoria was of particular importance to Dunstablians because she sold them the Town Hall in 1866 and then the whole Manor of Dunstable in 1870.

### The Dunstable Cemetery

The 'new' Dunstable Cemetery was opened during the reign of Queen Victoria in 1861. It is about three furlongs (600 metres) further along West St. from The Victoria pub and has a large Victorian entrance. The road opposite was called 'Cemetery Road', now 'Chiltern Road'.

# THE OLD MILL

*(Built 1839. Now Sea Cadet H.Q.)*

*The Old Mill*

## Introduction

The Old Mill can be seen from West St. at the end of a short rural lane. It was built in 1839 as a windmill, on the site of several previous mills, and was used as a mill for almost 100 years, ending its working life as a steam-mill.

During the Second World War the building was used as an observation tower by the local Home-Guard. Towards the end of the war it was acquired for the Dunstable Sea Cadet Unit. On the front can be seen the date '1942', in very large numerals, which refers to the year that the Dunstable Sea Cadet Unit was officially formed by Admiral Sir Lionel Preston, K.C.B. In 1945 the Old Mill was bought from the retired miller, Frank Simmons.

In 1948 it was named 'Training Ship Lionel Preston', after the Admiral who set up the Unit. The building is therefore sometimes referred to as 'The Ship without Sails'!

Over the years, the Cadets have added to the inside of their 'ship' fixtures and fittings from various Navy vessels. Hence, on entering the building today, one is immediately transported into a nautical world complete with a ship's 'galley', a radio room and much naval equipment. The floors (now called 'decks', of course) are connected by genuine metal-rung ship's ladders, set at near vertical angles. The Sea Cadets meet at the Old Mill on Mondays and Wednesdays. Occasionally, there are 'open days' when members of the public are shown around.

## Description of the Old Mill

The tower is 58 feet tall and 28 feet in diameter at the base; the walls are about 3.5 feet thick at the bottom and 2 feet thick at the top. It has six floors including a small floor in the copper covered cap. Inside the cap is a wooden observation platform from which it is possible to see out of the top, beneath the small perspex dome. The metal spike at the very top is a lightning conductor which runs down the side of the building.[i]

Ref: i TWADDLE (1975) p. 62

The tower is a rather unusual shape for a mill in that the first two floors were built with vertical walls, with the tapering starting at the second-floor. (The mill at Houghton Conquest, in North Bedfordshire, is of a similar shape but is smaller.) The building material is the local Caddington Grey brick.[i]

### The First Mill and the Young Family

There have been mills on this site since at least the 13th century when it was owned by the Young family. The Youngs were extremely wealthy: they owned most of West St. at that time, as well as farm land, and they exported Chiltern Wool to France and imported wine. One of their customers was Henry III (in 1242, John Young sold the King a goshawk). The Young family made many gifts to the Priory, including: houses, shops, money for the Leper hospital, and candles for the altars.[ii]

### Youngs v. Priory

However, the Youngs 'fell out' with the Priory when the Prior tried to go through their account books to claim a 'tithe' (a tenth) of the family business profits. The family simply refused to allow this. In addition, the Youngs asked for a parish church of their own. Eventually, as a compromise, a parish altar dedicated to St. John the Baptist was established at the Priory in 1220, and Alexander Young later agreed to pay some money towards the costs of parish priests. (There is still an altar dedicated to St. John in the Priory today.)

Even so, other disagreements between the Youngs and the Priory continued: John and Alexander refused to pay tithes on the work carried out at their West Street Windmill, and John's son refused to give hay that was part of his business (presumably as animal food). Even the Pope was asked by the Prior de Morin to sort out these difficulties! The problems persisted and other 'burgesses' (citizens of the borough) joined forces to protect their financial interests. These conflicts between the burgesses and the Priory continued, on and off, throughout most of the 13th and 14th centuries.[iii]

Refs: i HOWES (1983); ii EVANS (1980) pp. 19-30; iii (ibid)

### The Last Mill

The last windmill (i.e. the present building) was built in 1839 by Richard Gutteridge, a local landowner described as 'Gentry' and 'Maltster'. It had four double-shuttered patent sails and was winded (i.e. turned to face the wind) by an eight bladed fantail. Later, an engine-house with a tall square chimney was attached to the west side of the mill. The engine provided steam power when there wasn't enough wind.[i]

The mill passed from Richard to Matthew Gutteridge and was then sold for £850 in 1868 to a baker and corn dealer, William Rodwell. In about 1890 the mill was bought by Frederick Simmons. In 1908 the sails were removed but the mill continued using only the steam-engine driving three pairs of large stones. In the early 1920s, Frederick passed the steam mill on to his son Frank who ran it until just before the Second World War.

## THE SEA CADETS

### The Birth of the Dunstable Sea Cadet Unit

The 'father' of the Sea Cadet Unit was Admiral Sir Lionel Preston who came to live in Dunstable after retiring in 1935. At that time there was a thriving Pioneer Boys Club in the town so, from 1st April 1942, the Admiral negotiated with the Boys Club Management Committee to form a Sea Cadet Unit.

On June 15th 1942, the Admiralty granted official recognition and thus Sea Cadet Unit No. 115 was born. The new Unit was so popular with the youth of Dunstable that it quickly reached a complement of nearly 80 Cadets plus a waiting list. It soon became necessary to find an alternative meeting place so the Unit moved from the Pioneer Boys Club to various temporary 'homes', including the Fire Station, the Methodist Church and Britain Street School.

By the end of 1943, a total of 180 Cadets had enrolled with 92 of these already having left to join the Royal Navy and other Services. In 1945 a section of the Girls Nautical Training Corps (G.N.T.C.) was formed to cater for the town's female youth.

Refs: i HOWES (1983)

## The Launch of T.S. Lionel Preston

Since the West St. miller Frank Simmons had retired and the mill was no longer used, discussions took place about the possibility of acquiring the Old Mill for the Sea Cadet Unit. It was eventually bought with the conveyance of sale being signed on September 8th 1945. A Trust was formed to look after the Old Mill and four Trustees were appointed on 21st August 1946. In September of the same year the Unit was officially Registered as a Charity. It took two years for the Old Mill to be converted into a suitable permanent home for the Unit, most of the work being done by Cadets and Staff volunteers. In 1948, the place was finally commissioned and the Old Mill was officially named as 'Training Ship Lionel Preston' at a Champagne Launching Ceremony.

Major repairs were carried out to the roof in 1956. Now the cap is fixed in position: it no longer turns around as it did when it was necessary for the sails to point towards the wind.

## The Sea Cadets

The Unit is part of the National Voluntary Organisation of Sea Cadets. The main aims are to develop the qualities of leadership, devotion to duty, self-discipline and self-respect so that the Cadets will become reliable and useful members of the community. The Cadets pass through a training programme which is consistant with the training given to recruits in the Navy: they learn a wide range of skills related to seamanship and modern communication systems. The Dunstable Cadets own several small sailing vessels and canoes which are used at various lakes, reservoirs and rivers. (There aren't many Sea Cadets so far from the sea!) The Sea Cadets wear an authentic Navy Uniform, (the only group outside the Service allowed to do so) i.e. blue jacket and trousers with a white peaked cap. NB The Sea Cadets are not be confused with the Sea Scouts which are an entirely separate organisation.

## The Pitstone Windmill

A good example of a working mill, which is still used, can be visited at Pitstone Green near Ivinghoe about 6 miles west of Dunstable along the Tring Road (B489).

# ST. MARY'S ROMAN CATHOLIC CHURCH

*('Our Lady Immaculate': Built 1964)*

This unusual circular building was constructed between 1962 and 1964, at a cost of about £75,000, by Desmond Williams and Associates of Manchester. It is a large brick church with a lamella roof and a copper covered spire. Inside, the ceiling is painted in eighteen shades of blue (which took over 36 gallons of paint) and the floor is composed of 100,000 tiles in a diamond pattern. The altar is made of Italian marble.[i]

## The Social Club

In front of the new Church is the old Roman Catholic Church. This is now used as a Social Club and it contains a bar. (The ground was deconsecrated first, of course.)

Refs: i PEVSNER (1968) p. 78 & HICKENBOTTOM (1974) p. 142

### Before the Churches were built

In 1925 there was no place of worship in Dunstable for Roman Catholics. It was necessary for them (about 60 people then) to go to Luton for Sunday Mass. In 1927 a request was made to the Bishop of Northampton for a priest to visit Dunstable every Sunday. (The town was in the Diocese covered by this Bishop.) As a result a Priest-in-Charge, Father Gregory Tobar, was obtained from a community of Spanish priests in Potters Bar.[i]

### The First Meeting Place

At first a house in Regent Street was used for Sunday Mass. Before the end of 1927, the property in West St. was purchased and converted into a church.[ii].

### The old Roman Catholic Church

The property that was bought in 1927 was formerly the Church of England Rectory. To begin with, two rooms in the Old Rectory were made into an oratory where the Roman Catholics worshipped. After more changes the old Roman Catholic Church was formally opened in 1936. The number of Roman Catholics in Dunstable increased year by year. In 1957 a new Parish Priest, Father Maurice O'Neill, was appointed who undertook the task of building a new Parish Church and Presbytery.[iii]

### The new Roman Catholic Church

The Foundation Stone for the new Roman Catholic Church was laid in March 1962. The building took two years to complete. It was eventually blessed and opened on 15th March 1964, during a snow storm, by the Lord Bishop of Northampton.

The St. Mary's Church is unusual in that it is circular. It is believed to be the first circular church to be built in England since the Reformation.[iv]

### St. Mary's School

The building of the first Roman Catholic School in Dunstable was approved in 1964 by the Ministry of Education. The St. Mary's School was opened in the early 1970s on Downside Estate, next to the Manshead Upper School.

Refs: BROADFOOT in DBG (1965) p. 18; ii (ibid); iii (ibid); iv (ibid) & TURVEY (1977) p. ix

# THE VICTORIA STREET R.C. CHURCH

*(Built 1862)*

The church in Victoria Street is used by Roman Catholics, many of Polish origin. It was opened as a R.C. Church in 1968. Before then, this was the Victoria Street Methodist Chapel.

## The Origins of the Methodist Chapel

In March 1839 the Aylesbury Primitive Methodist Circuit decided to send missioners to begin new work in Dunstable and Luton. On 2 April 1839, Henry Higginson preached on the Market Square in Dunstable to a large crowd and then, the same evening, preached outside the Houghton Regis Parish Church. The Vicar, however, was not happy about Higginson's presence so he ordered the Church bells to be rung in an attempt to drown out the 'Ranter' (the name given to such energetic preachers.) In addition to this, Henry Higginson was faced with threats from a gang led by a local prize-fighter, called Odell, who also wanted to stop the Ranter. However, the Methodist was such a powerful preacher that Odell was not only converted but he became Higginson's protector. Furthermore, a few years later, Odell's son became one of the first Methodist Ministers in the District – the Rev. J. Odell![i]

## The First Primitive Methodist Meeting Place

The first meeting place in Dunstable was the bar of a disused public house, the 'Rising Sun', in Edward St. (then 'Mount St.') In 1852 a small chapel was built, in the same Road, which still stands today at the corner of the lane between Edward St. and Prince's St. A Sunday School also opened in connection with the chapel. The congregation grew rapidly – from 6 in 1852 to 100 in 1862. In 1862, the Victoria St. site was bought and the Foundation Stone was laid in July by Harpur Twelvetrees.[ii]

Refs: i BROADFOOT in DBG (1965) p. 20; ii (ibid)

# NO. 26 WEST ST.

*(Building with Totternhoe Stone)*
*Benning, Hoare and Drew Solicitors*

*Totternhoe Stone in West St. Buildings*

## Totternhoe Stone

On the corner of West St. and Matthew St. is the white fronted building, no. 26 West St., occupied by 'Benning, Hoare and Drew' solicitors, who are also next door at no. 24. On the east side of no. 26, facing the town centre, can clearly be seen blocks of Totternhoe stone within the exposed timber framework. This stone was probably taken from the Priory or the Friary buildings sometime after the Dissolution in 1540 (see 3.)

## Benning, Hoare and Drew

This Solicitor's Firm was originally founded c1783 by John Hooper; in 1839 it was transferred to John Pearse. In 1850 C.S. Benning took over and in 1880 it became Benning and Son followed by Benning and Hoare in 1929. In the early 1930s Joseph Arthur Ivor Drew joined. The firm was at no. 11 West St. (the site now occupied by 'Pay-less' and the South Beds Showcase – see 33) until it moved to the present address in the 1970s.[i]

Refs: i BEDS C.C. (1957) p. 97 & TRADE DIR.

### C.S. Benning and C.C.S. Benning

The first Benning in this firm was Charles Stockdale Benning, the son of Henry Benning of Barnard Castle. C.S. Benning was the town's first Mayor in 1865.

Charles Crichton Stuart Benning, the son of C.S. Benning, was born in Dunstable in 1854 and educated at the Royal Naval School, New Cross. He first joined his father as a solicitor in 1875 and later became the sole partner. He held several important positions including: Town Clerk, Receiver of Cart's Charity, Clerk to the Joint Hospital Board, and Steward of the Manor, C.C.S. Benning had four sons and six daughters, his eldest son, Arthur Crichton Stuart, became a solicitor in 1906. C.C.S. Benning died in 1925.[i]

### J.H. Hoare

John Henry Hoare, like his partner, held important posts including: Steward of the Manor, Clerk to the Managers of Dunstable Group of Council Schools, Clerk to the Dunstable and District Hospital Joint Committee, Receiver to Jane Cart's Charity, and Clerk to the Governors of Chew's Foundation.

(NB The Benning and Hoare Solicitors' Deeds, dating back to the 17th century, have been very useful as sources of historical information!)

### Matthew Street

This Street was named after Matthew Gutteridge, farmer, the son of Richard Gutteridge. The Gutteridge family owned much land in and around Dunstable, including this part of West St. Matthew Gutteridge owned the Old Mill until 1868.

NB Dunstable's last Town Crier, George White, lived at 10 Matthew Street.[iii]

Refs: i PIKE (1907) p. 244 & DERBYSHIRE (1882) p. 183 & HAYWARD (1973) p. 21; ii (CRO) DDBH; iii TRADE DIR.

# WEST ST. CHRISTIAN CENTRE

*(West St. Baptist Church)*

*West St. Baptist Church and School*

Built in 1847-8 by J. Clarke, this red brick church has decorative yellow brick corner-stones and tall, arched windows. It is three bays wide with the central bay 'pedimented', i.e. the middle section has a triangular top. In 1984 the wide single-storey entrance was added when the church was converted into a full-time day school. This church was founded by 'General' Baptists, as distinguished from the 'Particular' (or 'Strict') Baptists at the Old Chapel in St. Mary's Gate (see 37.) Both churches developed from fellowships that were much wider and which met outside the town. [i]

Refs: i PEVSNER (1968) p. 78 & BROADFOOT in DBG (1965) p. 19

### The Thorn Meeting House

In the 18th century, Baptists from Dunstable and the surrounding places met at a small meeting-house in Thorn, near Houghton Regis. The first recorded meeting was in 1720 and at this time the group was part of the Luton Baptist Church. In 1751 the church at Thorn separated from Luton. Some of these members then started other meeting places: at Houghton Regis in 1790, and at Dunstable in 1801. In 1803 the small building at Thorn was moved to Houghton Regis.[i]

### The First Dunstable Meeting House

The original Dunstable meeting-house was built in 1790 on a piece of land, given by Mr. R. Gutteridge, next to the present West Street site. The Dunstable and Houghton Regis groups shared pastors until 1836, when Dunstable amicably became separate under Rev. Daniel Gould who was a pastor from 1826 to 1881. The small Dunstable building soon became overcrowded and rather dilapidated so in 1847 the present church was built, to seat 700, opening for worship in June 1848. A Sunday-school, started in January 1807, was connected to the church and a 'British School', with Charles Lamborn (author of 'Dunstaplogia') as Headmaster, operated here until 1877.[ii]

### The West Street Baptist Church

The burial ground was in front of the church but the gravestones were moved in about 1945, during the ministry of Rev. Leslie McCaw. Some of them were used for pavings and some were erected in the area to the right (east) of the building. Members of the Chambers, Batchelor, Gutteridge and Osborn families were buried here. In February 1976, a new hall was built at the Church at a cost of £38,000. In 1984 the front extension was added and the Church was opened as a day school: the Pilgrims' Christian School of the new Covenant Church.

Refs: i BROADFOOT in DBG (1965) p. 19; ii BROADFOOT (ibid) p. 19 & LUNN (ibid) p. 27 & LAMBORN (1859)

## Maypole Yard

Immediately to the west of the Baptist Church and School is an area known as 'Maypole Yard', in recent years occupied by the 'Mark James' salvage business. Maypole Yard is reached from West St. via a short entrance which runs between two sets of old properties. On the left (west) of the entrance are two shops: 'Pat and Ray's Fruit Shop' (no. 20) and the 'Vanity Box (ladies) Fashion Shop' (no. 18). On the right (east) of the entrance are two smaller shops: 'Maggie's Fashions' ladies clothes shop (no. 14a) and the Crabtree Estate Agents (no. 12)[i]

## The Maypole

Maypole Yard is so named because it actually used to have a May Pole that was danced around by the girls of Dunstable in the May celebrations. However, the tradition died out in the middle of the 19th century and the pole was removed. (The May celebrations continued in some of the local villages, for example at Edlesborough, until the beginning of this century.)[ii]

## The Maypole Inn

Somewhere near Maypole Yard was an inn called The Maypole which was owned by the Chew Charity Trustess during the 18th century. It was mentioned in a Deed of 1724 as one of the four meeting places for the Trustees (the other three were: the 'Windmill and Still'; the 'Sugar Loaf' and the 'Black Lion').[iii]

Refs: i (MAP) GOAD (1974); ii SMITH (1904) p. 167; iii DERBYSHIRE (1882) p. 132

# THE PLUME OF FEATHERS P.H.

*Plume of Feathers P.H.*

The public house has old timber beams inside and an old gateway: it may have been a coaching inn. Before being named the 'Plume of Feathers', it was the 'Black Horse'.

## The Black Horse

In 1823 George Willmore was at the Black Horse, followed by John Willmore (by 1827), then James Varney (by 1839) and John Dawson (by 1847).

## The Plume of Feathers

By 1869 the Black Horse had become the Plume of Feathers with Mrs Francis Stanbridge as landlady, followed by George Barnes (by 1876). In 1877 George Rixson took over and then Mrs Eliza Rixson (by 1894). By 1903, Alfred Selley was landlord.

Refs: TRADE DIRECTORIES

# THE CROSS ROADS

The Cross Roads at the centre of Dunstable, where there is now a double roundabout, is the place where the ancient Icknield Way crosses the Roman Watling Street. It was largely due to the importance of these two roads as trading routes that Dunstable was established by King Henry I and developed over the centuries to be the town it is today: it was around these Cross Roads that the early markets and businesses were set up.

## Icknield Way

This is one of the earliest routes in the country. It was used by prehistoric traders, long before the Romans came, who travelled as far as The Wash in Norfolk (to the north east) and Salisbury Plain (to the south west). The Icknield Way may have been named after a tribe called the Iceni who lived in Norfolk. The term Iceni, however, may simply have meant any strangers who lived far away. The traders probably included people carrying tools made at the famous Grimes Graves flint mines, in Norfolk, who traded them for skins, woollen products and pots.

## Alternative Routes

The Icknield Way was not a single route in the sense that we think of roads today: it was more of a general track or way, across the country, which split into several routes in some parts. These alternative routes, all in the same general direction, were used partly to visit settlements off the main track but mainly to avoid hazards such as dense vegetation, where there might be thieves, or poor weather conditions. England at that time was covered in thick forest, therefore, depending on the time of year, it might be better to take a high route rather than a low one. Most travellers would probably have followed the lines along the tops of hills rather than take the generally slower and more difficult tracks in the valleys.

## The Half Moon Route

One alternative route through Dunstable was the track passing along the foot of Blows Downs which still exists today. This continued along the present Half Moon Lane and continued to the top of Dunstable Downs where it then joined up with the present Whipsnade Road. The Romans developed part of this route, as could be seen from the 'aggered' or rounded surface in Half Moon Lane before it was resurfaced in the 1960s.[i]

## Watling Street

Watling Street was built by the Romans during the 1st century to provide a route to the centre of England and to North wales. This road needed to be straight and well-made so that soldiers and supplies could move along it quickly. Staging posts were built about half a day's march apart, i.e. approximately every 12.5 miles (20km), to provide places for the soldiers to rest and eat. These also provided convenient points where messengers could change horses. That is why, 12.5 miles north of Verulamium (now St. Albans), the staging post of Durocobrivis was built where Dunstable is now. The meaning of Durocobrivis isn't clear since a literal translation is 'a fortified bridge' and there was no river or bridge here. One theory is that the name referred to the ancient fortified settlement which was at Maiden Bower, the large circular earthwork on the N.W. edge of Dunstable. Another theory is that the name was simply a Romanised version of an existing Celtic name, which the Romans could neither pronounce — because it was too guttural — nor even understand! (NB 'Durocobrivis' is now used instead of the plural form 'Durocobrivae'.)

## The Effects of the Motor Car on The Cross Roads

While the Motor Car industry has been beneficial to Dunstable, by providing many jobs and bringing money into the town, the effects of the Motor Car have in some ways been devastating.

Refs: i HAYWARD (1973) pp 2-3

The Cross Roads began to be regularly congested when the number of cars dramatically increased during the 1950s. Towards the end of the decade, plans were drawn up to improve the traffic flow by widening the streets near the Cross Roads.

When the M1 (the first motorway in Great Britain) was opened on 21 November 1959, with a junction halfway between Dunstable and Luton (J11), the volume of traffic though Dunstable was immediately reduced by about half. However, even this was not sufficient to relieve the congestion at the Cross Roads. The main problem for the traffic was Church St. because it was then less than half the width that it is today: on the corner of Church St. and High St. North was the Red Lion which actually stood where there is now road on the north side of Church St. The side of this old Inn was roughly where the island of the Pelican crossing is today. In the 1960s, the Red Lion was demolished along with many other old buildings and businesses in Church St. (NB The widening of Church Street is dealt with in more detail later (see 90).

## Site of the Eleanor Cross

Until the 17th century the Dunstable 'Eleanor Cross' stood on the Cross Roads. It was built in 1291 and destroyed in 1643. The exact location of this 'High Cross' isn't known: according to W.G. Smith (1904), 'It stood on the west side of the High Street, opposite the "Red Lion" hotel'; according to C. Lamborn (1859) it 'stood by the road-side, near the entrance of the public-house known by the sign of the 'Rose and Crown', south of the house called the Cross-house (which) stood opposite the Red Lion, the front of the house toward London'. Therefore, the Eleanor Cross was probably near to the present Keep's corner at the beginning of High St. South.

## Queen Eleanor

Queen Eleanor was the wife of Edward I. She died while they were staying at Hardby (Now 'Harby'), near Lincoln, on 28 November 1290. The King wanted his wife to be buried in Westminster Abbey, London, so a funeral procession started on 4 December 1290 following a route which stopped at several important religious houses – including the Priory at Dunstable. When it arrived in Dunstable, the coffin was placed near the Cross Roads so the local people could mourn the dead Queen. The coffin was then guarded inside the Priory by the Canons overnight before continuing on to St. Albans. In return, the Priory was given two precious cloths and 120 lbs of wax for candle-making. After a total of 13 days the long procession of coaches, horses, courtiers and servants, all dressed in black, arrived at Westminster.

King Edward I was deeply grieved so he ordered large crosses to be erected at each of the over-night stopping places. The Eleanor Cross at Dunstable was made by John Bello who also made the cross at Northampton. There was a figure of the Queen carved on the monument along with biblical characters. William Torel, a London Goldsmith, helped to decorate the work which was apparently very large. (Only three crosses still stand today: Waltham Cross in London; Geddington in Northamptonshire; and the Northampton Cross). The Dunstable Cross was smashed to pieces by Cromwell's soldiers in 1643 when they were destroying anything connected with Royalty.[ii]

## Queen Eleanor's School

The name of Queen Eleanor was given to the modern Girl's Grammar School, in Canesworde Rd, which combined with Kingsbury School in 1971 to form the present Queensbury Upper School.

## The Modern Eleanor Statue

In 1985 Queen Eleanor's name was also given to the shopping precinct in High St. North which has a modern statue of the Queen (see 64).

Refs: i SMITH (1904) p. 110; ii (ibid)

# SITE OF THE RED LION

The Red Lion stood on the corner of High St. North on what is today the north half of Church Street. It was demolished in 1963 during the Church Street widening programme.

## 15TH AND 16TH CENTURY: THE SWAN

The Red Lion is thought by Mrs Vivienne Evans to be the inn called the Swan which, in 1422, was listed with two others, the Lion and the Peacock. (This conclusion is partly based on the 1548 listings of property owned by the Houghton Fraternity.)[i] In 1422 the Swan was owned by Alice Petever, the wife of John Petever, daughter of Thomas Hobbes (who was the ringleader when the townsmen rebelled against the Priory in 1381).[ii] In 1502 the Swan was conveyed from John Dyve to John Parkyns when it was ambiguously (in Latin!) described as being in North Dunstable, in front of the Eleanor's Cross, with the Lion to the south and the Peacock to the north.[iii] These two inns are though to have been in the middle of the Cross Roads, in the small group of buildings later known as 'Cooke's Row'. The 16th century Swan would probably have been a fairly simple timbered room or rooms with trestles on a straw-strewn floor.[iv]

## 17TH CENTURY: THE RED LION

From about 1645, the increasing road traffic benefited the innkeepers and so the Red Lion (along with the Saracen's Head) was enlarged to become one of the leading inns.

## THE CIVIL WAR

During the Civil War in England, Royalists passed through Dunstable and raided it from time to time. In one raid, in June 1644, the host of the Red Lion, Mr. Plott, was killed by the King's men for being anti-royalty. (Many locals were against the King at this time.) It was during the same raid that the Priory Church suffered an attack and bullets were fired into the doors, the holes still being visible today.[v]

Refs: i EVANS (1985); p. 45; ii VCH 3:355; iii BNQ1: 259; iv WOODCOCK (1950-1) p. 328 & p. 286; v TIBBUTT in B. MAG 2:337

## King Charles Never Slept Here

After the battle of Naseby, in June 1645, the defeated King Charles I passed through Dunstable in August 1645 on his way back to Oxford, and called in at the Red Lion for about an hour or so. (The new host was obviously more hospitable this time!) This royal call led to the local tradition that King Charles actually slept at the Red Lion but it has since been shown by H.G. Tibbutt that this story is untrue.[i]

## 18th century: Red Lion Coaching Inn

When the first regular stage-coach arrived in 1742, it hailed a century of prosperity for the Red Lion and other inns. The 'Times' coach made its first call at the Red Lion, where the passengers required food, drink and accommodation. The Red Lion was refronted and it became a familiar landmark for travellers from London, Leeds and Birmingham.[ii]

## 19th century

When the railways arrived in the mid-19th century the Red Lion was badly hit. However, it managed to survive and retain its position as an important meeting place. In 1864, when the Dunstablians requested the status of Borough for their town, the main meetings took place in the Red Lion: Commissioner Donnelly heard the people's demands there and C.S. Benning (the 'Steward of the Manor Royal' of Dunstable) was elected Dunstable's first Mayor.[iii]

## 20th century

The Red Lion continued as a hotel, catering for travellers throught the town, until it was condemned by the Church Street widening scheme: on 17 March 1963, the Red Lion was closed down and, on 2 June 1963, the building was demolished.[iv]

Ref: i TIBBUTT in B. MAG 2:337; ii LAMBORN (1859) p. 138; iii DERBYSHIRE (1882) p. 108, iv TURVEY (1977) p. 18

## The Site of Cooke's Row

In the middle of High St. North used to stand a group of buildings known as Cooke's Row'. They were pulled down in 1804 to widen the road, so the stage-coaches could turn more easily into the inns on both sides, e.g. The Anchor and The White Hart. The gap between Cooke's row and High St. North was known as 'White's Lane' (as mentioned in the Augmentation Accounts of 1542), perhaps because of the Anchor's earlier name — the 'White Horse'. Cooke's Row was erected in the 16th century as the High St. North equivalent of Middle Row now in High St. South. (Cooke's Row was also known as 'Middle Row' while today's Middle Row was called 'Middle Rents'.)

Cooke's Row included the Lyon and The Peacock inns and The Cokerye (possibly a cook-house). The Lyon was owned by Richard Denton who died in 1564 and whose memorial brass used to be in the Priory Church. The name Cooke's Row may have come from a Houghton brewer. Cooke's Row also used to have the town market house where stalls could be held indoors. In 1804, after Cooke's Row had been demolished, the market house was moved next to The Crown where it became known as the 'Old Market House' and was later converted into the Town Hall (see 55).

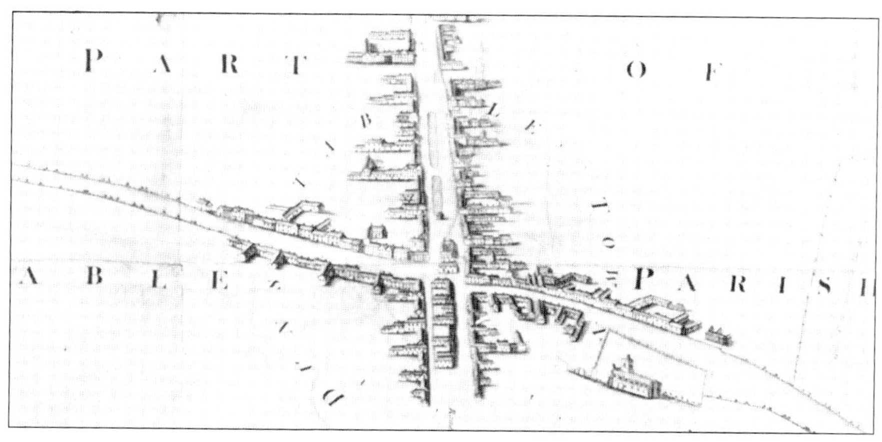


*Map showing Cooke's Row*

Refs: WOODCOCK (1950); VCH 3:355; BNQ 1: 259; BHR 63, 64

## The Nag's Head

The Nag's Head P.H. is on the corner of High St. North and West St. and it dates back to at least the 17th century when it was owned by the Settle family. One member of this family was Elkanah Settle who became a famous playwright. The Nag's Head was always known as being a good place for individual travellers to stay.

In 1904 The Nag's Head Hotel was advertised as having 'Good Accommodation for Motorists and Cyclists; Well-aired beds; Wines and Spirits of the Finest Quality; Dinners and Teas; and Moderate Charges'. The proprietor then was James Williams and the Hotel was 'in High Street and West Street, opposite the London and County Bank' with 'A Market Ordinary every Wednesday from 12 to 2'.[i]

---

### *ELKANAH SETTLE (1648-1724)*

*Elkanah Settle, the writer of plays and political works, was born in Dunstable on the 1st February 1648. His father owned the Nag's Head and at least one other Dunstable inn (The Bull). The Nag's Head is usually associated with Elkanah, although there's no evidence that he was actually born in this building.*

*Elkanah Settle went to Oxford and then on to London where he intended to make a living with his pen. He became famous during the reign of King Charles II, mainly as a rival to his contemporary, Dryden. In 1671 he had a success with his tragedy 'Cambyses' and, later, his play 'Empress of Morocco' was staged by the Earl of Rochester (notorious for his buffoonery and debauchery) at Whitehall, played by the lords and ladies of the court, in order to deliberately annoy Dryden. After Dryden had retaliated with 'Absalam and Achitophel', Elkanah lost popularity and settled into obscurity. He died at the Charterhouse in London.*[ii]

---

Refs. i SMITH (1904) advert., ii LYSONS p. 77 & CHAMBERS B10G. DICT. p. 1159;

# THE CROWN INN

*The Crown P.H.*

## THE CROWN P.H.

During the 19th century this old public house was called The Crow. According to Mrs Evans it may have been the Raven mentioned in 1692.[i]

## DUNSTABLE CROWS

Crows were associated with the town, as in the old saying 'As Black as a Dunstable Crow' which may have referred to the fact that crows look especially dark against the light chalky fields.[ii] According to one local, crows were trained to carry letters before pigeons were used![iii]

Refs: i EVANS (1985) p. 95; ii SMITH (1904) p. 160; iii WOODCOCK (1950) p. 328

## The Crow Pub

In the 19th centruy, Francis Ratt was the landlord at the Crow (e.g. 1839 & 1854) and Joseph Fearn was here in 1869. In 1870 The Crow changed its name to the Crown Inn.

## The Old Crown Inn

There used to be a famous coaching Inn in High St. North called The Crown but this was converted into a hat factory in 1847 (See 63). The owners of the Crow obviously wanted to capitalise on the name of the old Crown, which had built up a good reputation over many years, so it was used to replace the name of the Crow. There was also at this time a resurgence of patriotism under the Reign of Queen Victoria, so the Crown was an appropriate name for that reason too. (NB This name is not to be confused with the Crown that is mentioned in 1853 as the initial name of the Borough Arms pub in Albion St. — see 65)

## The present 'Crown Inn'

The present Crown was recorded with its new name in 1871 with Frederick Field as the landlord. Joseph Fearn, who was landlord when this was the Crow, had meanwhile moved to the new Globe pub in Winfield St. (see 72). By 1876 Frederick Field had also moved to another pub, the New Inn in Union St., and he was replaced by Lawerence Turner who was a butcher as well as a victualler.

Several landlords then ran the Crown (e.g. John Burnand in 1877 and Arthur Castle in 1885) but George Pleasant had taken over by 1894 and he remained there for many years until after 1924.

By 1928, William Hill was running the Crown and he too stayed for many years. Today's Crown is very popular, especially with younger people, and it retains its reputation for being patriotic. This was shown by the displays of Union Flags and red, white and blue bunting which decorated the whole pub for the recent Royal weddings!

Refs: (DIR)

# THE SITE OF DUNSTABLE TOWN HALL

The Town Hall stood between The Crown and the Anchor Gateway. The site is today occupied by the Abbey National Building Society which, as a piece of architecture, is unfortunately one of the most uninteresting buildings in Dunstable – in complete contrast to its predecessor!

## The Old Market House

In 1805 the Old Market House was built next to The Crown when the previous Market House was removed from the middle of the road (see 53).[i]

## The First Town Hall

In 1866 the Old Market House premises were bought from Queen Victoria (Lady of the Manor) by the new Borough Council, which was formed in 1864, for Council Meetings and for a Police Court. In 1869 a clock tower was erected and, in 1872, a corn exchange and plait hall were fitted behind the Town Hall in the Anchor Yard.[ii] The Fire Engines were also accommodated in this yard, a situation which proved to be inconvenient, to say the least, when the Town Hall caught fire in 1879 – the Fire Engines were unable to get out and so the Town Hall was destroyed! (NB Dunstable's first fire-engine, built in 1569, is the oldest in England – now in the British Museum.

## The Second Town Hall

The Town Hall was rebuilt in 1880. It included small municipal offices and a main hall which was used for meetings of all kinds (including indoor markets) and for entertainments. The new clock tower could be seen at quite a distance, from many angles, and it was very accurate. (Unlike the Quadrant Clock!) In November 1965 The Town Hall was sold to the Pearl Assurance Co Ltd, in an auction at The Old Sugar Loaf, for £35,000. (In 1964 the Queensway Hall opened as a 'replacement' – see 82.) The Town Hall was finally pulled down, in July 1966, to make way for the present offices.

Refs: i SMITH (1904) p. 185; ii (ibid) p. 186

# THE ANCHOR ARCHWAY

*The Old 'Anchor Archway'*

The Anchor Gateway has a round arch, supported by two columns, and a gabled upper floor with small mullioned windows above. This was the stone Gateway to a 16th century inn, the White Horse, which no longer exists. On the site of the White Horse was built the Anchor Inn, thus the gateway (the only surviving part of the White Horse) became known as the 'Anchor Archway'. In 1984 all the original early 17th century stonework on the front was replaced, giving the Gateway a rather bright and sharp 'brand new' appearance. However, the new stone will soon weather and The Anchor Gateway will then look old once more.

Ref: VCH 3:351-2

## The White Horse

On the site of the Anchor Inn was the White Horse Inn during the 16th century. It was at The White Horse that King Henry VIII stayed, in 1537, after he had refused an invitation from The Priory. (He was about to close all the monasteries in England so obviously didn't want to stay in one!) Later, King Henry VIII's daughter Queen Elizabeth was also accommodated at the White Horse.[i]

As one looks under the Archway today, the Baptist Church (and school) can be seen at the end of the alley. This stands on the site of the bowling green which was in existence at the time of the White Horse. King Henry VIII may have played bowls on this green when he stayed at the inn. The White Horse was mentioned in 1692, in the will of George Briggs, along with 'the Raven and the White Lion in Watling Street,' 'the Goat in Church End,' and 'The Woolpack in South End.'[ii]

## The Anchor

The name of The White Horse was transferred to a pub in Church St., behind The Red Lion (see 90), and the original White Horse was rebuilt as The Anchor which apparently became known as a poachers' tavern. The Anchor sign was probably symbolic of a safe 'harbour' and 'mooring' for the night, rather than have any direct reference to the sea.[ii]

## 19th century

In the early 19th century, the Anchor Inn was occupied by John Holmes who then moved to the Saracen's Head in the 1830s. John Watson was at the Anchor in 1839 followed by William Arnold. By 1864 John Holt was landlord followed by Martha Holt. In 1877, Edward Smith took over, followed by James Moore. By 1894 the Anchor Inn had closed down and the premises were occupied by Middleton and Gutteridge solicitors.[iv]

Refs: i VCH 3:355; (CAT) 1950 (CRO B3 153); WOODCOCK (1951) p. 328; (DIR)

### Middleton and Gutteridge

This firm consisted of Stephen Douglas Beckley Middleton and Albert Gutteridge.

S.D.B. Middleton lived at 'Evansville' (now 'St. Mary's Court') West St. (in 1885) then at 'The Cedars' High St. South (in 1898). He was 'solicitor and clerk to the Borough Magistrates, Steward of the Manor of Markyate Street (now Markyate), perpetual commissioner, solicitor to the local branch of Bassett and Co. Bank and to Dunstable and Markyate Street Building Societies'.

Albert Gutteridge, who lived at 'North House' High St. North, was 'solicitor and commissioner for oaths and certified bailiff under the Law of Distress Amendment Act'.[i]

### Bennett's Hat Factory

In the 19th century, next to the Anchor Inn (now Halifax Building Society) was Benjamin Bennett's private residence (now John Wilkinson Estate Agents and Stevens). Benjamin Bennett owned the large Bennett's Straw Hat Factory next to his house. Today, by walking under the Anchor Archway and turning right before the end of the alley, the rear of Bennett's house can still be seen along with the extensive factory premises behind the 'Town Hall Chambers' and a stable block.

At the end of the last century, Bennett's house was occupied by Thomas Weatherill who used part of Bennett's old factory as his own factory.

There were two Benjamin Bennetts: the son ran the Bennett's straw hat factory while his father ran the Bennett's Brewery much further down High St. North (where the Chiltern P.H. is today).

### Oliver's/Milligan's Hat Factory

Next to Bennett's Hat Factory was the smaller hat factory of Oliver which was taken over by Milligan & Co. The building is now Connells Estate Agents.

Refs: (DIR) & (CEN) 1851

# THE BANKS

*High St. Banks*

The east side of High St. North is today dominated by three major Banks: (from south to north) National Westminster, Lloyds, and Barclays.

## NATIONAL WESMINSTER BANK

Since 1964, when the Red Lion was pulled down, this bank has been on the corner of High St. North and Church St. The earlier bank, on the same site, was rebuilt during the redevelopment of the 1960s. The Westminster Bank took over the small local Barnard's Bank at the beginning of this century. Between the National Westminster Bank and Lloyds Bank are the Palmers Estate Agents and the Woolwich Building Society.[i]

## LLOYDS BANK

Lloyds Bank was built in 1923 on the site of an old ironmonger's shop which Lloyds bought in 1920 from Wood and Co. The shop's address was 80 High St. North or Market Place, as it was then called, and it was at one time occupied by J. Chambers and Son as tenants of the Trustees of the Charity of Jane Cart. It was large, with extensive outbuildings, and it had been estalished since 1763. The old shop was soon demolished, however, and the present bank was built in its place, opening in November 1923 as 12-14 High St. North.[ii]

Refs: i GODBER (1969) p. 553; ii BAGSHAWE (1967) p. 9

### The Chambers Family

In 1906 John Mellor Chambers, son of John Chambers, was occupying the shop. The Chambers family had a long history in this town: there was a John Chambers living in Dunstable in 1573! John Mellor Chambers married Mary Scroggs whose ancestors also had long local connections, especially in the hamlet of Sewell. This couple had a son, Alec, and two daughters, Evelyn and Maud. Evelyn taught children at home and also became part-time governess at The Grove House.

### Aberfeldy

In 1909 the ironmonger's business was sold to H.W. Cash and Co. and the Chambers family moved to 'Aberfeldy' — a large house at 31 High St. North, opposite to The Grove House. Evelyn Chambers established a successful and popular Kindergarten school at Aberfeldy which grew larger and employed several teachers, including Maud.

## BARCLAYS BANK

### Dunstable's First Main Post Office

The modern Barclays branch was built on the site of Dunstable's first main Post Office. This Post Office moved in 1912 to what was then a new building in High St. North, later known as the old Post Office (now DHSS — see 70).

### Bassett's Bank

Barclays Bank took over the local Bassett's Bank which was a typical example of a small family bank. Like many banks, Bassett's started in the early 19th century in a market town when a business man acquired enough capital to begin banking transactions. Bassett's began in 1812 when Peter Bassett, a Quaker Draper, opened a bank at Leighton Buzzard. He retired in 1813 so his son, John Dolin Bassett, took over the £9000 capital and a partner brought in another £3000. In 1823 a branch of Bassett's was opened in Dunstable which remained a steady, although smaller, competitor to Barnard's Bank.[ii] In 1826 there was a 'run', when a rumour that the banks were short of money caused people to panic and rush to their banks demanding the gold that was 'promised on demand' on the bank notes. The smaller banks couldn't cope with this sudden demand so they went out of business. Locally, only Bassett's withstood the pressure.[iii]

Refs: i BAGSHAWE (1967); ii GODBER (1969) p. 448; iii LAMBORN (1859) p. 173

## BANK NOTES

There were two types of bank: 'banks of deposit,' which would look after cash and return it when asked, and 'banks of issue,' which kept deposits and issued bank notes of their own.

The local bank of issue was the 'Dunstable and Luton Bank' which, according to Lamborn, 'occupied the spot now filled up by the shop of Mr Chamber grocer.' Lamborn also wrote 'It is believed that there are but two £1 notes remaining in Dunstable, of this issue, the one in the possession of Humphrey Brandreth and the other of Mr Johnson, postmaster. One . . . bears the date Dec. 17th, 1802; its registered number is 10,800, was entered by G. Taylor, signed by D. Queenborough; payable to Messrs. Buttton and Son, Paternoster Row, London, on Gutteridge, Butterfield and Co., Dunstable and Luton bank.'[i]

## TRADE TOKENS

In the reign of Charles II, tradesmen were allowed to issue their own coins and several of these Dunstable 'Trade Tokens' have survived. Some of the issuers and brief descriptions of both sides, front (O) and back (R) are, in alphabetical order:

### Barret

O: THOMAS.BARRET.CARRIER = a pack horse pannier
R: IN.DUNSTABLE.1669 = HIS HALF PENNY[ii]

### Chester

O: EDWARD.CHESTER.BAKER.IN = 1667
C
R: DUNSTABLE.HIS.HALF.PENY = E E between 2 roses, the stems entwined[iii]

NB This Edward Chester is probably the Quaker baker who formed a Society of Friends group in Dunstable c1654 and was jailed in 1660 (see 33).

### Chew

O: WILLIAM CHEW = 1667
R: DUNSTAPLE HALF-PENNY[iv]

NB Chew's School, built 1715, was named after William Chew, 1656-1712 (see 16 & 17). This token was probably issued by another William Chew.

Refs: i LAMBORN (1859) pp. 172-3; ii BLUNDELL (1928) p. 19; iii (ibid) p. 21; iv LAMBORN (1859) p. 101

### Element

O: WILLIAM ELEMENT = an angel with hands clasped in an attitude of prayer
R: IN DUNSTABLE 1667 = two flowers, the stems entwined between W.E.[i]
NB Blundell mentions 2 others and states that all 3 types were poor specimens, difficult to read. This William Element is probably the same as 'William, son of William Element, baptised Nov. 8th, 1641'. Lamborn mentions a Brass ELEMENT token (no date) with a 'figure in armour'.[ii]

### Finch

O: DANIELL.FINCH = 'The Merchant Tailors' Arms' on a shield
R: IN DUNSTABLE 1668 = HIS HALF PENY D.S.F.[iii]
NB Blundell mentions 3 others, including one dated 1666 from 'EDLESBORO'. The Finch family was of long standing in Dunstable. A Daniel Finch was buried on 12 Aug. 1589.[iv] This Token was probably issued by Daniel Finch mentioned as son of Roger Finch in his will 27 Dec. 1652. Daniel Finch's will, 7 Sept. 1672, included property in South St., Church St. and Icknield Way left to wife Sarah, son Daniel and two daughters. A Finch token was mentioned by Lamborn.[v]

### Fossey, Daniell

O: DANIELL FOSSEY = a greyhound carrying a hare, between two tobacco pipes crossed
R: OF DUNSTAPLE 1668 = HIS HALFE PENY over F
D E
NB Lamborn mentions similar token of 1638 (but date could be misprint);[vii] presumably an inn, perhaps called 'The Greyhound' or the 'Hound and Hare' (location unknown).

### Fossey, William

O: WILLIAM FOSSEY = a swan with a chain
R: IN DUNSTABLE 1667 = W.F. between three roses, stems entwined[viii]
NB another version of this, which is more common, has no chain, This token was presumably issued at an inn called 'The Swan' (perhaps the inn later called the Red Lion — see 51). The Fossey family

Refs: i BLUNDELL (1928) p. 21; ii LAMBORN (1859) pp 101-2; iii BLUNDELL (1928) p. 23; iv BLAYDES (1890) p. 92; v (as iii); vi (ibid) p. 24; vii (as ii); viii (as vi & vii)

was recorded in Beds in the 13th century. A Daniel Fossey was buried on 27 Aug. 1635; another was baptised on 24 Oct. 1641; and yet another was born on 25 Jan 1657. A William Fossey was born on 2 July 1658, son of William and Deborah; and William and Martha Fossey had a daughter, Martha, who was baptised on 8 June 1683. William Fossey, a yeoman, was buried on 19th Dec. 1689.[i]

### Tiplady

O: EDWARD TIPLADY OF = 'The Grocers' Arms' on a shield
T
R: DUNSTABLE HIS HALF PENY = E M between two flowers, stems entwined[ii]

### Whitley

O: JOHN WHITLEY = 'The Drapers' Arms' on a shield
R: IN DUNSTALE = W
I M

NB According to the Parish Register, John Whitley and Mary Sear were married on 5 May 1658.[iii]

### Wimpew

O: NATHANIELL WIMPEW = a hart lodged
R: IN DUNSTABLE HIS (HALF) = a Mitre over W
N I

NB On the North Wall of the Priory Church is a Monument to Nathaniel Wimpew, son of Richard, who died 13 Feb. 1705 aged 63.[iv]

Trade Token:
Edward Chester 1667

Trade Token:
William Fossey 1667

Refs: i BLUNELL (1928) p. 25; ii (ibid); iii (ibid) p. 27; iv (ibid)

# CHARLIE COLE'S OLD SHOP

The Nationwide Building Society branch now between Curry's and Halford's was Charlie Cole's bicycle shop from 1925 to 1985, until he moved to the present position in High St. South (see 21) Charlie's penny farthing bicycle, which is today above his new shop, used to protrude at right angles to these old premises and was a well known local landmark in the centre of town. The shop was almost totally rebuilt in 1985 but it was based on a very old timber framed building which dated from the 16th century. At one time it was a pub (perhaps The Bear).

The most striking thing about this shop was the collection of wall paintings which were discovered on the first floor in 1954 during alterations. One of the pictures showed a man dressed in Tudor clothes, smoking a long clay pipe, which dates from about 1580. Some of the paintings were removed from the wall in 1985 and are now displayed on the ground floor.

*16th Century Wall Paintings*

# SITE OF THE WHITE HART

*(now the corner of Nicholas Way)*

The White Hart, an Elizabethan tavern, used to stand on what is now part of the Quadrant in High St. North. The White Hart was closed down in July 1965 and was demolished, along with adjacent buildings, in order to build the modern shops. [i]

### The White Hart

There was a White Hart at the beginning of the 16th century. A record in the Parish Register, written c1500, states that a stranger was buried in Dunstable after he died of the plague at the 'White Harte'. In 1606 the White Hart Inn and its garden were bought by William Bennett, a yeoman. In 1785 the White Hart was occupied by Mark West.[ii]

### The Maddocks Family

In the 19th century, this inn was owned for many years by the Maddocks (or Maddox) family who ran carriers to London. James Maddocks was occupying the White Hart in 1823, followed by Mrs Elizabeth Maddocks by 1847, then William Maddocks by 1862. By 1869 Charles Horn had taken over, followed by: William Dally (1885), William Robbins (1894), and Walter Peirce (1898).[iii]

### 20th Century

The landlord and landlady who ran the White Hart for its last three years (1962-5) were Jim and Betty McNamara. They transferred to the new Winston Churchill pub when it opened in Church St. on 9 August 1965 (see 90).

Refs: i TURVEY (1977) p. 18 ii (DIR) 1785 p. 15 & (CAT) 1950 iii WOODCOCK (1950) p. 328 & (DIR) iv TURVEY (1977) p. 19

# FLEMONS AND MARCHANT CHEMISTS

*(now the corner of Nicholas Way)*

Standing on the left (northern) corner of Nicholas Way, is the pharmaceutical business of Flemons and Marchant. This modern chemists shop, built with the rest of the Quadrant, stands approximately where the previous Flemons and Marchant premises were. The business is one of the oldest in Dunstable, dating back over 100 years to its founder Joseph Flemons.

## Joseph Flemons

Joseph Flemons was a pharmaceutical chemist who ran the business (then at no. 73 High St.) which had been established in 1881. He was known as a man of personality and culture who, dressed in a sombre frock coat, apparently gave the impression of being some sort of alchemist. The Felmons' business was taken over by Mr Marchant, the eldest son of John Albert Marchant who owned the West St. Temperance Hotel (see 35), and so the shop became known as Flemons and Marchant's[i]

After retiring from the shop, Joseph Flemons continued to deal in herbs, with his son's help. This successful business was carried out behind the shop in part of an old malting house. Women and children were regularly seen walking through the town pushing old prams, or soap-boxes on wheels, full of herbs that had been gathered in the local fields and hedgerows — to sell to Mr. Flemons![ii]

Refs: i BAGSHAWE (1967) p. 227; ii (ibid)

# OXFAM SHOP

*(was Woolley Sanders Hat Factory)*

The Oxfam Shop moved into this building, 40 High St. North, in 1986 from the previous premises which were on the opposite side of High St. North, in Warren's (see 63). The main advantage of the new shop is that furniture can be stored and sold in its large warehouse.

## Woolley, Sanders & Co.

The large premises (which today also contain the Gateway Building Society) were built c1863 for the Woolley, Sanders & Co. Ltd straw hat manufacturers who also operated at Cheapside, London. Woolley Sanders closed in 1924.[i]

## The Dunstable Museum

Between 1935 and 1939 The Dunstable Museum was housed at 40 High St. North after being moved from Kingsbury Barn (now the Norman King P.H.). These premises were provided by the Borough Council and they also contained the Beds C.C. Library. However, the library moved in 1938 to High St. South (now the 'Little Theatre') so the Museum lost its County Council support, Unfortunately, the Museum contents deterioated while they were here (and were nearly destroyed by a fire in 1936!) so, in the absence of local support, the collection was transferred in March 1939 to Wardown Park Museum, Luton, where it can still be seen today.[ii]

## Electrical Shop

Before Oxfam moved in, this shop was for many years an electrical shop. Its last name was 'Rediffusion' and before that it was 'Wetherheads'. The original electrical shop was set up c1935 by Arthur L. Chattell who also ran a bicycle business, hence the shop was called 'Cycles and Wireless Ltd.' Arthur Chattell was very active locally: he was Chairman of the Dunstable Pioneer Boys Club which met in Manchester Place (see 68), and was also Secretary of Dunstable Rotary Club.[iii]

Refs: i (DIR); ii DUN. LIB. & MUSEUM REPORTS; iii TURVEY (1977) pp 46-7

# THE OLD SUGAR LOAF

*(Built c 1717)*

*The Old Sugar Loaf Hotel*

The Sugar Loaf has been a 'Berni Inn', previously a Schooner Inn, since 1972. It was built in about 1717 as a luxury hotel and it proved to be a good business investment for Jane Cart.[i]

## 18TH CENTURY

In the early 18th century, the country as a whole had experienced uncertain times. The Scottish Jacobites rebelled in 1715 and it was generally unsafe to invest in business. However, after King George I (who reigned 1714-27) had been on the throne for a couple of years, the country became more stable, allowing people such as Jane Cart to develop new businesses.[ii]

Refs: i TURVEY (1977) p. xiii; ii WOODCOCK (1950) pp 325-6

### The Origin of the Name

The Sugar Loaf's name probably derived from a Grocers' Arms. There was one recorded in Dunstable in the 16th century when 'ingrossers' or 'monopolisers' advertised their wares by a loaf of sugar. The word grocer derives from 'gross', i.e. one who deals in large amounts of food, such as sugar. (The term 'Grocer's Itch' refers to the eczema or irritation of the skin that can be caused by handling sugar.)[i]

### An Exclusive Inn

The Sugar Loaf soon became known as a place to stay, on the important Watling Street, for the nobility and the gentry. For being so exclusive, the inn had to pay a heavy duty to the Inland Revenue – six hundred pounds a year. During the American War, however, this duty was suspended and The Sugar Loaf had to billet soldiers along with the other Inns in Dunstable. It lost the profits but managed to survive by building a special house for the soldiers next door, later known as the 'Sugar Loaf Tap' (see below).[ii]

### Famous People

Many famous people stayed at or visited the Sugar Loaf. According to Daniel Defoe, Moll Flanders stayed there in 1750. Visitors included the Marquis of Waterford (a.k.a. 'Spring-heeled Jack' because of his habit of jumping out and frightening people!) and Lord Byron.

Queen Victoria and her husband Albert visited the Sugar Loaf in 1841 and inspected a display of straw plait and bonnets, including the well-known 'Seven-Ends Dunstable' and 'Bedford Leghorn' plaits as well as the famous 'Dunstable Bonnet.'[iii]

### The Coaching Trade

Business at The Sugar Loaf was at its peak during the Coaching Era when there was a demand for good food, accommodation and stabling facilities.

One popular speciality was Lark Pie made from Skylarks that had been caught on Dunstable Downs – local people where employed to catch these birds. The water supply to the Inn, though, was still drawn from the ponds in the road outside![iv]

Ref: i WOODCOCK (1950) p. 325 & O.E.D.; ii GREGORY (1952) pp. 211-2; iii (ibid) & WOODCOCK (195) p. 326; iv (ibid) p. 325-6

The stables included a stud of greys and up to 40 pairs of horses. Even after the coaches had stopped, the stables were continued for many years: the last ostler (stableman) was Mr. J. Christmas Willimot who retired in the 1920s.[i]

### The 20th Century

A locally well-known proprietor for several years was Mr. Peter Allen who was a former councillor and Alderman. He died suddenly in April 1965. In 1972 the Old Sugar Loaf was closed in order to make the extensive internal alterations to convert it into a Schooner Inn. Mrs Joan Allen, the proprietress, had been there for 22 years when it was taken over.[ii]

In April 1976 the Sugar Loaf Hotel had a special guest: a lion stayed overnight while travelling from Edinburgh Zoo, where it had been on loan for one year, back to Longleat in Wiltshire.[iii]

### The old Sugar Loaf Tap

The old Sugar Loaf Tap is the building adjoining the Sugar Loaf, now occupied by a ladies fashion shop. Until 1985, F.L. Moore's Record Shop was in this building before moving into High St. South.

The Sugar Loaf Tap was built in 1861 as a place where soldiers could stay during the preparations for the American War of Secession. These red coated soldiers were billeted in Dunstable as they passed through on their way to the Weedon Barracks. Accommodation was commandeered in the town at various places, including the Sugar Loaf and The Saracen's Head Inns.

The Sugar Loaf was well-known for being an expensive and private Inn, catering for the most wealthy travellers. Therefore, in order to keep the soldiers separate from the other clientele, the proprietors quickly had the extension specially built, hence it was known as The Soldiers House or The Soldiers Tap. After the last soldiers had left, the building was kept as The Sugar Loaf Tap, i.e. as a Public Bar.[iv]

Refs: i TWADDLE (1975) p. 53; ii TURVEY (1977) pp xiii-ix; iii (ibid) p. xv; iv WOODCOCK (1950) pp. 325-6

# 'WARRENS'

*(was Crown Inn/Hat Factory)*

In recent years, the ground floor of this large building has contained two separate shop premises. On the right (north) side was Oxfam until it moved across the road in 1986. The shop on the left (south) side has been empty since the tobacconist, 'Peter Graham', moved out.

## Windmill and Still Inn

On this site was the 'Windmill and Still Inn' which was mentioned in the 1724 Deeds of Chews School as being one of the meeting places for the Chews Trustees belonging to the Ashton/Cart/Aynscombe families. (The other meeting inns mentioned were: the Sugar Loaf, the Black Lion and the Maypole.)[i]

## The Crown Inn

In the middle of the 18th century, the Windmill and Still became the famous 'Crown Inn' (not to be confused with the present 'Crown Inn' in High St. North). The subsequent 18th century history of the Crown Inn can be traced from the solicitors' Deeds of Albert Gutteridge: In 1757, a Dunstable innholder named Henry Norman was at the Crown Inn. In 1772 a Deed of Conveyance stated that a third part of the Crown Inn owned by Henry Norman, deceased, was transferred by his widow Hannah Norman (of Ampthill) to a gentleman named Richard Dickenson (of Ware).

In 1773 the Crown Inn was conveyed from Richard Dickenson to Alex Jeffreys, a Dunstable innholder. In 1794 the Inn was conveyed from the son and heir of Alex Jeffreys, William Jeffreys (a yeoman of Bruton Street, Middx.), to Jerimiah Fossey, a Dunstable gardener.

In 1795 the Crown Inn was conveyed from Jerimiah Fossey to James Smith (of Bishops Hatfield, Herts.), a carpenter[ii]

Refs: i DERBYSHIRE (1882) p. 132; ii (CRO) DDGT 90-105

### The 19th century Crown Inn

By 1823 John Gilbert was at the Crown Inn, succeeded by Daniel Gilbert who was at the 'Crown Inn and Posting House' by 1827. (William Gilbert was at the Swan in 1827). Daniel Gilbert remained at the Crown until at least 1839.[i] In a Deed dated 1841, Thomas Burr was recorded as the property owner of 'a messuage formerly called 'The Windmill and Still' and now 'The Crown' Inn in Dunstable.'[ii] In 1847, the Crown Inn was converted into a large straw hat factory.[iii]

### The 19th century Crown Hat Factory

The straw hat factory was started by 'Forfar and Milligan Straw Bonnet Manufacturers' who became 'Milligan, William and Co.' by 1853. In about 1885 Milligan and Co were replaced by the straw hat business of Alfred Warren who had started in Albion St. and who had a private residence known as 'Tressillian House' in High St. North.[iv]

### The 20th century Crown Hat Factory

The hat company continued into this century as 'Alfred Warren and Sons' who by 1910 were producing felt hats as well as straw hats. The hat factory closed in 1928 by which time it was known as either the 'Crown Factory' or simply 'Warrens' — the name which is still used to describe the building today.[v]

Refs: i (DIR); ii (CRO) DDBH 407; iii DERBYSHIRE (1882) p. 100 iv (DIR); v (DIR)

# THE ELEANOR CROSS SHOPPING PRECINCT

This modern shopping precinct, which extends from High St. South through to Albion Street, was opened in 1985. It was developed by Robinsons Ltd who also designed the Ashton Square precinct (see 31). The interesting shop fronts create an almost medieval atmosphere around a small square.

At the focal point of the precinct is a statue of Queen Eleanor which was specially commissioned for this building project.

The precinct is named after the Eleanor Cross which used to stand at the Cross Roads (see 50.)

*The Modern Eleanor Statue*

# ALBION STREET

Albion Street, along with the other streets in the N.W. quadrant of Dunstable, was owned by the British Land Company during the Victorian Era, hence the patriotic names: Victoria St., Princes St., Edward St., and Regent St. ('Albion' was the Roman word for 'Britain'). Albion St. developed during the 19th century from east to west: the road beyond Matthew St. and Edward St. was developed last and was originally known as 'Upper Albion Street.'

## The Hat Factories

Hat Workshops were on both sides of Albion St., with some on the site now occupied by the Eleanor Cross Precinct which were demolished in the 1970s when the Precinct was first developed. The workshops were erected in the middle of the last century, when straw plaiting was the main trade in Dunstable, and they were used to make felt hats as well as straw products. As with other hat factories, production ceased at the end of the 19th century when businesses moved to Luton.

## The Corners

At the High Street end of Albion St., on the southern corner, used to stand the 'Stone House' private residence. The opposite (nothern) corner contained the Dunstable Borough Gazette offices until August 1986 (see 66).

On the corner of Albion and Edward Street is the 'Borough Arms' P.H.

# THE BOROUGH ARMS P.H.

The Borough Arms stands on the right (northern) side of Albion St., on the corner of Edward St.

### The First Pub: 'The Crown'

In 1850 the site where the Borough Arms is was sold by Edward Burr to Frederick Burr, who built a small coaching inn called 'The Crown' with adjoining stables (still there today). NB This 'Crown Inn' is not to be confused with the Old Crown Inn, which closed in 1847 (see 63), or the present 'Crown Inn' (see 54) In 1853 the Albion St. 'Crown' was advertised as an inn and posting house occupied by Henry Lockhart, beer retailer and coach proprietor. By 1862 Henry Lockhart had moved on to the Red Lion Hotel.

### The Borough Arms

By 1871 the 'Crown' had become the 'Borough Arms', with Henry Walter as landlord who was followed by Frederick Rossiter (by 1876), Henry Bedford Reason (in 1877), John De Vulder (by 1885) and James Franklin (by 1894). In 1903 Joseph Sermon was at the Borough Arms, then Hamilton Dealtry (by 1910), and Edwin Tilley (by 1914) who stayed there until the early 1930s.

### The Modern Pub

In August 1986 the inside of the Borough Arms was altered, by Whitbread and landlord Paul Hearty, which included extending the pub into the old stables next door to form a games room (for pool and darts). The bar is now twice the size it was. The pub sign still shows the Arms of the Borough.

Refs: (DIR) PIGOT, KELLY, SLATER, CRAVEN, etc.

### The Arms of the Borough of Dunstable

The conical shape in the middle of the shield represents a wooden stake. At the top of this stake are two interconnected circles which symbolise a gold ring attached by an iron staple to the wooden post. This image derives from an old legend about King Henry I fixing a gold ring to a post in Dunstable in order to lure and catch a notorious thief called Dun the Robber. Dun was supposedly a Saxon outlaw who, refusing to accept the Norman rulers, lived with a gang of followers in the local woods — a bit like Robin Hood, but a lot less chivalrous!

### Variations on a Theme

The legend (in its various forms) and the Borough Arms make up a curious collection of puns, which can become confusing: Dun is supposed to have given his name to Dunstable, which was known first as Dunstaple; Dunstaple is supposed to derive from Dun and the staple which held the King's ring; a staple is also an old word for a post (or pole or pile) such as the posts which mark out a market place; Dun is also supposed to have been a horse thief or at least had a stable, hence the naming of Dun's Stable — Dunstable etc.

In fact there is no reliable record of any King fixing a ring to a post or even of the existence of a man named Dun. One version of the legend was recorded in verse form in the Church Register in 1600 by the curate John Willis, but even this early story would have been several hundred years after any Saxon outlaw could have survived.

### Etymology

The most commonly accepted explanation of the naming of Dunstable, originally Dunstaple, is far more mundane: 'Dun' means a hill or downs, and 'staple' comes from 'estaple' meaning a market place with wooden posts, i.e. 'Dunstaple' was the market place by the hills.

Further Reading: SMITH (1904); COX (1957) Refs: SMITH (1904) pp. 10-11 108-9; SMITH (1906) pp. 150-2

# MATTHEW STREET

Matthew Street was built in the mid 19th century when it was first known as 'Edward Street'.

### Wheelwrights' Arms

On the corner of Albion St. and Matthew St., diagonally opposite the Borough Arms, stands a building at an odd angle to the road. This is now 'Plus Business Systems Ltd' (15 Matthew St.) but in the 19th century it was the Wheelwrights' Arms P.H. and it was the first building in this area, being put up before either Matthew St. or upper Albion St. existed, hence its unusual position.

In 1864 the Wheelwrights' Arms was occupied by William Marshall (previously at the 'Shoulder of Mutton') who was actually a 'coach and cart wheelwright' as well as the pub landlord. In the 1870s (e.g. 1871, 1877) it seems that William Marshall was still operating from here as a 'coachbuilder and wheelwright' but the public house was run by William Pantling. This arrangement continued until about 1885 when William Marshall returned to running the pub. By 1894 John Flecknell was the landlord.

By 1903 Samuel Marshall was at the Wheelwrights' Arms and he too operated for a short time as both beer retailer and wheelwright. By 1910 the Wheelwrights' Arms had closed but Samuel Marshall continued to work there as a wheelwright until the start of the First World War in 1914. NB at 10 Matthew St. lived the last Town Crier, George White, who was last recorded in the Directories in 1914.

## EDWARD STREET

Edward St. was developed in the mid 19th century when it was originally known as 'Mount Street', probably because there was an old burial 'mound' at the northern end which was flattened when the road and houses were built. There are some quite interesting houses along Edward St., many of which were involved in the straw trade.

### East Side

On the 'Borough Arms' side of Edward St. used to be a large area owned by Burr's Brewery (the site now includes the Bingo Hall in High St. North, see 68). Burr's Brewery became Cooper's Hat Factory which eventually employed 300 workers, some of whom lived in this area e.g. Manchester Place.

### West Side

Pickering's Hat Factory: the shop on the corner of Albion St. and Edward St. (now a specialist dry cleaners) was the factory of John Pickering who took it over c1871 and expanded it from 10 to 50 workers.

Langridge's Bonnet Rooms: 23 and 25 Edward St. were the bonnet sewing rooms of Arthur Langridge. At 25 (then no. 11) lived 'forewoman' Sarah Bass. Johnson's Hat Factory: 31 (then no. 17) Edward St. was the small factory of Edwin Johnson and his son John.[i]

### The United Reformed Church

The United Reformed Church stands on the west side of Edward St. in the building that was originally a School Hall attached to the Congregational Church, which stood next to it until recently. The School Hall was built adjoining the church in 1856 and was first known as 'Osborn Hall' in memory of Mr Joseph Osborn the founder member. Today, the words 'Memorial Bicentenary School A.D. 1862' can be seen on the front of the United Reformed Church, which has the Rev. Bevan Bird as minister.[ii]

### Site of The Congregational Church

The Congregational Church was built in 1853-4 in an Italian style, with grey brick and Corsham stone dressings, and was nearly 60 feet long, over 40 feet wide and 26 feet high. The building accommodated 700 people and was erected by 'Congregational' or 'Independent' worshippers who had previously used a temporary wooden building, the 'Tabernacle', in Edward St. The Tabernacle was built in 1852 and used by the Rev. Henry Perfect while the brick building was being constructed. On 9th August 1853 the Foundation Stone of the Congregational Church was laid by Mr Joseph Osborn and the building work was begun by John Marshall. The church opened on the 12th January 1854 and the first pastor, James Lyon, was appointed on 9th November 1854. The building was sometimes called 'The Tabernacle' (after the temporary building).[iii]

Refs: i EVANS (1985) 104-5; ii DBG (1965) p. 20; iii (ibid)

# THE DUNSTABLE GAZETTE OFFICES

Until August 1986, The Dunstable Gazette Offices were on the corner of Albion St. and High St. North, with the main entrance in Albion St. (originally it was in the High Street). Now the Dunstable offices are in much smaller premises, opposite the former Dunstable Grammar School, at no. 83.

The *Dunstable Gazette* is part of the Luton News/Dunstable Gazette newspaper which belongs to the Home Counties Newspaper Group. The main editorial offices of the Luton News/Gazette are in Luton, while the Dunstable office contains a sub-editor with a few staff. Printing is no longer carried out at either Dunstable or Luton.

The editor of the newspaper is John Buckledee who was educated at the Dunstable Grammar School and has been working on the *'Gazette'* since the early 1960s.

Both newspapers are issued on Thursday: the *Dunstable Gazette* (about 7,000 copies) and the *Luton News* (about 30,000 copies).

## The First Dunstable Newspaper

The 'father' of newspapers in Dunstable was James Tibbett, a Wesleyan lay preacher who strongly supported the temperance movement. James Tibbett started the first Dunstable newspaper, the *'Dunstable Chronicle,'* in 1855. It was produced by his small printing business called the Albion Press in his shop in High St. South (now Moore's Clothes Shop — see 10). The Dunstable Chronicle ended on 28 July 1860.

## The Start of the Gazette

In 1865 Daniel Tibbett, the son of James Tibbett, started *'The Dunstable Borough Gazette,'* at the age of 26 years. Daniel had a total of seven brothers and sisters, including two brothers who also became printers: James Jnr. (1841-1921), who took over his father's business, and Tom (1851-1941), who owned the Enterprise Printing Works in High Street North.

Refs: (DBG) 1965 pp. 7-11

In 1871 Daniel Tibbett died when he was only 33 years old, after what the black-bordered Gazette described as a 'protracted and severe illness'. His widow, Kezia, died a month later aged 29 years, leaving two orphans.

### The Early Gazette

At first The Gazette was published on Saturday mornings, price one penny, As with most early local newspapers, it received much of its material from a firm supplying newsheets which included national and international news, e.g. stories about the American Civil War. A typical *Gazette* consisted of four pages: local advertisements on page one, national news on pages two and three, and local news and advertisements on page four (the back page).

### Henry Ballans

After Daniel Tibbett died, *The Gazette* was run by his father James until he died in 1876. By then, *The Gazette* was actually owned by Mr. Henry Ballans, who bought it in July 1875 from the previous owner, Mr. William Etchells.

### The Move into The Gazette Offices

In June 1879 Mr. Ballans moved *The Gazette* from 71 High St. North (now part of Nicholas Way in the Quadrant) to the building on the north corner of High St. North and Albion St.

### Competition

When *The Gazette* started, there were no other papers in Dunstable but there was some competition from Luton e.g. *The Luton Times and Dunstable Herald*,' which printed a full column of Dunstable news. However, on 2 August 1884, another Dunstable Newspaper started as a rival to the Gazette. This was the *'Dunstable Advertiser and Weekly Reporter'* and it was printed at the Albion Press by none other than James Tibbett Jnr, — the brother of the Gazette's founder. The *'Advertiser*,' as it was called, eventually finished on 23 September 1905, when it was incorporated into the *'Luton Reporter'* (which, in turn, closed in 1926).

Refs: (DBG) 1965 pp. 7-11

In order to cope with the competition, Mr. Ballans made many improvements to the efficiency of the business, including the installation of a gas-powered faster printing machine.

### Miles Taylor

After Mr. Ballans died in 1892, *The Gazette* was published for a short period by Martha his widow. In 1895 Mr. Miles Taylor bought the firm after moving to Dunstable from Guisborough in Yorkshire, where he had managed a printing business.

### A. W. Mooring

Miles Taylor appointed Mr. A. W. Mooring as editor and together they wrote and compiled the newspaper, causing a steady increase in circulation. In June 1909, Mr. Mooring left the *Gazette* to become the editor of the new *'Biggleswade Chronicle'.* (Mr. Mooring wrote a novel called *'Dunstaple'* which was loosely based on the legend of Dun the Robber. Mr. Mooring's son, incidentally, was Sir George Mooring, British Resident of Zanzibar.)

### W.H. Press

Mr. Mooring's post was filled by Mr. W. H. Press, who had previously been editor of the old 'Leighton Buzzard Reporter'. Mr. Press was an 'absent editor', i.e. he worked as a freelance journalist from his home in Great Northern Road. He had a vivid imagination and wrote articles which were highly fictitious, e.g. *'How I spent Christmas in the Southern Seas'* and *'A Night in Dunstable Priory Church'.* These stories can be found in the old Dunstable Town Guides, published by Miles Taylor, e.g. the 1910 issue contains the 'Southern Seas' fantasy.

### Miles Taylor's other publications

Miles Taylor had other printing commitments in addition to the Gazette, e.g. School Magazines (including that of the Dunstable Grammar School), Parish Magazines (including Houghton Regis and Kensworth) and his own town guide, the *'Dunstable Year Book and Directory',* which was regularly issued between 1910 and 1925.

Refs: (DBG) 1965 pp. 7-11

## The Albion Street Offices

On the same premises as the Gazette Offices, Miles Taylor also ran a stationer's shop, a travel agency and a lending library. The Albion St. editorial and advertising offices were then used as the Taylors' home. On the top floor of the building, Miles' son made a living by giving piano lessons and, later, he too was increasingly involved in the Newspaper as a writer.

During th 1920s, Miles Taylor suffered more and more from the blindness that was affecting him, and, finally, he was forced to sell the business. Mr. C. W. Clarke took over in 1928, having just returned to this country from Australia.

## Poor Circulation

Mr. Clarke decided to create a new image for the Gazette and he used bold banner headlines as part of his changes.Unfortunately, his adventurous moves, coupled with a lack of sensitivity for the local people, resulted in very poor circulation and sales dwindled to less than 100 papers per week!

## The Agreement

The Gazette was on the point of closing when it was taken over by Gibbs, Bamforth and Co Ltd, the proprietors of *'The Luton News'* (who later became the present Home Counties Newspapers Ltd). The take-over happened on the understanding that the Dunstable Gazette would not be merged with any other Newspaper. This agreement was actually negotiated, not by the Gazette's owner, but by Mr Percy Lockhart (Town Mayor 1928-9) who acted as a spokesperson for the local people by saying: 'The Gazette is our own Newspaper, it has always championed Dunstable. If you take it over, let it continue as our Newspaper, devoted as it always has been to our Borough'. This policy was accepted by the new owners and it is still followed today.

Refs: (ibid)

### THE 1930s

After extra staff and modern equipment were used, and more pages and pictures were included, the circulation of the Gazette increased again. In October 1930 *The Gazette* was praised for its improvement by *'The Newspaper World,'* a journal of the newspaper and printing industry.

During this transformation, Mr. Earnest Buckman was in charge of *The Gazette.* He had been a *'Luton News'* reporter and had run their offices in High St. North (later occupied by Geary's Central cafe, now P. G. Allder the optician).

### D. S. McREATH

In June 1931 Mr D. S. McReath became editor of the Gazette, having served under Mr Buckman as a member of staff. Mr McReath helped the circulation to increase rapidly, remaining editor until 1945 when he took over a Watford Newspaper. (Later, he became editor of the *'Beds and Bucks Observer.'*)

### SINCE 1945

Since the Second World War *The Dunstable Gazette* has continued to grow under the successive editorships of Mr H. A. Franklin, Mr J. D. Lewis, Mr Donald Birdseye and now Mr John Buckledee.

### THE NEW TECHNOLOGY

The printing is now done using some of the latest facilities, including computerised typesetting — vast technical improvement from the days when each page was printed from a tray containing thousands of individually placed letters! The introduction of new technology has, as with other newspapers, meant radical changes including the closing of the Luton Castle Street print works in 1985, when all the print workers were made redundant. Printing is now carried out by a separate firm in Bicester.

### THE MOVE FROM ALBION STREET

In August 1986 the Albion St. Offices were finally closed down and the team of Dunstable staff moved into much smaller offices in 83 High St. North. This marked the end of an era for the Albion St. building.

Refs: (ibid)
177

# QUEENSWAY

Leading north-eastwards off High St. North is the modern Queensway road, at the end of which can be seen the car park (where the Market is held) and beyond that the large Queensway hall. Queensway is on the site that was previously the entrance to Park Farm which had farm land extending eastwards to the railway line and northwards to Dog Kennel Lane. When the building works of the 1960s began, most of Park Farm was grazing land, including Dunstable Park, of which a small portion remains as 'Grove Park.'

At the beginning of this century Dunstable Park was owned by Mrs. Malden, of the Isle of Wight, including the large houses known as the Grove House, the Beeches and the Lawn. Arthur Bagshawe acquired the Grove House and the adjoining Beeches which still survive, but the Lawn (last occupied by Dr. Pinkerton) was destroyed when the modern shops were built.

## The Co-op Site

The land on the south of Queensway was for several years an unsurfaced car park belonging to the Co-op. In 1986 this area, including the Co-op's old shop in High Street North, was built up into the new shopping block. Until the 1960s, the Fire Station watchtower used to stand on this site with a loud siren which, whenever a fire was sighted, could be heard all over Dunstable!

North House was here which was the home of Albert Gutteridge, a solicitor with the firm 'Middleton and Gutteridge' next to the 'Anchor Gateway' (see 56).

## The 1960s Development

The shopping block on the north of Queensway is a flat roofed collection of concrete boxes, unfortunately characteristic of the 'sixties' architecture which devastatingly consumed most of the north-east quarter of the town. This unpleasant and uninteresting architecture contrasts with the more imaginative 1986 building work opposite.

Refs: BAGSHAWE (1967) p. 224; (DIR)

# THE BINGO HALL

*(was Cinema)*

*The Bingo Hall*

The large building which stands on the west side of High St. North, opposite Queensway, is the Bingo Hall which was built as a cinema in 1937.

Next to the Bingo Hall is Manchester Place which is a short lane leading behind the Post Office to the halls used by the Pioneer Boys Club and the Dunstable Young Peoples Club.

Before the cinema was built, this was the site of Cooper's Hat Factory and before that it was the site of Burr's Brewery.[i]

Refs: i (MAP) O.S 1880; 1901; 1924; 1937

## Burr's Brewery

Burr's Brewery occupied this site in the 18th and early 19th century. Thomas Burr ran the brewery until he died in 1835, then Edward Burr took over until he retired and the 'Dunstable Brewery' closed in 1843.

The 'Dunstable Brewery' was sold in 1844 along with other properties, including no less than 43 pubs! Nine of these were in Dunstable:

The Bull; The Crown (formerly The Windmill and Still); The White Hart; The Wagon and Horses (formerly The Cow and Hare); The Anchor (formerly The White Horse); The Swan With Two Necks (formerly The Lion and The Lamb); The Yorkshire Grey Horse; The Shoulder of Mutton; The Sawyers.[i]

## Cooper's Hat Factory

Cooper's Hat Factory took over Burr's premises in 1847. The Coopers had come from Manchester and consisted of John, James and George Cooper. They built a row of cottages in 'Manchester Place' (named after their home-town) at the back of the factory for some of their workers. The name 'Manchester Place' is still used today for the lane which is now beside the Bingo Hall. The J.J. and G. Cooper hat and bonnet factory lasted until at least 1877 but it had closed by 1885.[ii]

## The Cinema

The cinema was built in 1937 when it opened as 'The Union', being initially owned by Union Cinemas Ltd. The Company was taken over in the same year by Associated British Cinemas, so the name was officially changed to 'The ABC'. However, the 'Union' sign which was on the front of the building was not changed to 'ABC' until April 1960.[iii]

Refs: i (CRO) DDBH 369-400; ii (DIR); iii PECK (1981) & TURVEY (1977) p. 49

The cinema held 1,048 patrons in the stalls and 384 in the circle and it had an orchestra pit in front of the screen. Behind the cinema was a car park. One particularly busy year was 1953 when many children saw the Queen's Coronation film here. (Few houses had television sets then!) In 1955, 'Cinemascope' was introduced.[i]

During the late 1950s, a Christmas Tree was annually erected in the foyer of the cinema and local people placed toys beneath it for sick children. The cinema was well used during the 1950s and 1960s – especially by children on Saturday mornings! The Pakistani Film Society held their meetings here until 1963, when they went to the Ritz in Luton. However, the effects of television were eventually felt and, as in many other towns, the attendances became less and less. In the late 1960s, in an attempt to attract more customers, amusement machines were tried and so were special family shows.[ii]

### Bingo

Bingo was first tried in January 1969 on three days a week and it was gradually increased, over the following four years, to two sessions every weekday and one on Sunday. Finally, in 1973, the cinema closed down completely and the premises were adapted totally for Bingo. This meant that films could not be shown and so the special licence was withdrawn by the Stage Plays Performance Committee. The Bingo Hall is now run by Star Cinemas (London) Ltd., a subsidiary company of ABC.[iii]

### The Other Cinema

Next to the cinema, on the right (north) side, used to be another Cinema: the two stood side-by-side until the area was redeveloped in the early 1960s. The site of this second cinema is now occupied by the modern shops between the Bingo Hall and the new Post Office.[iv]

Refs: i PECK (1981); ii (ibid); iii (ibid) & TURVEY (1977) p. xi; iv TURVEY (1977) p. 92

# THE POST OFFICE

*(Site of Manor House)*

The main Post Office opened on 8 July 1963 next to the old Post Office, now the DHSS offices, at a cost of about £80,000. The modern building was about three times larger than the old building and it had an unusual lighting system and a sound-proof ceiling.[i]

## The Manor House

The General Post Office was built on the site of the Manor House. In 1885 the Manor House was occupied by Dr. George W. Murphy B.A., M.B., M.Ch., who was the Medical Officer of Health to Dunstable Urban District, and Medical Officer and Public Vaccinator to Dunstable District, Luton Union. At the end of the 19th century the Manor House was used as a Girls' Boarding and Day School, called 'The Manor House School', run by the Misses Mein. At the beginning of this century, the Manor House was converted back into private residences.[ii]

NB Some writers have erroneously stated that the Post Office is on the site once occupied by the Cooper Hat Factory: comparison of the O.S. Maps (e.g. 1880 with 1937) makes the true position clear.

*The Main Post Office & The DHSS Offices*

Refs: i TURVEY (1977) p. ix & HICKENBOTTOM (1974) p. 142; ii (DIR)

# DHSS OFFICES

*(was Old Post Office)*

Since 1986, when the whole of the premises behind the frontage were rebuilt, this has been the centralised Dunstable DHSS offices. Previously, this was known as the Old Post Office. After the present Post Office opened in 1963, the Old Post Office was still used for sorting until 1984 when the sorting was transferred to Milton Keynes and it was put up for sale. The building was purpose built as a Post Office in 1912 when it was known as the 'New Post Office' because it replaced the earlier Office, opposite the old Town Hall, where Barclays Bank is today. The building was designed in a style similar to late 15th century Gothic, with a frontage of about 65 feet. The facade consists of dark red brickwork with Monk's Park stone used for most of the windows, doorways, mouldings and dressings. The roof is steeply pitched with two gables projecting from the front. The larger gable has a wall, filled in with a chequered pattern of white stone and flints, which is surmounted by a moulded stone coping. As well as being used as a Post Office, this building contained the Dunstable Telephone Exchange.

## The Telephone Exchange

The Dunstable Telephone Exchange started, in 1897, in the old offices of The Dunstable Borough Gazette on the corner of High St. North and Albion St. (see 66). In 1912, when the G.P.O. took over from the National Telephone Company, the Telephone Exchange moved into this Post Office. Apparently, most people were very cautious about telephones and many people wanted nothing to do with them, so they were very slow to be accepted. By 1916, for example, there were still only 58 telephones connected to the Dunstable P.O. Exchange – only some of the local businesses and a few prominent people had telephones. The exchange in 1916 had one operator plus a part-time and a night caretaker operator. The number of telephone lines eventually increased, especially after the Second World War. On 8 December 1960 the exchange went automatic and later was taken over by Luton Telephone Exchange.

Refs: (DBG) 1965 p. 25; TURVEY (1977) p. viii

# THE GAS BOARD

The local Gas Board, Eastern Gas, is in the premises next to the Old Post Office. The building itself is unremarkable, being little more than a glass fronted showroom. However, the gas supply has played an important part in the town's development and has a history of almost 150 years.

## Dunstable Gas and Coke Co.

Dunstable possessed a gas-works, the 'Gas-House', from 1836 when the Dunstable Gas and Coke Company was formed. In 1837 the gas cost 7s for 1,000 feet. Gas Lighting was available for homes from this time and by 1865 there were 94 gas lit street lamps in the town.

## The Dunstable Gas and Water Company

In 1872 the business was extended at the Brewers Hill Road site and the Dunstable Gas and Coke Co became the Dunstable Gas and Water Company. By the turn of the century, most houses and streets in Dunstable were lit by gas. Despite the change in name the Gas Works still produced coke, of course, which local people bought and collected in their wheelbarrows.

## Water Supply

Until the 19th century, water was obtained from wells and from long ponds in the four main streets. In High St. South the pond was in front of the Saracen's Head; in High St. North there were two ponds, one near the Sugar Loaf and one nearer the Cross Roads. The well water was very pure, for which Dunstable had a good reputation, but the pond water was very unhygienic. The last ponds were filled in during the 19th century and two deep wells were sunk on Half Moon Hill to supply fresh water: both are 8 feet in diameter; one is 192 feet deep and the other is 203 feet deep.

## Eastern Gas

The water interests were disposed of in 1960 to the Luton Water Company. The gas supply was then taken over by Eastern Gas. On 2 February 1971, Dunstable changed to Natural Gas from the North Sea and new appliances had to be fitted in every building that used gas. Today there are no more gas lights left but gas is still very popular for heating and cooking .

Refs: BAGSHAWE (1965) p. 92; (DBG) 1965; TURVEY (1977) p.xii; (DIR) 1974

# THE GLOBE P.H.

*The Globe P.H.*

This 19th century public house has undergone major internal alterations in the last ten years, mainly by converting small separate bars into one large bar. The outside of the building, however, has changed little. The name of the pub was first advertised in 1876 when Joseph Fearn was occupying the 'Globe' as a victualler and cooper (a barrel maker). He moved here in about 1871, having previously been at the 'Crow' (now the Crown Inn). By 1885, Henry North was at the Globe P.H., followed by Francis Ashplant (1894). At the beginning of this century, Patrick Kelly was landlord (1903, 1914) followed by Frederick Kelly (1920) and Mrs Kelly (1921). By 1924, the Globe was occupied by Robert George King who had moved from the 'Rifle Volunteer'.

Refs: (DIR)

# MANSHEAD ARCHAEOLOGICAL SOCIETY H.Q.

*(was The Sportsman P.H.)*

5 Winfield St. is the H.Q. of the Manshead Archaeological Society. Until 1984 it also housed the Women's Voluntary Service (the WVS), now at 46 Edward St. The WVS and the Manshead Society previously shared premises at no. 9 West St., next to Ellis' Shop, before those buildings were pulled down. This used to be The Sportsman P.H., which was known for its skittle alley.[i]

## THE SPORTSMAN P.H.

The pub name was first advertised in 1903 when Walter Cardell was at the 'Sportsman P.H.' By 1910, Sydney Buckingham was here followed by Mrs Rose Jane Buckingham by 1920 who was still here in 1940. By 1951, Archibald S. Bliss was landlord. In the early 1960s the Sportsman closed and the name was transferred to a new pub in Katherine Drive.[ii]

## THE MANSHEAD ARCHAEOLOGICAL SOCIETY

The Manshead Society is a voluntary group of extremely dedicated and hard-working local people who, guided by some of the country's top experts, have provided a great deal of information about Dunstable's past. The MAS was formed just after the Second World War by Mr Les Matthews. For a few years before the war he carried out some field explorations at Totternhoe with a group of Rover Scouts. This turned out to be a Late Bronze Age site and the results were published in the 'Antiquaries Journal.' After the war an Oxford University Tutor, Dr John Morris, helped the newly formed amateur society to pursue 'digs' scientifically and produce professional results. Since 1958 the Manshead Society has published the annual 'Manshead Magazine' about its research. There are also several books and articles about their work, by the Society and by others (see list below). It would be impossible here to even begin to summarise the vast amount of findings of the Manshead Society, so a small sample of their work is mentioned and readers are urged to read the publications themselves.

Refs: i WOODCOCK (1950) p. 323; ii (DIR) & TURVEY (1977) pp. 96-7

### Puddle Hill

Puddle Hill is on the N.W. edge of Dunstable, on the west side of the A5 at the Chalk Cutting. The Manshead Society members were digging here, non-stop, for 17 years! They found evidence of several early occupations, including Early Iron Age (i.e. Iron Age A, from about 550 B.C.), Belgic (i.e. Iron Age C, from the 1st century B.C. up to the Roman invasion), Roman and late Saxon.

### Maiden Bower

Maiden Bower is a large circular causewayed camp enclosing over 10 acres of land on the western edge of Dunstable. It is reached either by the Green Lanes off West St., or by the Sewell Road at the Chalk Cutting. The ditches of this camp were discovered at the beginning of this century by Worthington G. Smith, including a westerly ditch over 20 m. long and up to 3.6. deep. Maiden Bower was probably originally Neolithic (i.e. early New Stone Age, from 3,000 B.C.) and later occupied as an Iron Age Fort. Some of the pottery found here is thought to date from before 3000 B.C.

Near to Maiden Bower was found a 'Beaker Burial' that appeared to be an important Chieftain of the early Bronze Age (about 1750 B.C.) A bronze pin in the burial was the earliest piece of pure bronze to be found in Britain!

In Dunstable town itself there have been several major digs, including: a Saxon Cemetery at Marina Drive (excavated from 1958); the Friary Field (where Maxene Miller found the White Swan Jewel); a Roman Cemetery near the site of the Friary (excavated 1967-1981) and the Priory Meadow.

### Recommended Reading:

Matthews, C.L. Ancient Dunstable. Manshead Archaeol. Soc. of Dunstable. 1963.

Matthews, C.L. Occupations on a Chiltern Ridge Part 1 Neolithic, Bronze Age and Early Iron Age. Brit. Archaeol. Reports 29. 1976.

Matthes C.L. The Roman Cemetery at Dunstable, Durocobrivae. Beds Archaeol. Soc. Jour. Vol. 15. 1981.

The Manshead Magazine (1958-)

# THE BULL P.H.

This old pub on the corner of High St. North and Union St. was called the 'Prince's Arms' and then the 'Red Hart'. For a short time it was the 'Rose and Crown' before becoming the 'Bull' or the 'Black Bull' in the 18th century. A large coaching yard still exists (now a car park).[i]

NB In the 16th century a 'Bull' existed in High St. South (possibly where the Victoria Bun House was).

### 17TH CENTURY: PRINCE'S ARMS/RED HART/BLACK BULL

A Deed dated 4 July 1649 refers to 'the Prince's Arms, now the Red Hart in the North end and North St. of Dunstable.'[ii] Another Deed, dated 16 October 1663, refers to 'the Red Hart Inn in North St. Dunstable occupied by William Neale' being conveyed to William Ketteridge, innholder, of Dunstable. Also mentioned is '15.5 acres of land in Dunstable and Houghton Regis' which is bounded by 'Deadman's Hill' and 'Leighton Gap' (sic) and the 'Icknield Way.'[iii] (NB The 'Leighton Gap' path is still off West St.) In 1679 the inn was transferred from William Ketteridge to Henry Earle, a coachman, of London.[iv] By 1690 the inn was called the 'Black Bull' and it was leased by Henry Earle to John Bissaker, an innholder from Dunstable, after being occupied by Robert Wintour.[v] (NB John Bissaker died 9/4/1712 and his black marble monument can be seen in the south aisle of the Priory.) The Bull Close adjoining the inn was then 30 acres 'in the fields of Dunstable and Houghton Regis.'[vi] By 1697, Henry Earle had died and the Bull had transferred to his son and heir Henry Earle, coachman, of Chester. It was mortgaged by Ann Wright of St. Martin's in the Field, London.vii

### 18TH CENTURY: THE BULL

In 1710 the mortgage was taken over by John Wright, cutler, who had previously lived at Birmingham.[viii] In 1711 Henry Earle of Chester became bankrupt, and in 1713 the Bull was transferred to John Wright as part of a marriage settlement when he married Henry Earle's daughter, Sarah.[ix]

In 1785 William Palmer was at the 'Bull'.

Refs: i (CRO) DDBH 407; ii (CRO) DDGA 702; iii (ibid) 703; iv (ibid) 710; v (ibid) 711; vi (ibid) 711; vii (ibid) 712; viii (ibid) 714; ix (ibid) 715-7;

### 19TH CENTURY

A Deed of 1841 states that Thomas Burr (the owner of Burr's Brewery) died owning 'a capital messuage called 'The Red Hart', since 'The Rose and Crown' and then 'The Bull' Inn in North Street'.[i] By 1869 George Olney was at the 'Bull' (when Thomas Olney was at the 'Swan') and he remained there until at least 1885.[ii]

### 20TH CENTURY

William Robbings was in the Bull P.H. from about 1898, followed by Walter Cuell (1910), Thomas William Ivens (1913), Charles Martin (1914, 1933). Before the street numbers changed in 1921, the address was 52 High St. North. By 1936, William John Ives was at the Bull Inn, 115 High St. North, remaining until the 1950s.[iii]

### THE DUNSTABLE-HOUGHTON BOUNDARY

Before 1907, the land to the north of Union St. (including the north side of Union St.) was called 'Upper Houghton Regis' because it belonged to the Parish of Houghton Regis. This boundary went along the middle of Union St. and Chiltern Rd. down to West St., i.e. the western part of West St. was also in Houghton Regis. Under a Provisional Order of the Local Government Board, dated 28th August 1907, Upper Houghton Regis was transferred to the parish and municipal borough of Dunstable.[iv]

Refs: i (CRO) DDBH 407; ii (DIR); iii (DIR); iv (DIR) 1910

# THE WHEATSHEAF

The name of this pub was first advertised in 1894 when Thomas Buckingham was at the 'Wheatsheaf P.H.' He was previously here for several years as a 'beer retailer'. By 1936 William Arthur Smith was at the Wheatsheaf followed by Horace H. Crew by 1951. In the 1970s this pub was taken over by Terry and Jenny Walker-Spiers.[i]

## Other Wheatsheafs

The 'Wheatsheaf' name was also used by earlier Dunstable pubs, e.g. an 1813 Deed describes 'a messuage with yard' on the east side of High St. South 'formerly known as "The Wheatsheaf"'. Another 'Wheatsheaf' existed in 1839 in West St., where Princes St. now is.[ii]

## Terry Walker-Spiers

In the 1970s the present Wheatsheaf was taken over by Terry and Jenny Walker-Spiers and it became very popular with younger people, especially because of the juke-box containing an unusual selection of 1960s music! Terry and Jenny started a Folk Club in a small hall behind the pub which became famous for its high standard of performers, both local and international. Alex Campbell once said the Wheatsheaf Folk Club was the best in Europe! By the end of the 'seventies' this type of entertainment was no longer as popular so the Folk Club closed and was converted into a 'Pool Hall'. Live music soon returned, however, in the form of 'rock' bands which now play in the recently extended main bar.

Terry and Jenny have been involved with other local pubs, e.g. the Farmer's Boy (Kensworth,) the Chequers (Caddington), the Greyhound in High St. South, and the Harvest Home (Houghton Regis). In 1979 Terry Walker-Spiers organised a bizarre and unforgettable event in Dunstable: having decided that he didn't want to miss his own funeral, he held it prematurely! Black invitations were sent out and, a few days later, a long funeral procession walked through the town following a coffin containing the (not yet) deceased Mr Walker-Spiers. Afterwards, he was also able to enjoy the 'wake' held at the Wheatsheaf 'in his memory'!

Refs: i (DIR); ii (CRO) DDBH 458

# THE OLD GRAMMAR SCHOOL

*(now Ashton Middle School)*

*Illustration of Old Grammar School*

### The Old Grammar School

This school was built between 1887-94 by E. R. Robson in a Tudor Style using plum brickwork. It consists of two distinct sections, each in itself symmetrical, which are joined together at the main front entrance. Above this entrance is a square tower, set asymmetrically. The left (north) section, containing the hall, is Late Perpendicular in style; the other section is Jacobean.[i] Since 1973, this has been the Ashton Middle School for children aged 9-12 years. Before then it was the Dunstable Grammar School.

### The Dunstable Grammar School

Above the front door can still be seen an inscription which reads:

DUNSTABLE
GRAMMAR SCHOOL
FOUNDED A.D. 1728 BY
MRS. FRANCES ASHTON
BUILT A.D. 1887

Despite the wording on this inscription, Frances Ashton was not directly responsible for the establishment of the school. The date, 1727, is the year Mrs. Ashton died, leaving her estate for various charitable purposes including some provision for education. It was the group of Trustees of the Almshouse Charity who decided to build the Grammar School in 1887. This happened after The Charity had increased its funds through the sale of land and interest. The Trustees found that there was still plenty of money after they had built the Boys and Girls Elementary Schools in Church St. (now the Ashton St. Peter Lower School) so this school was built and opened in 1888.

### County Council

In 1948, as a result of the 1944 Education Act, Ashton Grammar School was taken over by the Beds C.C., so it ceased to take fee-paying pupils and the school leaving age was raised to 15 years.[ii]

### Past Pupils

Some well-known ex-pupils include: Gary Cooper, who starred in many films; Mr. Khaja Nazimuddin, the Prime Minister of Pakistan (who visited his old school dormitory in 1952); and Sam Kydd, another actor who appeared in many films and on T.V. (e.g. as Mr. Walton in 'Crossroads') – he opened a fete in Dunstable on 18 March 1961.[iii]

Refs: i PEVSNER (1968) p. 79; ii LUNN in (DBG) 1965 p. 27; iii TURVEY (1977) pp vi, xiii, 91

## GARY COOPER

Gary Cooper, the famous film star, was educated at the Dunstable Grammar School. His real name was Frank Cooper and he was born in Helena, Montana, USA in 1901. Gary's father, Charles Henry Cooper, originally lived in Houghton Regis but emigrated to America with his wife, Alice, at the age of 22. The Houghton Regis home of Charles was 'The White House' at 131 High St. which no longer exists, having been recently demolished to provide factory buildings. In America, Charles Cooper became a judge, and had two sons: Arthur Le Roy, born on 15th January 1895, and Frank James, born on 7th May 1901.[i] When Arthur and Frank were old enough, they were sent with their mother to England to be educated at the Dunstable Grammar School between 1910 and 1913.

### Gary Cooper lived here

While they were here, the Coopers stayed with their father's cousin and her husband, Mr and Mrs Walter Henry Barton, at 238 (renumbered 157 in 1921) High St. North. Walter Barton helped to run the business where his brother Frederick lived, called the Barton Brothers (provision merchants) shop, at 23 Winfield St. The house where Gary Cooper lived is therefore now the grocers shop called 'Lombardos', 157 High St. North, owned and run by an Italian family of that name.[ii]

### Friends

Mrs Cooper was apparently strict with Frank and Arthur and they made few friends while in Dunstable. However, they were allowed to frequently visit Mrs Barton's sister, Miss Laura Freeman, who lived in Houghton Regis at 129 High Street – next to The White House. Laura Freeman was Godmother when the boys were Baptised at Houghton Regis Parish Church on 3rd December 1911. The brothers also cycled to visit their grandfather, John Cooper, who had left The White House and moved into Manor Farm at Tingrith. At the Coopers' temporary home in High St. North, Frank and Arthur used to play with the Bartons' daughter Dorothy. (Dorothy Barton later married Bert Adams and went to live in Houghton Road, Dunstable.)[iii]

Refs: i (CRO) PARISH REGISTER FOR H. REGIS; ii (DG) 31.07.86 p. 14; iii (ibid) p. 14

### Neighbours

The boys also played with some of the neighbours' children. These included members of the Mead family — Jack, George, and Kitt — who lived at 2 Waterlow Road. The Meads' back garden gate opened onto a passage and faced the gate leading to the rear garden of the Barton-Cooper residence. George later moved to Borough Road, in Dunstable, while Jack went to London Colney and Kitt (now Mrs Wright) moved to Australia. It was George and Jack who, in 1986, helped to confirm the location of Gary Cooper's Dunstable home so that it could be commemorated.[i]

### Bagshawe and Cooper 2

The most interesting memories of Gary Cooper in Dunstable were written by Thomas W. Bagshawe. He was the son of Arthur Bagshawe who came to Dunstable in 1907 to start the Bagshawe Company in Church St. The Bagshawes lived at the Grove house, next to the Grammar School, and Thomas Bagshawe attended the school at the same time as the Cooper brothers. Since it was always customary at the Grammar School for boys to be called by their Surnames, Arthur Cooper (the older brother) was known as 'Cooper 1' while Frank was called 'Cooper 2'. 'Cooper 1' was apparently good at many things, both academic and athletic. 'Cooper 2', on the other hand, was shy, awkward and less capable in all aspects of school life. (He wasn't even noted for being good at drama!) In later years it was Arthur who was remembered, but very few people could remember Frank at all! Thomas Bagshawe recalled that he and Cooper 2 sat side-by-side at a desk in the lowest form (seated according to their adjacent names in the alphabetical register). Bagshawe described himself and his desk-mate as being 'two nervous boys, neither very good at school lessons'. He explained: 'In those days scholastic ability was much dependent on a parrot-like memory which neither had'. The young Gary Cooper was, according to Bagshawe, good at drawing. During lessons, Cooper 2 would draw pictures of ships and railway engines and show them to Bagshawe — which sometimes got them both into trouble![ii]

Refs: i (DG) 31.07.86 p. 14; ii (ibid) & BAGSHAWE (1966) p. 222

## Cowboys and Indians

Next to the Grammer School, in Grove House gardens, was a small wood called 'The Spinney'. Thomas used to play 'Cowboys and Indians' here with Frank and they sometimes used an airgun as a realistic 'prop'. On one occasion Thomas was playing an Indian when he was (as he put it) 'so stupid as to disobey orders from a cowboy and get shot in the leg with a slug'.!

## Cooper Goes West

In 1913 at the age of 12, Frank Cooper returned to his father's ranch in Montana with his mother and elder brother. Frank first worked as a Commercial Artist (his drawing practise at the Dunstable Grammar School no doubt helped!). His film career began as an 'extra' in some early Westerns and he eventually became contracted to Paramount in 1927, aged 26, after changing his name from Frank to Gary.

## Films

Gary Cooper's first success was with the 'The Virginian' made in 1929. Some of his other well known films include:
* *'Morocco'* (1930) — with Marlene Dietrich
* *'Today We Live'* (1933) — with Joan Crawford
* *'Beau Geste'* (1939) — with Ray Milland
* *'For Whom The Bell Tolls'* (1943) — with Ingrid Bergman

Gary's Directors included: Capra, Hawks, Lubitsh, Mann, von Sternberg, and Vidor. By the end of the 1930s Gary Cooper was reputed to be the highest wage earner in the United States! He married Veronica 'Rocky' Balfe, a New York Socialite, and remained happily married throughout his life. Gary Cooper's most outstanding film performance was in 1952, towards the end of his career, as the town Marshall in 'High Noon'. For this he received his second Academy Award. In 1961 when Gary Cooper was dying of cancer, he was honoured by the Film Industry for his outstanding services. Less than a month after this ceremony, he died aged 60 years. Today, Gary Cooper is a movie legend whose films are enjoyed by millions throughout the world. He's the most famous person to have been educated at the Grammar School and to have lived in the town. Perhaps one day there'll be a suitable commemoration to remind people of this fact.

Refs: BAGSHAWE (1966) p. 222; CAROL SMITH

# DOG KENNEL LANE

This ancient public footpath starts next to the old Grammar School, in High St. North, and leads to Houghton Regis. It is named after the Dog Kennels which used to be kept at Houghton Hall for hunting purposes. The land that this footpath crosses used to be known as 'Dog Kennel Closes', e.g. on the 1840 Tithe Map and on a Deed dated 6th February 1794. Previously, the land was known as the 'Duke of Bedford's Closes' since it belonged to the Duke during the 18th century. In 1907 the part of the footpath nearest the High Street was diverted to its present position.[i]

## The Walk to Houghton Regis

Today, the Dog Kennel Lane is still a useful short-cut for pedestrians between Dunstable and Houghton Regis. On the left (north) are the grounds of the Ashton Middle School and on the right (south) are the Grove House Gardens. Beyond the School grounds, on the left, is the back of Waterlows printing Works. The path then crosses the footbridge over the railway line. Over the bridge, on the right, is the recently expanded Vauxhall Motors plant which usually contains many newly made vehicles. Houghton Regis is then reached by walking downhill to the lower land in the north.

Refs: i BAGSHAWE (1966) pp. 133-7 & (idem, 1965) p. 97

# OLD FIRE STATION

*(built 1939)*

*Photograph of Old Fire Station*

The building next to Dog Kennel Lane was the Fire Station between 1939 and 1965. It is built with local Kensworth Grey bricks; the keystone (with the Borough Arms) and the door opening margin, front cornice, piers and wall copings, are all made from Clipsham stone. Today the building is used by the St. John's Ambulance Brigade.

## The Old Fire Station

This was Dunstable's first purpose built Fire Station which housed the two Fire Engines previously kept at the old Town Hall (see 55). The building was designed by Mr W. F. Wilkins and the contractors were Robinson and White. The Station was formally opened on 28th January 1939 by the Rt. Hon. Lord Luke of Pavenham KBE, along with the Public Conveniences at the rear.[i]

## The Present Fire Station

By the 1960s a larger Station was required for the modern appliances, so today's Station on the corner of High St. North and Brewers Hill was built at a cost of over £100,000. It was opened in October 1965 by the Rt. Hon. Lord Stonham, Under-Secretary of State for the Home Office, and the Mayor and Mayoress of Dunstable, Ald. and Mrs Walter Creasey.[ii]

Refs: i OFFICIAL OPENING (28.01.39); ii (DBG) 08.10.65 & 16.06.67

# THE GROVE HOUSE

*(mid 18th C)*

*Grove House*

This white building was built in the mid-18th century as 'The Duke of Bedford's Arms' inn. It is a well proportioned Georgian style house, fronted by a porch with two pairs of thick Tuscan columns. The building consists of two halves – as can still be seen from the front. In fact, after it ceased to be an inn, the property was rented out as two houses: 'Grove House' (the left half) and 'The Beeches' (the right half). At the beginning of this century, the building became the home of the Bagshawe family and the building was converted back into one private residence. In 1936, Grove House and its land were bought from the Bagshawes by the local council. They turned the house into Municipal Offices and opened the gardens to the public. Today it houses the S.B.D.C. offices.

Refs: BAGSHAWE (1966) p. 134; (idem) (1965) pp. 95-8; PEVSNER (1968) p. 78

*The 18th century*

The Grove House was originally 'The Duke of Bedford's Arms' inn, later abbreviated to 'The Duke's Arms'. It was named after the Duke of Bedford who was then the 'Lord of the Manor' of Houghton Regis. (This part of Dunstable was then in Upper Houghton Regis.)[i]

The inn was built c1750 according to a will dated 1759 made by the first owner, John Swindall, who left to his children the 'inn known by the Sign of The Duke of Bedford's Arms which I lately built'. John Swindall also owned the Saracen's Head in High St. South.[ii]

A map dated 1762 shows that the land in this area, known as 'The Duke's Arms Closes', belonged to John Miller. It seems, therefore, that initially the land was owned by John Miller while the Swindall family owned the inn itself. However, in 1773, John Miller bought the Duke's Arms as well and made it his own Mansion House.[iii]

## 19TH CENTURY

At the end of the 18th century and the beginning of the 19th century, the house was let to several people, including: H.J. Hichen (in 1797); Daniel Parken, a brewer (1801); James Buttfield and, later, Mrs Buttfield (from 1805 to 1812).

In 1813, John Miller sold the property to Frederick Brown who then occupied the house and land himself.[iv]

(NB There is a pencil drawing by Thomas Fisher of the 'Lawn Part of Mr Brown's house, Dunstaple', c1813, in the Cecil Higgins Museum, Bedford.)[v]

## W. F. BROWN

The next owner was William Frederick Brown (probably the son of Frederick Brown) who lived at the house from about 1830. He is recorded as being a regular attendant at church vestry meetings, sometimes acting as chairman. He also served as churchwarden between 1832 and 1842.[vi]

Refs: i BAGSHAWE (1966) p. 134; ii (ibid) p. 134; iii (ibid) pp. 134-6; iv (ibid) p. 136; v (ibid) p. 136; vi (ibid) p. 136

### Two Residences

Shortly before 1840 the building was divided into two residences, each with a garden, and rented to tenants. The 1840 Tithe Map shows that Henry Heulett was the tenant of the northern half (later 'Grove House'), while Elizabeth Budd rented the southern half (later 'The Beeches'). The whole property was still owned by William Frederick Brown, hat manufacturer, including: part of Dog Kennel Close; a garden (later called 'The Lawn'); a plantation; and part of The Park.[i]

NB Local Tithe Maps are very useful but they lack information, only listing the property on which tithe was payable. Much of Dunstable was tithe free.

According to several deeds, William Frederick Brown continued to own the property in 1868-85.[ii]

### The Rev. Macaulay and The Dunstable Riot

Between 1890 and 1903, Grove House was lived in by the Rev. Canon Heyrick Macaulay, M.A., Rector of Dunstable. He was quite wealthy and, like his predecessor, did much to improve the Priory Church. The Rev. Macaulay was a very determined man which was to his cost when, on 25th June 1902, over 50 panes of glass in the house were smashed by a crowd of locals! The people were angry because they wanted to celebrate the Coronation of King Edward VII but the Coronation was postponed, due to the King's illness, until the 9th August. Rev. Macaulay wanted to postpone the Dunstable celebrations as well, but the crowd had already built a large bonfire on Dunstable Downs and they wanted to light it and drink the free beer they'd been promised. After smashing the Grove House windows, they went off down West St. and carried on with the bonfire party regardless of the Rector's instructions![iii]

### 20th century: The Bagshawe Family

In 1906 Arthur Bagshawe rented the Grove House from Mrs Mary Elizabeth Maulden of Sandown Bay in the Isle of Wight, who also owned The Beeches, The Lawn and Dunstable Park.[iv]

Refs: BAGSHAWE (1966) pp. 136-7; ii (ibid) p. 137; iii (idem) (1965) pp. 94-5; iv (ibid) p. 95

In 1914 the tenancy was extended to The Beeches and so the two adjoining houses were made into one residence again. Both the Grove House and The Beeches were finally purchased by Arthur Bagshawe by a conveyance dated 13th October 1920.

At this time there was evidence that the northern end of the house and the yard had once been a brewery: in the extensive cellars was brewing equipment (vats, etc.) and wine vaults, and in the yard was a 'malt-house' or 'malting' — the upper part being a pigeon-loft accessed via a ladder. (This was all destroyed when it was bought by the Borough Council in 1936.)

In 1926 Arthur Bagshawe died and his various properties — including Grove House, and Kingsbury House and farm — were gradually divided between his sons. The eldest son, Arthur William Gerald Bagshawe, took over Grove House, while Thomas W. Bagshawe moved from Grove House (when he was married) to The Grey House (see 14) and then into Kingsbury House (see 97).

On 9th July 1936 the property and about five acres of land (formerly part of Dunstable Park) were passed by conveyance to the Borough of Dunstable. Grove House has been Municipal Offices ever since.[i]

### The Bagshawe Business

Bagshawe and Co Ltd was started in London in about 1880. Its main business was the importation of mechanical chains, carborundum grinding wheels and steam packings. From 1897 it also imported American-made bicycles. The owner, Arthur Bagshawe, decided that he wanted to make the iron chains himself, so he began to look for land on which he could build an iron foundry and engineering works. Arthur Bagshawe also wanted to live outside London, in a place which would be healthy for his wife and three children. The ideal location was therefore somewhere in the country, near a railway line, and within easy reach of London offices and warehouses.[ii]

Refs: i BAGSHAWE (1965) p. 95-8; ii (ibid) p. 93-4

## The New Industries Committee

Arthur Bagshawe was persuaded to come to Dunstable by two Councillors: James Field (who owned a photographic studio in High St. North) and Arthur Nash (a builder and contractor in Princes St.). These men were part of a 'New Industries Committee' which was formed to attract new businesses to the town. (There was unemployment in Dunstable due to the effects of industrialisation in general and the decline of the straw hat trade in particular.) These men, therefore, regularly visited London and arranged for advertising. The name of Dunstable was even featured in Piccadilly Circus![i]

## Bagshawe's Factory

Arthur Bagshawe consequently established a factory, built by Arthur Nash, on the land known as 'Backfields' alongside the Great Northern Railway, between Church St. and Dunstable Park. The family moved from Norwood in Surrey into The Grove House, which was conveniently available for renting, in 1906.[ii]

Bagshawe's Engineering Works grew in importance and, during the First World War, made tracks for the new military tanks.

The factory near to the railway bridge in Church St. was acquired by Thomas Tilling Ltd. in 1953. It was particularly well-known for the production of conveyor belts, which were of central importance to many manufacturing industries, including the local:
Vauxhall Motors Ltd (e.g. an 'Escaveyor' which elevates tyres to an overhead gravity roller conveyor); Electrolux Ltd (e.g. 5 types of Conveyors in a circuit to handle refrigerators); AC-Delco Division of General Motors Ltd (e.g. a minitrack to carry electric horns); Commer Cars Ltd (e.g. a Truck Haul Conveyor handling van bodies); The Associated Portland Cement Manufacturers Ltd (e.g. a Bucket Elevator).[iii]

In 1972 the business, still known as 'Bagshawes', eventually closed and in 1977 the firm's mock Tudor building was destroyed by fire.

Refs: i BAGSHAWE (1965) p. 93-4; ii (ibid); iii (DBG) 1965 (ADVERT)

### The Bagshawe Collection

Thomas W. Bagshawe took over, and built up, the large family collection of antiques and items of historical importance. He displayed some of the items of local interest to the general public when he opened the 'Dunstable Museum' (1927-34) in his barn (now The Norman King pub — see 98) in Church St.

The Bagshawe Collection was donated to the Wardown Park Museum, Luton, where it can be seen today.

Thomas W. Bagshawe also wrote many articles on local history (e.g. for The Bedfordshire Magazine and for The Dunstable Gazette) which have been of immense value.[i]

### The South Beds District Council

The Grove House is the main Dunstable offices of the South Beds District Council (the SBDC). These offices include:
Publicity and Information; Administration (e.g. Councillor services, electoral registration, land charges, cemeteries); Chief Executive's Department (e.g. Public Relations and Personnel and Management Services).

The other three main SBDC offices are:

1. Council Offices, Sundon Rd., Houghton Regis. (a) Development and Works & (b) Housing: e.g. housing, development control and building regulations, planning and architectural services, inspection of highways, street cleaning and lighting, car parks, drainage, parks, recreational facilities, conservation, listed buildings.

2. 5 Regent St., Dunstable. Environmental Health: e.g. refuse collection, markets, pest control, control of infectious diseases, home safety, clean air, inspection of food, offices shops & railway premises, noise abatement.

3. The White House, Hockliffe St., Leighton Buzzard. Finance: e.g. rates.[ii]

Refs: i SEE BIBLIOGRAPHY; ii (DIR)

# THE GROVE HOUSE GARDENS

*Grove House Gardens' Gates*

The Grove House Gardens were made public in 1936 when they were acquired from the Bagshawe Family by the Council. The original large iron gates were presented to the town in 1939 by A.F. England to form an impressive entrance to the Gardens.[i]

### Inside the Gardens

By entering the Gardens and taking the path to the right, one soon reaches the Market area in front of the Queensway Hall (82). However, if the path straight ahead is taken then, after walking through the Gardens, Grove Park is reached where there is a children's recreation area with swings and slides (81), and the Recreation Centre (83).

Refs: i BAGSHAWE (1965) p. 98

## The Park Estate

By leaving the Grove House Gardens on the south side (having taken the right hand path) the new Market Place and surrounding modern buildings can be seen. This whole area was part of the Park Estate which was developed during the 1960s and 1970s. The buildings around the Queensway Hall (82) and Market Place are, from left to right:

The Recreation Centre (83)
The Dunstable College of F.E. (84)
The Magistrates Court (85)
The Ambulance Station, behind the Hall (86)
The County Council Offices (87)
The Library (88)
The Quadrant Shopping Precinct (89)

The Market Place has markets on Wednesday, Friday and Saturday. At other times it is used as a car park. Further car parking exists on the south side of the Queensway Hall.

## The Planning of Park Estate

It is perhaps hard to believe that in 1960 this was over 22 acres of undeveloped land containing fields, a few allotments, and some old army Nissen huts left over from the Second World War! The whole Civic Centre Plan for Park Estate was conceived in 1959 by a group of local men including: the Town Clerk, Jack Smith; the County Council Clerk, George Brewis; the Town Borough Surveyor, Ron Carrington; and a member of Dunstable Borough Council, Michael L. Kilby. They met to discuss the idea on the railway bridge in Dog Kennel Lane, from where they had an uninterrupted view across the empty fields of Park Estate, as far as the buildings in Church St.

After the plan was approved, the 22.06 acres of Park Estate land was purchased by the Council in January 1960 for £137,876 and building started in 1961.

Refs: i TURVEY (1977) p. vii

# GROVE PARK

*Grove Park Recreation Area*

This Recreation Park is behind (i.e. east of) the Grove House Gardens. There are swings and a slide, etc., for children to play on and tennis courts for adults. The grass area extends beyond a row of huge horse chestnut ('conker') trees up to the new indoor Dunstable Recreation Centre (see 83).

This area was once part of the large Park Farm Estate, purchased by the Council in 1960.

# THE QUEENSWAY HALL

*The Queensway Hall*

The Queensway Hall is the building which looks like a huge 'flying saucer' trapped in a square enclosure of concrete and glass. It was built between 1962-4 by Desmond Williams and Associates of Manchester, who also built the circular Roman Catholic Church in West St. (see 45). The initial cost of the Hall was £320,000.[i]

Inside, the Main Hall is oval with wood-slat walls and a floor area of 8,800 sq. ft. This is surrounded by the restaurant and other ancillary rooms. The Vernon Room, on the first floor, is now used as the District Council debating chamber.

Refs: i PEVSNER (1968) p. 78 & TURVEY p. ix

## The Queensway Hall

The new 'Civic Hall' (later renamed 'The Queensway Hall') was opened on the 16th April 1964 by the Lord Mayor of London, Sir James Harman.[i] He told the assembled dignitaries that the new building was "bold and dramatic".[ii]

The first Catering Manager was Mr. Peter Aitken who ran the restaurant and bars for 13 years before leaving in 1977. The Catering Manager today is David Surgenor.[iii]

The Queensway has been used for many formal functions, including the annual Mayor's Balls. On the 24th March 1966, the Prime Minister, the Rt. Hon. Harold Wilson delivered his election speech here.[iv]

There have also been a wide variety of weird and wonderful events at the Queensway, including the European Weight Lifting Championships held in April 1977 which were attended by more than 80 of Europe's strongest men. A Cat Show is held here every year.[v]

In the early seventies this was a regular venue for major musical groups and artistes including Roxy Music and David Bowie. A few years later there were memorable concerts by bands such as The Clash and Blondie.

The Queensway is also used by local groups for their meetings e.g. the Dunstable and District Flower Club which meets every third Monday in the month in the Vernon Room.

The Hall Manager is Frank Daley and the rooms that are available for hire are: the Main Hall (max. 1000 people), Vernon Room (max. 100), Centenary Room (max. 200), Ground Floor Foyer, and First Floor Foyer.[vi]

Refs: i TURVEY (1977) p. ix; ii (DG) 25.04.85; iii; TURVEY (1977) p. ix; iv (ibid) p. x; v (ibid) p. xvi; vi ADVERT IN 'LEADER' 25.08.83 p. vii

# THE RECREATION CENTRE

*The Recreation Centre*

This indoor recreation centre was opened on 18th January 1975 by Olympic Gold Medallist Mary Peters, OBE, and Major Simon Whitbread, Lord Lieutenant of Bedfordshire. The building cost nearly £1,000,000 and it is maintained by the SBDC.[i]

The Recreation Centre includes a swimming pool, squash courts, badminton courts, table tennis, roller skating, weight and fitness training facilities, trampolines, and a cafe and bar.

Refs: i TURVEY (1977) p. xiv

# DUNSTABLE COLLEGE OF F.E.

*Dunstable College*

This College of Further Education was opened in September 1961 to provide mainly post Secondary classes, i.e. education for those above school leaving age as recommended in the 1944 Education Act. Since then the college has been greatly extended and it now provides a wide range of vocational and non-vocational courses.[i]

The Dunstable College is particularly notable for being the main centre in Bedfordshire for Nursery Nurse training (N.N.E.B.) and courses for the printing industry.[ii]

Refs: i LUNN in (DBG) 1965 p. 27; ii HICKENBOTTOM (1974) p. 142

# THE MAGISTRATES COURT

*(Built 1963)*

This rectangular two-storey Court House has a facade of blue-grey Welsh slate beneath the windows, and cobbled ground work (to discourage people from walking too close to the windows). In the main entrance are some distinctive fossil patterns in Derbydene marble. The Magistrates Court was opened in July 1963.[i]

## The County Court

The County Court House, the Crown Court, is in Bedford – as is the County Prison. Dunstable once had a Jail in Middle Row but this was destroyed long ago.[ii] Today there are, of course, cells in the Police Station in West St.

## 18th Century Justice

In the 18th century the Justices of the Peace were responsible for both administration and justice in Bedfordshire. In Bedford, a Session House was built in 1752 as the main venue for the County Sessions. Subsidiary meetings, called Quarter Sessions, were held in towns and villages in any convenient buildings e.g. the Black Bull Inn (see 74).[iii]

## Market Trouble

Being a market town, Dunstable attracted thieves and swindlers on market days, and the large numbers of people that gathered on these occasions meant that there was often trouble. Dunstable had two Constables to help catch offenders (there was no Police Force then).[iv]

## Whipping

Sentences frequently included whipping which, in the early 18th century, was always carried out in public: both men and women could be stripped naked to the waist and beaten, combining "justice" with "entertainment"! (sic). The whipping post and stocks at Dunstable were in front of the Ashton Almshouses, near the market.[v]

## Transportation

More serious offences were dealt with by transportation to the colonies – a useful way of ridding the county of further responsibility.[vi]

Refs: i HICKENBOTTOM (1974) p. 142 & TURVEY (1977) p. ix; ii SMITH (1904) pp. 101 & 182 & DERBYSHIRE (1882) p. 80; iii GODBER (1969) pp. 328-30 & (ibid) pp. 370-3; iv (ibid) p. 329; v (ibid) p. 373; vi (ibid) p. 373

## Hanging

The ultimate sentence was, of course, hanging. The main Dunstable gibbet was just outside the north end of town, beside the Watling St., on Puddlehill. The dead man's body was sometimes left for days or even weeks on the gibbet to act as a warning for travellers entering the town from the north. This gibbet was removed in 1803. Hanging is also recorded to have taken place on Pascombe Hill, Dunstable Downs.[i]

## 19th Century Justice

In the early part of the 19th century, before Dunstable obtained a regular court house and an official police force, justice was still carried out in the Inns. One local constable was John Franklin who was also an innkeeper at the White Horse, Church St. In 1819, he took two people out of the 'Shoulder of Mutton' (Middle Row) on suspicion of theft, and hauled them up in front of a J.P., Edward Tanqueray, at the Sugar Loaf. On another occasion, John Franklin rounded up a jury at the Saracen's Head Inn when he was trying 'to find out how Lucy Lakin came to her deathe'.[ii] The stocks were still used in the 19th century: in 1826, a travelling carpenter who had beaten his wife in Church St. was put into the stocks for a couple of hours.[iii] Whipping ceased in about 1850.[iv]

*The County Emblem on the Magistrates' Court with the motto 'Constant Be' from Bunyan.*

Refs: i SMITH (1904) p. 185 & DERBYSHIRE (1882) p. 81; ii WOODCOCK (1950) p. 288; iii GODBER (1969) p. 425; iv (ibid) p. 530

# THE AMBULANCE STATION

*The Dunstable Ambulance Station*

The Ambulance Station is next to the Magistrates Court, opposite the College, at the end of Kingsway. It was built at the same time as the Court House in the 1960s. The Ambulances stationed here are able to quickly transport people from Dunstable to the nearest General Hospital, the 'Luton and Dunstable', which is about three miles away. The Hospital is on the Dunstable Road, Luton, next to the M1 (Junction 11). NB For detailed information see 'Hospitals in Luton and Dunstable' by Margaret R. Currie.

# THE COUNTY OFFICES

*The County Offices and Dunstable Library*

The four-storey County Offices are on the left (east) of the two-storey public library. The two buildings are externally connected by a low linking section which contains the library's front entrance doors. The County Offices have a separate entrance to the library and contain various administrative offices plus a Probation Officers' Headquarters.

### The County Council

The main responsibilities of the County Council are: education, environment, recreation, large scale planning, refuse disposal, highways and transport, libraries and museums, social services, county records, fire service, police service, trading standards, and consumer protection.

Most of the Beds. C.C. Offices are at County Hall, Bedford. Apart from the Dunstable Offices, the only other County Offices outside Bedford are the Education Offices in Old Bedford Rd., Luton.

The Dunstable County Offices also contain the 'Births and Deaths Registrar'. ('Marriages' are at the District Council Offices, Sundon Rd., Houghton Regis). The Trading Standards and Consumer Protection Office is at the rear of the County Offices.

88

## THE DUNSTABLE LIBRARY

The public library is next to the County Offices, facing the Market Place, in a two-storey square block with large windows connected by concrete strips. It was purpose built in a typically uninspiring sixties style, at a cost of £75,000. (The previous library was in the building now occupied by the Little Theatre — see 18).

The interior is of the 'open plan' design which, topologically, is a single space containing: an exhibition foyer, a computerised book lending desk, a children's book section, a music library, a computer section, the Dunstable Museum Trust's exhibition area and the recently added Tourist Information Centre.

The library is unfortunately not conducive to serious study, being sometimes noisier than the Market Place outside! (NB Luton library has good facilities.)

### The Electronic Information Unit

Outside the library is the electronic information unit (a VDU with simple keyboard) which was installed in June 1986. It provides information about tourist attractions and amenities in the area.

# THE QUADRANT SHOPPING PRECINCT

The Quadrant is a pedestrian only shopping area designed by Willoughby Fletcher and Associates. It was formally opened on 3 June 1966 by the T.V. personality Bob Monkhouse. The two shopping lanes, set at right-angles to each other, are called 'Broadwalk' (off Church St.) and Nicholas Way (off High St. North).

## The Quadrant Clock

At the focal point of the T-shaped precinct is the three-faced Quadrant Clock designed by Robin Cameron Don of Scotland. The clock is suspended high in the air by a network of curved tubular steel and translucent coloured fibre-glass panels. This piece of abstract scaffolding is supported by three thick concrete columns. The clock has rarely worked properly, which is not suprising since the mechanism is so exposed to the elements. Dunstablians who remember the reliable clock that used to be on the Town Hall have been particularly displeased with this 'replacement'. Furthermore, the old Town Hall clock could be seen in the middle of town from a long way down the High Street. The Quadrant Clock, however, is visible from only a few positions. It's never been popular and, hopefully, it will be removed one day!

## The Quadrant Mural

The abstract mural in the Quadrant, above 'Boots' the Chemists and the adjacent shop, was designed by William Mitchell and Associates.

## The Electricity Board

The Eastern Electricity Board showrooms are in Nicholas Way, the Quadrant. Dunstablians were suprisingly slow to accept electricity: it wasn't supplied until 1925 because local people didn't see the need for it! (Gas and coal were considered to be sufficient for all domestic and industrial requirements.) Luton Council supplied the electricity until 1948 when it was 'Nationalised'. In 1955 the 168ft. pylons were erected across Blows Bowns.

Refs: TURVEY (1977) pp. vi, x, xi; HICKENBOTTOM (1974) p. 141

# CHURCH STREET

At the south end of the Quadrant, where Broadwalk finishes, is Church St. This road is part of the A505 and is usually very busy with traffic travelling to and from Luton and the M1. Suprisingly, perhaps, this road was only made up in 1784 when the road from Oxford to Cambridge was built through Dunstable. During the 18th and 19th centuries Church St. was called 'East Street'. Previously, however, this road was the site of part of the ancient Icknield Way which connected Norfolk (and the north-east) to Salisbury Plain (and the south-west).

## Church Street Widening

During the 1950s there was a huge increase in the volume of traffic passing through Dunstable as the motor car became more and more popular. The building of the M1 helped reduce the north-south flow of vehicles but the east-west route was still very busy.

At the centre of Dunstable the problem was particularly acute because Church St. was very narrow and it was not directly opposite West St., so the traffic couldn't move across easily. The only apparent solution was to widen the top end of Church St. Consequently, during the early 1960s, the Council put Compulsory Purchase Orders (C.P.O.s) on many of the properties lining the street and then demolished them. Some of the businesses that were closed in this drastic move were family concerns, built up over several generations (e.g. Baker's Hardware & Furniture shops).

The part of the Street most affected by the Church St. widening was the north side which had some very old buildings, including the White Horse P.H.

## Site of the White Horse (King's Head)

The White Horse stood where there is now road on the north side of Church St., opposite the Book Castle. The White Horse was originally named the King's Head.

### 16th century King's Head

The King's Head inn dated from the middle of the 16th century when a house owned by the Houghton Chantry (which owned most of the north side of East St.) was converted shortly after 1542. The inn may have been named in honour of King Edward VI (1547-53), although he closed the Chantries in 1548. The King's Head was later conveyed to John Wingate of Harlington.[i]

### 17th century King's Head

During the Civil War (1650-9) the 'King's Head' name could obviously have been dangerous, or at least unpopular, so it may have been renamed then.[ii]

### 18th century King's Head Inn

The King's Head was recorded at the beginning of the 18th century, e.g. Deeds dated 1705 and 1732.[iii]

### 19th century White Horse

The King's Head was renamed the White Horse at least by 1819 when the landlord was Mr. Franklin. The 'White Horse' name was taken from the inn in High St. North which had changed its name to the Anchor (see 56). Trade directories record the White Horse under the name of John Franklin from 1823 to 1876. By 1885, Mrs Elizabeth Franklin was running the inn, followed by Septimus Franklin from at least 1894.[iv]

### 20th century White Horse

During the first part of this century, Septimus Franklin remained in charge of the White Horse P.H. and then Mrs Elizabeth Franklin took over by 1936. By 1952, Maude E. North was occupying the White Horse but it eventually closed on 4 March 1963, with Mr. E.S. Reid as the last landlord.[v]

### The White Horse Stone

Outside the White Horse used to be a large stone which had been near the steps of the old inn for many years. It was worn and had probably been used to tether horses and as a stepping stone to climb into horse-drawn carriages. When the Church St. widening started, the White Horse stone was rescued and moved to the front of Beecroft School by Mr. John Lunn (then Headmaster), where it can still be seen today.[vi]

Refs: i EVANS (1985) p. 93; ii (ibid); iii (CRO) DDGT 28, 41; iv (DIR); v (DIR) & TURVEY (1966) pp. ix, 66; vi JOHN LUNN

# THE WINSTON CHURCHILL P.H.

The Winston Churchill P.H. was opened on 9 August 1965, after Church St. had been widened. The first landlord and landlady, Jim and Betty McNamara, had previously run the 'White Hart' in High St. North (see 59) until it had closed. This pub is noted, among other things, for its wide selection of Scotch! The pub was named, of course, after Sir Winston Churchill who had died on 24 January 1965, the same year the pub was opened. The 'Winnie' is the meeting place for Dunstable Rotary Club which organises many charity fund-raising events each year. Other organisation also meet here, including the Manshead Archaeological Society.

NB Next to the Winston Churchill P.H. is the tallest building in Dunstable, 'Quadrant House', which contains the local Tax Office.

Refs: TURVEY (1977) pp. ix, x, 19

# 'GIBBS AND DANDY' SHOP

The Dunstable Branch of Gibbs and Dandy, Builders' Merchants and Ironmongers, opened at 6 Church St. in 1910. Today, in addition to this shop and entrance, there are adjoining premises with an entrance round the corner in High St. South.

## The origins of the business

The Gibbs and Dandy business originated in Luton, in 1840, when Frederick Brown and Joseph Green established an ironmongery in a yard on Market Hill. This was so successful that the business soon moved out of the rather obscure yard into Luton's main road, George St., in 1842. In 1844 the two founders decided to become manufacturers as well as merchants and consequently set up Luton's first ironfoundry. Since this new venture was also very successful, Messrs. Brown and Green soon sold the ironmongery side of the business to Mr. C. F. Gibbs and continued as Green and Brown Ltd. (which still exists today).

## The origins of the name

Mr. Gibbs eventually sold out in 1894 to two brothers, William and Percy Dandy, who moved to Luton from Peterborough. Since the name of Gibbs was already well known and respected, the Dandy brothers decided to keep it and add their own – hence 'Gibbs and Dandy', even though there was never actually a Gibbs and a Dandy in business at the same time. Mr William and Mr Percy Dandy kept the business, until 1920, when a private limited company was formed. After the Dunstable branch was opened in 1910, there continued to be a steady growth in trade. In 1923, therefore, the original Church St. premises were extended by acquiring the adjoining shop, and other premises were added more recently. Today, the Dunstable shop stocks a wide range of commodities and many local firms have regular accounts there.

Refs: BANFIELD (1963) (ADVERT)

# THE BOOK CASTLE

*(Built 1872)*

*The Book Castle Book Shop*

The Book Castle is the only book shop in Dunstable and its customers come from many miles around. There is a very large stock of titles covering a wide range of subjects. As well as selling books, the shop has a computer section (hardware and software) and a classical music section (records, C.D.s and cassettes). The Book Castle also publishes books by local authors, including 'Dunstable in Detail'.

The Proprietor of the Book Castle, Mr Paul Bowes, chose the shop's name which aptly suits the architectural design of the frontage – with its hints of military fortification. The building dates from 1872 and it was, in fact, used as a Drill Hall by local volunteer soldiers for many years.

In 1985 the premises' long-disused and sealed basement was re-opened and converted into the music and computer department.

# LITTLE ALLEY

*Little Alley*

## Little Alley

The 'Little Alley' connects Church St. with Church Walk, joining it near the Priory Health Centre.

This illustration shows the view down the alley looking towards Church St. and it corresponds to the one drawn by Worthington G. Smith, in 1887, which shows a woman and a pig in the alley. The right (east) side has changed little in the past hundred years: the roof and jettied (i.e. overhanging) section looks similar, and so does the guttering and some of the brickwork. The left (west) side, on the other hand, has been totally rebuilt, leaving us with a plain vertical wall and metal gate which contrasts sharply with the interesting shapes and patterns opposite.

The land on the left, which is directly behind Woolworths, used to contain straw hat work-rooms and a tall chimney stood here until recently. The old building on the right is no. 26 Church Street.

*Passage from High Street to Church 'Church Alley'* | *Passage between Ashton and High Street* | *Passage between Ashton and High Street* | *Passage in Church Street 'Little Alley'*

*Worthington Smith's Alleys*

# 26 CHURCH STREET

No. 26 Church Street, which was sometimes known as "Mentmore House", is now an Italian Restaurant called "La Vecchia Capanna". Before being converted for its current use, this old building was very nearly pulled down. (The row of buildings which used to stand to the east were demolished during the 1960s.) Mentmore House was eventually saved after a local pressure group formed to protect it. Mentmore House was considered to be particularly important because, as John Bailey discovered, it was a typical example of a timber-framed building which had jetties on two adjacent sides. Inside, there was a "dragon beam" which spanned diagonally across the building to receive the floor joists.[i]

Renovation and modernisation has caused many changes to the front and interior of the restaurant. Fortunately, though, much of the building's interesting character is still there and the remaining jettied side also helps "Little Alley" to retain some of its old world charm.

### Rixson's Antiques

26 Church Street used to be Rixson's Antique shop and 12 Church St. (now the Book Castle) was once an additional showroom. Rixson's business was established in 1865.

Ref: i BAILEY

## Priory Church Car Park

Adjoining the east side of Mentmore House is the modern 'Eastgate House' office block.

The rest of the land to the east and south-east of Mentmore House is now mainly occupied by the car park (for about 75 cars) in front of the Priory Church. On this site were many buildings until the sixties demolitions.

## J. & W. Baker

The row of shops which used to be along this section of Church Street included the business of Joseph & Walter Baker, established in 1902, which had an ironmongers shop at no. 32-34 and a furniture shop on the other side of Church Street at no. 25.

## The Horse and Groom P.H.

Until the beginning of this century, the Horse and Groom stood on the corner of Church Street and the short road leading to the Priory Church. The site is today the corner of the Priory car park, opposite the Church Hall.

The Horse and Groom was known by various related names which changed erratically throughout the 19th century: in 1823 it was the 'Yorkshire Tavern'; in 1827 the 'Grey Horse'; in 1839 the 'Yorkshire Grey'; in 1853 the 'Horse and Groom'; in 1862 the 'Yorkshire Grey'; and in 1864 the 'Horse and Groom'! From 1864, however, the name remained constant as the 'Horse and Groom' until it closed down shortly after 1903. (NB The pub was also sometimes erroneously called the 'White Horse', an understandable mistake since a white horse is known as a 'Grey' in equestrian terms.)

Ref: (DIR)

# PRIORY CHURCH HALL

*(Built 1839)*

*The Priory Church Hall*

This Hall was originally built in 1839 as the National School for Infants. The school closed in 1922 and the building was formally opened in 1926 as the Church Hall, which it has been ever since.[i]

## The Founding of the National School

In 1833 the Government decided to give annual grants towards education. However, there was very little support for any kind of national education policy so the grants given were small: in 1833 there was only £20,000 for the whole country![ii]

## 'National' and 'British' Schools

Due to the lack of Government action, two groups set themselves up to organise schools and use the little amount of money that was available: the Anglican 'National Society' (for 'National Schools') and the Non-Conformist 'British and Foreign Society' (for 'British Schools').[iii]

Refs: i (DIR); ii GODBER (1969) p. 506; iii (ibid)

Since Dunstable had both Anglicans and Non-Conformists, both 'National' and 'British' schools were established. (The two types also existed in other towns but in Bedfordshire, generally, the Anglican contribution to education was the largest.) Consequently, the 'National School' was founded in Church St. and the 'British School' was founded in West St. (at the Baptist Church).[i]

## The National School

The National School opened in 1839 for 250 pupils and was especially intended to provide education for the poor. Initially, the infants received no more education after leaving this school. From 1864, however, infants from the National School were able to go on to the Ashton Junior Schools opposite (see 96). Attendance was purely voluntary until the 1870 Education Act was passed after which, in theory, all infants should have been at school. In practice, many parents kept their children at home (e.g. to plait straw to earn money!) so the attendance figures fluctuated. In 1894 the National School was advertised as being designed for 140 pupils with 'an average attendance of 101' and Miss S. Sibley as Mistress. The National School finally closed in 1922 when infants went to the Burr St. and Chiltern Rd. Schools.[ii]

## The Priory Church Hall

In 1926 the National School building became the Parish Hall of the Priory Church. Since then, the Hall has been used by many different organisations e.g. 'Sunday Schools', Scout and Guide Groups, Mothers' Union, Youth Clubs. As well as being used for meetings, it is used for social and fund raising events, e.g. dinners, dances, bazaars, jumble-sales, auctions. During the day the Hall is frequently used by Play-Groups for young children.

Refs: i GODBER (1969) pp. 506-8 & (DIR); ii LUNN in DBG (1965) p. 27

# ASHTON ST. PETER'S LOWER SCHOOL

*(Built 1864)*

*Ashton St. Peter's Voluntary Aided Lower School*

This Lower School, for children aged 5-9 years, is on the north side of Church St., opposite the Priory Hall. It is church aided and run by the County Council, and was originally founded by the Frances Ashton Charity, hence the long name.

## The Founding of the Ashton Elementary Schools

The Ashton School in Church St. was founded as a result of Frances Ashton's Almshouse Charity accumulating money through the sale of land in the mid 19th century. (The Ashton Almshouses were in West St. — see 33.) In 1859 the Master of the Rolls agreed that the extra money acquired by the Almshouse Trustees could be used to build a Church of England Elementary School. In 1861 the plans were drawn up and in 1864 the building was completed. It opened in 1865 as two separate schools, one for boys and the other for girls, with about 90 pupils in each.

## The Two Schools

The first Headmaster of the Boys' School was Mr Frederick Hatt who had two pupil teachers (trainee teachers) to assist him. The Girls' School had Miss Page in charge, with three pupil teachers to help her. The Boys' School consisted of two classrooms: one large (about 100′ × 20′) and one small (about 15′ × 20′). The Girls' School had three rooms: one medium (about 50′ × 20′), one small (about 15′ × 20′) and a small classroom which was also used as a committee room.

## The Early School Years: 19th Century

During the life of these schools, from 1865 to 1935, logbooks were kept by the Heads and they give a fascinating insight into the daily life of the institution. On some mornings, for example, the rooms were apparently so cold that the ink was frozen solid in the inkwells!

## Attendance

One of the greatest problems, though, was the poor attendance record. In 1871, an Inspector reported that, despite excellent teaching, the average attendance for each child was only 2.6 days per week! Sometimes children were kept at home by parents to work in the house or on the farms. Some children continued to work in the fields long after the official Harvest Holidays were over. Other absences were due to events such as local weddings, the Statute Fair, Church Outings, etc. In winter many children didn't have weather-proof clothing, particularly during the times of recession when the straw trade was poor.

## The 20th Century

Until the beginning of the 20th century, the school was still aided by the Ashton Almshouse Charity which had originally supplied the money. In 1903 (as a result of the 1899 Board of Education Act) the money for education was separated from the Almshouse Charity to form a distinct education charity, the 'Ashton Schools Foundation', which funded both the Ashton Elementary Schools in Church St. and the Ashton Grammar School in High St. North.

In 1911, a further distinction was made when the Ashton Schools Foundation was divided into two independent charities with separate Governing Bodies: the Ashton Elementary Schools Foundation and the Ashton Grammar School Foundation.

### The start of Ashton Primary School

In 1935, after 71 years, the separate Boys' and Girls' Elementary Schools were combined to become the Ashton C. of E. Primary School. This catered for children up to 11 years old, beyond which they were sent to local senior schools. The Ashton Primary School continued to be under the Ashton Elementary Schools Foundation.

### The New Governing Body

In 1958, the Elementary Schools Foundation was again combined with the Grammar Schools Foundation to re-form the 'Ashton Schools Foundation'. The separate Governing Bodies were then replaced by a single Governing Body to run both the Primary and the Grammar Schools as voluntary schools (as defined by the 1944 and 1953 Education Acts), in which 'religious instruction shall be given in accordance with the doctrines of the Church of England'. The two Ashton schools continued to have close links with each other and the Priory Church.

### The Comprehensive System

In 1971, the Comprehensive System was introduced. The pupils of Ashton Grammar School were moved to new premises at the southern end of Dunstable to establish what is now Manshead Upper School. The vacated Grammar School building in High St. North was immediately taken over by Ashton Middle School for pupils aged 9-13 years. The Ashton Primary School in Church St. consequently became Ashton St. Peter Lower School for 5 - 8-year-olds, which it remains today.

Refs: DERBYSHIRE (1882) pp. 176-80; LUNN in DBG (1965)

# OLD PALACE LODGE

*(Site of Palace)*

*Kingsbury Court & Old Palace Lodge Hotel*

Looking at the front of the building in Church St., the Old Palace Lodge Hotel is on the right and the private residence called 'Kingsbury Court' is on the left. Before the hotel was established this was all one property known as 'Kingsbury' which also included the building that is now the Norman King P.H. (see 98). The Kingsbury Court part is much older than the Hotel end. The name 'Kingsbury' derives from the fact that on this site a Palace was built by King Henry I.

## The King's Palace

Dunstable as a town owes its origins to Henry I: the 1086 Domesday Book records nothing here since it was just part of Houghton Manor covered in trees. King Henry I ordered the land near the Watling and Icknield junction to be cleared, so it would be safer for traders, and arranged for a Royal Residence to be built c1120. This Manor House or 'bury' therefore became known as 'Kingsbury' and it provided a convenient Palace for the King and his guests to stay when in the district, especially when hunting.[i]

Unfortunately, it is not known exactly where this Palace stood, what materials it was made of, or what it looked like. W. G. Smith's plan includes a moat and drawbridge, but this is based on what other Manor Houses looked like: no evidence has ever been found that the house was either fortified or moated.[ii] It is known that Henry I stayed here in 1122 to celebrate Christmas and that among his guests was the Count of Anjou.[iii] In about 1132, Henry I founded the Augustinian Priory opposite his house and gave most of the manor and borough, except for his Palace, to these Priors. The last king to stay at Kingsbury was Stephen who spent Christmas there in 1137. Both Henry II and Richard I reserved the Royal house for their own uses but didn't stay there.[iv]

## Conversion to a farm-house

In 1204 King John gave the Royal building and land to the Priory, making the Priors responsible for the whole town. Kingsbury may not have been used much after then since, in 1277, the Priory built a new place for Royalty to stay (next to the Prior's Chamber). It may even have been destroyed when Dunstable, among other places, was hit by a large fire in 1213. Later Kings, including Henry III, Edward I, Edward III, Henry VI and Henry VIII stayed at the Priory (except for Henry VIII's last visit when he stayed at the old White Horse).[v]

In the 13th century, therefore, Kingsbury ceased to be a Royal residence and was probably converted to a farm house soon afterwards. The Priory disposed of the property before the Dissolution and Kingsbury is recorded as being a farm in 1542 and at several dates after that throughout the 17th and 18th centuries.[vi]

Refs: i BAGSHAWE (1968) p. 213; ii (ibid) & SMITH (1904) p. 101; iii BAGSHAWE (1968) p. 215; iv (ibid); v (ibid) p. 216; vi (ibid) p. 237

### The Oliver Family

In 1789 Kingsbury Farm was sold by auction (by Mr Christie in Pall Mall, London). The occupant was James Oliver who was also the proprietor of the 'Sugar-Loaf' in 1785. James Oliver died in 1821 at the age of 82. His son, James Hopkins Oliver, lived at Kingsbury until he died in 1839 aged 59. Alfred Oliver, son of James Hopkins Oliver, lived at Kingsbury until 1892 when he died at the age of 75. Other members of the family lived there until at least 1894. NB A tombstone can still be seen in the old cemetery, opposite, engraved 'James Oliver of Kingsbury' along with other family names.[i]

### The Freeman Family

In 1898 Edward Holloway lived in Kingsbury House and, between 1901 and 1906, Frederick Freeman leased the house and outbuildings from Henry Brown ('Farmer Brown'), who also owned Park Farm to the north of Kingsbury. Fred Freeman was the son of Henry, a boot and shoe dealer and a carrier, with a shop in Church St. Fred set up a cab driving business in London, starting with one horse and cab and gradually building up with 'hansom cabs', 'broughams', 'brakes', 'four-in-hands', and then horse-drawn buses.

Fred's first wife died after having five children and he later married Louisa Mary Darby, the daughter of Polly Darby. (Polly Darby was the daughter of James Tibbett, see 10.) Mr F. Freeman was the Proprietor and Coachman of 'The New Age' long distance coach which ran the 94 miles from London to Coventry via Dunstable.[ii]

Fred lost his best horses when they were commandeered for the Boer War in S. Africa between 1899 and 1901. So, leaving his depleted business in the hands of his two sons, he moved to Kingsbury House where he lived with his second family until 1906. He died in 1919 aged 74.[iii]

### The First World War

Between 1906 and 1914, Kingsbury became a farm again when Henry Brown lived there (after moving from Park Farm) farming the land behind the house. During the 1914-18 war Kingsbury farm was kept by Redhead Estates Ltd as part of the war effort. Local people queued outside Kingsbury barn (now the Norman King) to be given food![iv]

Refs: i BAGSHAWE (1968) p. 238-40; ii (ibid) & ROBERTS (1968) pp. 306-313' iii (ibid); iv BAGSHAWE (1969) p. 353

## The Bagshawe Family

Soon after the First World War Arthur Bagshawe acquired Kingsbury House and farm. The house was occupied by his elder son, Arthur William Gerald Bagshawe, while the land was let to George Woodham Pratt, a cattle-dealer who already rented Park Farm from him. In 1924 extensive alterations were made to the house, mainly the extension to the east end. Second-hand Caddington bricks were used to match the older walls and old hand-made tiles were used for the roof. In 1927, when Kingsbury belonged to T. W. Bagshawe, the barn was restored and used as a museum and library (see 98).[i]

## The division into two premises

In 1934 the new (east) end of the house was sold as a private residence which, in 1936, became known as the 'Old Palace Lodge'. The barn and stables were sold off at the same time to become 'Kingsbury Stables'. In 1937 the west end of the house was sold and it became a doctor's house and surgery known as 'Kingsbury Court' (still lived in by Dr Ashton and his wife). In 1950 Kingsbury Court became a 'listed' building.[ii]

## The Old Palace Lodge

In November 1959 the Old Palace Lodge was acquired by Creasey Hotels Ltd and it opened as the 'Old Palace Lodge Hotel' in February 1960. Few alterations were made so the general style of the house was not affected: the main additions were a two-storey wing (for bedrooms) and a restaurant.[iii]

## Walter Creasey

The proprietor of the Old Palace Lodge, Walter Creasey, was a Mayor of Dunstable (1965-66) who died in February 1967 aged 57. "Wally", as he was affectionately called, had been a licensee for 33 years and had taken over the 'Halfway House' in 1939, and later the 'Glen Eagles' Hotel at Harpenden. In August 1967, the Dunstable Town Football Club at Brewers Hill was renamed 'Creasey Park' in his memory.[iv]

Refs: i BAGSHAWE (1969) p. 354-5; ii (ibid); iii (ibid); iv (ibid) & TURVEY (1977) p. x, 63, 128

# THE NORMAN KING P.H.

*The Norman King P.H.*

## The Norman King P.H.

The Norman King opened in 1961. The building is L-shaped: the main section along Church St. was an old barn belonging to Kingsbury Farm, while the section along Kingsway is the modern restaurant. The pub name refers to King Henry I, son of William the Conqueror, the founder of Dunstable.

## The Totternhoe Stone

The front wall lining Church St. looks as though it could be very old masonry since it contains large pieces of Totternhoe Stone. This material may have come from demolished Priory buildings or even the original Kingsbury Palace itself. However, the present wall was probably actually built in the 18th century re-using earlier stone.[i]

## Kingsbury Farm

The Kingsbury Farm occupied this site for several centuries until the Bagshawe family bought the property soon after the First World War. The farm house is now Kingsbury House, attached to the Old Palace Lodge (see 97).

## Museum and Library

In 1927 the barn was restored and converted into a town museum and library, the first branch of Beds County Library in Dunstable. The museum and library closed in 1934 when the building was sold for use as riding stables. Both library and museum were moved into 40 High St. North (now the Oxfam shop — see 61) but in 1938 the library was moved to High St. South (now the 'Little Theatre' — see 18). The museum contents, including part of the "Bagshawe Collection", went to the Wardown Park Museum in Luton where they are still looked after by the professional Museum Staff. (Dunstable Borough Council refused to house and maintain the museum, because of the expense, so it was very fortunate that Luton Council accepted and kept the collection.)[ii]

## Public House

In April 1960 the Kingsbury Stables were purchased by Flowers Breweries Ltd of Luton. The Norman King public house opened in October 1961.[iii]

Refs: i BAGSHAWE (1968) p. 243; ii BAGSHAWE (1969) p. 355-6; iii (ibid)

## The Original Norman King P.H.

When the barn was converted into a pub, a great deal of trouble was taken to keep the traditional style and good taste: stone was brought from the Norman Picot's Castle (built 1069) at Bourn near Cambridge and clunch blocks from a 12th century Cambridge cottage site were used. Panelling came from a former medieval inn, "The George" at Caxton, Cambs. The original Beds. Wheat Straw Thatch was replaced with reed thatching by specialists from Abbott's Ripon, Hunts.[i]

The interior used to have bare stone walls with oak beams and simple decorations in the style of a traditional English pub. Church pews formed much of the seating from which the interesting conversation pieces could be seen (and old boar's head, deer's heads, pieces of armour, etc.).

## The Present Pub

In 1984 the interior was completely gutted and replaced with white plastered walls covered in brightly coloured plastic fittings. The old world setting of stone, wood, copper and brass was totally destroyed and the inside now looks like a 'Habitat' cocktail bar. The outside, however, remains attractive and still complements the Priory Church opposite.

## Kingsway

Kingsway is the road which leads northwards, next to the Norman King. At the far end is Dunstable College (84), the Ambulance Station (86), and the Court (85) where it joins at right-angles onto Court Drive. Kingsway was built in the 1930s when Kingscroft Estates Ltd was developing this part of Park Estate for residential use. The first Dunstable Clinic was in Kingsway, on the east side, until replaced by Priory Health Centre (6).

## Dunstable Football Club

The Dunstable Football Club had its first pitch in Kingsway when it started in 1950 with a seven year lease on Gerald Bagshawe's land. Then, all players were amateurs and teams were often made up from whoever was available! In 1960, after the club had moved to its present site at Brewer's Hill, several local businessmen gave their support. Among these was Wally Creasey, of the Old Palace Lodge Hotel (see 97), whose name is now used for the present site: "Creasey Park".[ii]

Refs: i BAGSHAWE (1969) p. 356; ii (DBG)

# THE LADIES LODGE

*(Built 1743)*

*The Ladies Lodge Almshouses*

## The Ladies Lodge Almshouses

The Ladies Lodge was built between 1740-43 to provide homes for 'six maiden gentlewomen,' and they are still used as almshouses today for 'six elderly single women of limited means.' The Ladies Lodge was established by two local sisters: Blandina Marshe and Mary Lockington. (See Chew Family Tree — 16).[i]

Refs: i DERBYSHIRE (1882) pp. 164-8 & (VCH) 3:367-8;

### Blandina Marshe and Mary Lockington

Blandina Marshe (1663-1741) was the unmarried daughter of John Marshe (1617-1700) and Blandina (nee Iremonger). Mary Lockington (1663-1730) was the sister of Blandina Marshe and the wife of Thomas Lockington. Blandina and Mary made provisions in their wills (dated 1 June and 25 November 1730 respectively) for Charities to be set up to help the poor. Since then, the Marshe and Lockington Charities have been continued for this purpose by a group of Trustees.

Blandina Marshe's Charity included the support of 'six maiden gentlewomen' and she also left an annual sum of £5 to be paid from her Kingsbury Farm estate to poor people who attended church. The Charity continued through money which was gained from land and property whch had been left for this purpose, including a farm at Toddington and two cottages.

Mary Lockington's Charity included money for poor maids, poor clergymen and clergymen's widows. The money was also gained from land, including: 102 acres at Totternhoe, 95 acres at Toddington, 59 acres at Hockliffe and Eggington, 3 acres at Stanbridge and 61 acres at Soulbury in Bucks.[ii]

### The Site of the Royal Oak P.H.

The Royal Oak, which stood at 125 Church St. opposite the end of Priory Road, was demolished for the 1960s Church St. widening scheme. This pub dated from at least 1853 when the beer retailer was John Langley who was still at the Royal Oak in 1877; by 1885 Mrs Ann Langley had taken over. Later occupiers included: James Olive (1898), Mrs Deborah Olive (1903), Thomas William Thompson (1910), Jonathan Read Brown (1912, 1924), Arthur Kibble (1928 onwards).[iii]

ii (ibid); iii (DIR)

# THE PRIORY CHURCH CEMETERY

*Priory Church Cemetery*

## The Priory Church Cemetery

This very old Parish Cemetery, attached to the Priory Church of St. Peter, dates from at least the 12th century and was in use until about 1861 when the present Town burial ground was laid out in West St.

The footpath through the cemetery runs parallel to Church St., from near the end of Priory Road to the front of the Priory Church. The path is lined with various deciduous trees and it provides a comparatively peaceful walk away from the noise of Church St. The cemetery is particularly beautiful in the Autumn when the ground is carpeted with gold and brown leaves and long shadows are cast across the graveyard.

The Priory Cemetery contains several gravestones of interest, including the horizontal stone of the Oliver family which is positioned on the right (north) of the path and "overlooking" Kingsbury – where they once lived.

The cemetery path passes by the long north side of the Priory Church and past the large doors of the old Parish entrance, beneath the Church Clock. This northern doorway was once used by the local Parishioners and it faces the site, on the other side of Church Street, where nearly 900 years ago King Henry I built his Palace and founded the town.

*This is, therefore, an appropriate place to end a guided tour of Dunstable: in the old cemetery, beside Dunstable's oldest building, near the spot where the town was founded and where the tour began!*

# ACKNOWLEDGEMENTS

Inevitably, there are many people who have contributed towards this book. I would particularly like to thank and acknowledge the following:

Special thanks to:

Vivienne Evans ('Mrs Dunstable') for her assistance and for being an inspiration to so many through her talks and lectures.

Also thanks to:

INDIVIDUALS (Alphabetical order)

John Bailey (Architect & Historian)
Jimmy Breed (of Dunstable Rep., D.I.T.A.)
John Buckledee (Editor of Dunstable Gazette)
Stephen Bunker (Keeper of Local History, Luton Museum)
Betty Chambers (Beds. Historical Records Society)
Cherry Crawford (Graphic Designer)
Jim Eldridge (Writer & Broadcaster)
Elizabeth Fish (Local Historian)
Mike J. Gibas (Designer & Illustrator)
Cllr. Nicholas Goodman (Dunstable Town Mayor, 1985-6)
Bob Harwood (Composing Room Manager, Turners)
Jacquie Holdstock (Salvation Army)
Barry Horne (Archaeologist & Historian)
Pauline Keen (of Moore's Clothes Shop)
Peter Kewley (Head Librarian, Barnfield College)
Reg Lewis (Lecturer in Computers, Luton College)
John Lunn (Local Historian)
Ron Marsh (Proof Reader, Turners)
Les Matthews (of Manshead Archaeological Society)
Maxene Miller (Archaeologist & Historian)
Frederick Moore (of Moore's Clothes Shop)
Cllr. Bil Musannif, J.P. (Dunstable Town Mayor, 1986-7)
Elizabeth North (Latin Translater)
Chris Pickford (Head of County Records Office)
Clive Rawlings (Studio Manager, Turners)
Ernest Richardson, Peter Richardson & Maureen Richardson, (Bakers, Victoria Bun House)
Tania Sawkins (Typesetter, Turners)
Joan Schneider (Archaeologist, Historian & Artist)
Carol Smith (Researcher)
Peter Smithers (of Graphic Store Ltd)
Les Soan (Computer Expert)
Lee Stanley (Photographer & Printer)
Rose Stripp (Designer, Turners)
Beverly Stott (of Stott's Shop)
David & Sue Turner (of Turner Typesetting)
Sharon Valentine (of Graphic Store Ltd)
Richard Walden (Dunstable Town Clerk)

ORGANISATIONS:

Bedford Central Library
Bedford County Record Office
Bedfordshire Historial Records Society
British Broadcasting Corporation
Chiltern Radio
Dunstable Gazette
Dunstable Town Council
Luton Museum
Sea Cadets at T.S. Lionel Preston
South Beds District Council

Finally, a big thankyou to my parents, Ralph and Heather, for their continued help and encouragement.

# THEME TRAILS

By using the map symbols, trails on specific themes can be followed, e.g. buildings of STRAW HAT TRADE; old inns and public houses of COACHING ERA; main CHURCHES AND CHAPELS. To assist with such trails the following key places are listed:

### Straw Hat Trade

12 Priory Gardens Gate (Site of Munt & Brown)
14 The Grey House (Site of Hat Factory)
27 52 High St. South (Site of Stuart & Co)
55 Site of Town Hall (Site of Plait Market)
56 Anchor Gateway (Site of Bennett's Hat Factory)
62 Old Sugar Loaf Hotel (Site of Displays)
63 Warren's (Site of Warren's Hat Factory)
64 Albion St. (Sites of Workshops: Straw & Felt)
65 Edward St. (Sites of small factories)
68 Bingo Hall (Site of Cooper's Hat Factory)

### Coaching Era

13 The Saracen's Head (Oldest inn – 17th C)
20 The White Swan (Small inn – 17th C)
51 Site of Red Lion (Site of famous inn)
52 Site of Cooke's Row (Demolished for coaches)
56 Anchor Gateway (Only surviving part of inn)
62 Old Sugar Loaf Hotel (The best inn – 18th C)
63 'Warren's Site of Crown Inn (a well-known inn)
65 Borough Arms P.H. (a small inn with stables)
74 The Bull P.H. (with Coaching Yard – 17th C)
79 Grove House (was 'Duke of Bedford's Arms' inn)
90 Church St. – Site of White Horse inn

### Churches and Chapels

Dunstable has several different religious groups, including many 'Non-Conformist' worshippers (e.g. Quakers, Methodists, Baptists).

1 Priory Church (founded c1132; memorials of C. of E. members, e.g. members of Chew, Cart, Marshe families – see also 16, 17, 31, 41, 76, 96, 99).

28 Methodist Church, (Wesleyan: 3rd on this site)

33 Site of Quaker Meeting House.

37 Old Baptist Chapel (Particular) built 1849 on site of previous Ebenezer Chapel.

45 St. Mary's R.C. Church built 1964 (first round church built in England since Reformation).

46 Polish R.C. Church, Victoria St., (originally built by Primitive Methodists).

48 West St. Baptist Church (General) built 1847.

65 United Reformed Church, Edward St., built 1857, next to Congregational Church (Independent)

# BIBLIOGRAPHY

*Abbreviations:*
BHRS = Bedfordshire Historical Records Society
BNQ = Bedfordshire Notes and Queries
CAT = Catalogue: Sales, Auctions, Exhibitions
CEN = Census Returns
CRO = County Record Office, Bedford.
DBG = Dunstable Borough Gazette
DG = Dunstable Gazette
DIR = Directory or Guide Book (chronologically)
GM = Gentleman's Magazine
MAS = Manshead Archaeological Society
MAP = Maps: including O.S. and Sale Catalogues
VCH = Victoria County History

**The Dunstable library and museum:** museum annual reports . . . 1925-32. (Typed until 1939.) Dunstable Mus. & Lib. 1925-39.

**Official Opening.** New Public Pleasure Grounds (Grove House Gardens). New Fire Station and Dedication of Entrance Gates to the Grounds. Sat. 28 Jan. 1939. By the Rt. Hon. Lord Luke of Pavenham, K.B.E.

**Dunstable and district trades council:** thirty years of progress. Dunstable. 1941.

**Dunstable Charter Centenary 1964:** Dunstable's Past for the Young of Today. (By Dunstable T.C.) 16pp. Dunstable. 1964.

**'Topic'** The Magazine of the 'Friends' for the 'Friends'. (NB 'Friends' of 'Dunstable Museum Trust') Issued annually.

## Major Sources

**(BHRS)** Tractatus de Dunstaple et de Houcton. BHRS. 19:1-97, 1937.

**(BHRS)** BHRS 63: Court of Augmentations Accounts for Bedfordshire I (Part 1 of 2). Ed. Yvonne Nicholls. 276pp.

**(BHRS)** BHRS 64: Court of Augmentations Accounts for Bedfordshire II (Part 2 of 2). Ed. Yvonne Nicholls. (contains index for I and II)

**(BNQ)** BNQ 1:258-9, 1886. (Conveyance in 1502 of a 'Swan' inn.)

**(CAT) Sale Catalogue: 1894.** The Garden Estate, Dunstable. 82 plots of free-hold building land, 74 in Garden Road and 8 fronting the High Street (South). Sold by Auction on Wed. 20th June 1894. (NB Includes map and 5 photos of Dunstable by P. Vlako Turner.)

**(CAT) Sale Catalogue: 1917.** 1066 Acres of Freehold & Tithe Free Estate including four farms, 'Kingsbury', Chalk Hill Marl Works, Market Garden Allotments, Building and Factory Sites. Sold by Auction on Mon. 20th August 1917. Vendors: Messrs. Redhead and Gray Ltd., Kingsbury. (NB Inc. map.)
**(CAT) Catalogue of Exhibition** of Documents relating to Old Dunstable at The Town Hall, Dunstable, Beds. Thurs. 4th May, 1950. Historical Manuscripts Commission, National Register of Archives, Dunstable Area. 22 pp.
**(CAT) Catalogue of Exhibition** of Historical Documents of Bedfordshire and Dunstable at the Town Hall, Dunstable. Arranged by the County Record Office. Thurs. 20th September, 1951. 18 pp.
**(CAT) An Exhibition of Maps** showing the Growth of Dunstable over the Ages. Dunstable Public Library 11th April-4th May, 1968. Presented by Dunstable Historical Society.

(CEN) Dunstable Census 1851
(CEN) Dunstable Census 1861
(CEN) Dunstable Census 1871
(CEN) Dunstable Census 1881

**(CRO) DDBH** (Deposited Deeds of Benning & Hoare Solicitors):
293-304 Cott. in Hollowicke (Chapel) Lane 1812-56.
305-312 (NB West St. land 1853; 'Crow Close' 1860)
313-328 (NB West St. land of Jos. Darby 1854; 'The May Pole' occupied by Cheshire, etc. 1854; property of C.C.S. Benning)
355: 1-15 (NB Kingsbury Farm, Snoxall's Farm, 1893; property of late Joseph Shepherd in High St. South 1894)
369-400 (NB Chew's Foundation; Star Close etc.)
401-413 (NB Dunstable Brewery; Cap. Mess. 'called "The Red Hart", since "The Rose and Crown", & then "The Bull", in North St. of Dunstable'.) (458 Including Map of West St. 1839)
**(CRO) DDGA** (Deposited Deeds of Garrard and Allen, Solicitors):
702-726 (NB Saracen's Head 1648; Red Hart (Bull 1649, 1678 etc.)
**(CRO) DDGT** (Deposited Deeds of Gutteridge, Solicitor):
1-105 NB King's Head 1705; George Fossey owned Red Lion 1787; Richard Gutteridge West St property 1795; Crown Inn 1771 etc.
**(CRO) The Poor Law.** Beds Archive Teaching Unit No. 1. Peter GREY. (NB A folder of photocopied extracts and manuscripts.)
**(DBG) Re-opening of the northern aisle and the organ.** DBG. 2.10.1878.
**(DBG) Article on John Heyrick Macaulay,** b. 1831-d. 1914, rector of Dunstable 1883-1903.) DBG. 28.10.1914.

**(DBG) Who was who, 1929-40.** DBG 19.11.30., 1930. (Inc: Canon W.W.C. Baker, rector of Dun. 1903-24.)
**(DBG) 18th century punishments in Dunstable.** DBG. 24.6.31.
**(DGB) An enlarged borough of Dunstable. DBG. 4.1.32.**
**(DBG) Founded Sixty Years.** Origin of Dunstable Schools. DBG. 10.5.33.
**(DBG)** The Dunstable Borough Gazette. **Silver Jubilee Supplement.** DBG. 1.5.35. (Historical matter.)
**(DBG) Great Dunstable fire of 50 years ago, (13 Sept. 1908.) DBG. 1.8.58.**
**(DBG) Grammar School, 70 years old.** DBG. 24.5.58.
**(DBG) Dunstable Borough Centenary Souvenir,** June 1964. DBG. 5.6.64.
**(DBG) Dunstable Borough Gazette Centenary Souvenir.** June 1965. DBG. 26.6.65. 36 pp.
**(DBG) How Dunstable gained — and lost — a museum.** Bagshawe. 16 Feb. 68.
**(DBG) The Gazette's ABC of Dunstable Street Names.** DBG 18 Apr. 69. (NB Computer Typesetting used for first time in that particular newspaper: an ICI 1901 computer.)
**(DBG) A Society in Need of a Home of its Own** (Manshead Society). David Orr. 25 Jan. 74.
**(DBG) One Man Won't Forget.** (Recollections of the changing traffic scene in Dunstable by 92 yr old former Mayor). Ben Scott. 15 Mar. 74.
**(DG) Dunstable Borough Dies:** Reorganisation of Local Government on 1 Apr. 74. DG 29 Mar. 74. NB Includes comments by some past Mayors.
**(DIR) Directory for Bedfordshire 1785** by J.F. Henington. Facsimile Reprint by F. Hockliffe. Bedford 1885. (NB Dunstable only: no H. Regis)
**(DIR) PIGOT 1823/4.** Beds. Dir. Pigot & Co. (Dunstable pp 116-7)
**(DIR) PIGOT 1827.** Beds. Dir. Pigot & Co. 1827 (Dunstable & Hockliffe pp 16-17)
**(DIR) PIGOT 1830/1.** Beds. Dir. Pigot & Co. 1830 (Dunstable & Hockliffe pp 16-17)
**(DIR) PIGOT 1839.** Beds. Dir. Pigot & Co. 1839 (Dunstable & H. Regis pp 22-24)
**(DIR) ROBSON 1839.** Commercial Directory of London and the nine counties of Beds . . . William Robson. 1839. (Dunstable pp 18-21; Hockliffe pp 22-23)
**(DIR) KELLY 1847.** Post Office Directory of Norths., Oxford., Beds., Bucks., Hunts. (1st Edition). W. Kelly & Co. London. 1847. (Dunstable pp 1724-1726)
**(DIR) SLATER 1850.** Dir. of Beds. Issac Slater. London. (Dunstable & H. Regis pp 16-18) (NB Slater took over from Pigot, hence 'Pigot 1850' = Slater 1850.)

**(DIR) CRAVEN 1853.** Commercial Directory for the County of Bedford and the towns of Hertford, Hitchin and Baldock. Craven and Co. Nottingham, 1853. (H. Regis pp 67-68; Dunstable pp 108-117)
**(DIR) KELLY 1854.** Post Office Dir . . . Beds. Kelly & Co. 1854. (Dunstable pp 24-25)
**(DIR) CASSEY 1862.** Beds. and Hunts. Dir. Edward Cassey & Co. London. (Dunstable pp 94-99; H. Regis pp 117-119)
**(DIR) KELLY 1864.** Post Office Dir . . . Beds. Kelly & Co. 1864. (Dunstable pp 320-323, H. Regis pp 330-331)
**(DIR) KELLY 1869.** Post Office Directory . . . Beds. Kelly & Co. 1869. (Dunstable pp 344-347; H. Regis pp 355-356)
**(DIR) MERCER & CROCKER 1871.** Gen. Top & Hist. Dir. Beds. Mercer & Crocker. Leicester. 1871. (Dunstable pp 183-185; H. Regis 210-211) (NB This is the earliest Trade Directory with street numbers)
**(DIR) HARROD 1876.** Royal County Directory of Bedfordshire, Bucks, Berks, Oxford., Hunts, & Norths. J.G. Harrod and Co., Norwich, 1876. (Dunstable pp 63-69; H. Regis pp 84-85)
**(DIR) KELLY 1877.** Post Office Directory of Beds. Kelly 1877. (Dunstable pp 42-47; H. Regis pp 57-58)
**(DIR) KELLY 1885.** Dir. of Beds. (Dunstable pp 50-55; H. Regis pp 66-67)
**(DIR) KELLY 1894.** Dir. of Beds. Kelly & Co. Ltd. London. 1894. (Dunstable pp 63-68)
**(DIR) KELLY 1898.** Dir. of Beds. Kelly & Co. Ltd. London. 1898. (Dunstable pp 66-71; H. Regis pp 84-85)
**(DIR) KELLY 1903.** Dir. of Beds. Kelly & Co. Ltd. London. 1903. (Dunstable pp 86-91; H. Regis pp 104-105)
**(DIR) Dunstable. (Guide.)** 'With the compliments of the mayor and corporation.' (Dunstable) 1905.
**(DIR) MILES TAYLOR'S The Dunstable Year Book and Directory for 1910.** (NB Contains complete Street Directory. Taylor's Year Books are also available for 1908, 1911, 1912, 1913-15, 1916)
**(DIR) KELLY 1910.** Dir. of Beds. Kelly & Co. Ltd. London. 1910. (Dunstable pp 90-97; H. Regis pp 110-111)
**(DIR) JAMES TIBBETT'S Annual Dunstable Almanack and Local Directory** for 1913. (NB Tibbett's are also available for 1912, 1915, 1921, 1922, 1923)
**(DIR) KELLY 1914.** Dir. of Beds. Kelly & Co. Ltd. London. 1914. (Dunstable pp 93-100; H Regis pp 113-4. NB Has street numbers for commercial premises)

**(DIR) A guide to Dunstable.** No. 435 of the 'Borough' guides. E.J. Burrow & Co. Ltd (Chelt.) **1919.**
**(DIR) KELLY 1920.** Dir. of Beds. Kelly & Co. Ltd. London. 1920. (Dunstable pp 90-96; H. Regis pp 109-110)
**(DIR) The New Dunstable Handbook and Directory.** Publ. by William MARCHANT. No. 1. Dunstable. **1921.** (NB Marchant was a 'chemist')
**(DIR) KELLY 1924.** Dir. of Beds. Kelly & Co. Ltd. London. 1924. (Dunstable pp 93-99; H. Regis p 114)
**(DIR) Dunstable: Official Guide and Directory** (By Dun. T.C.) Brit. Pub. Co., Glos. **1924.** (NB Arts. by T.W. Bagshawe & Gurney)
**(DIR) KELLY 1928.** Dir. of Beds. Kelly & Co. Ltd. London. 1928. (Dunstable pp 92-99; H. Regis pp 110-114)
**(DIR) The Official Guide to Dunstable and District** with local directory for **1933, 1937, 1940** and **1941.** Index Publishers. (Dunstable) Ltd.
**(DIR) KELLY 1936.** Dir. of Beds. Kelly & Co. Ltd. London. 1936. (Dunstable pp 93-99; H. Regis pp 114-115)
**(DIR) KELLY 1940.** Dir. of Beds. Kelly & Co. Ltd. London. 1940. (Dunstable pp 92-99; H. Regis pp 114-115)
**(DIR) Dunstable Directory and guide, 1951/52. 185pp. Leagrave Press, Luton. (Arch. & Hist. material.)**
**(DIR) Dunstable Official Guide and Directory,** Brit. Pub. Co., Gloucester. **1965.**
**(DIR) Dunstable Official Guide with folding street plan.** (By Dun. T.C.) 80pp. Brit. Pub. Co. Ltd. Gloucester. **1974.**
**(DIR) Pictorial Guide to Bedfordshire.** White Crescent Press Ltd. Luton. 144 pp. **1975.** NB Dunstable p 6; pp 47-51.
**(GM) Epitaphs in churchyard (Dunstable).** GM. 76(1):216, 1806. (by 'D.H.').
**(LN) Legend of the Dunstable Witch (Sally). 28 Sept. 1933.**
**(LN) Nearly 200 years of brewing** (inc. Green, Flower, Whitbread). 10 June 1965.
**(MAS) The Manshead Magazine** (Journal of the Manshead Archaeological Society of Dunstable) Excavation of a Roman Inhumation Cemetery at Dunstable. No. 25 January 1979.
**(MAP) Survey of Houghton Regis Parish. 1762.** (NB The oldest known detailed map of Dunstable.)
**(MAP) Tithe Map. 1840.** Surveyed 1822 by John Durham, revised 1840, for Commissioner of Tithes. (NB This is first 'proper' map of Dunstable.)
**(MAP) O.S. 1834 1″ = 1 mile).** Sheet 62. Woburn and Aylesbury. Facsimile Reprint of First Edition of One Inch Ordnance Survey. David & Charles, Brunel House, Newton Abbot. Devon.

**(MAP) O.S. 1880 Scale 1:500** Surveyed 1878. (on 8 sheets).
**(MAP) O.S. 1880 Scale 1:2500** (apprx 25″ = 1 mile) Surveyed 1878-9.
**(MAP) O.S. 1901 Scale 1:2500** (apprx 25″ = 1 mile) Surveyed 1878-9. Revised 1900.
**(MAP) W.G. SMITH 1903** (Scale apprx. 3.66″ = 1 mile) 'Map of Dunstable and Neighbourhood: showing old and new roads, lanes, footways and antiquities.' NB This map was issued with Smith's 1904 book.
**(MAP) O.S. 1924 Scale 1:2500** (apprx 25″ = 1 mile) Surveyed 1878-9. Revised 1922.
**(MAP) O.S. 1937 Scale 1:2500** (apprx 25″ = 1 mile) Surveyed 1878-9. Revised 1937.
**(MAP) O.S. 1976 TL 0122 SW** Scale: 1:1250 (apprx 50″ = 1 mile) Surveyed 1962. Revised 1975. (NB Covers NW Dunstable: High St. North, Union St., Chiltern Rd., Victoria St., etc.
**(MAP) O.S. 1968 TL 0122 SE** Scale: 1:1250 (apprx 50″ = 1 mile) Surveyed 1962. Revised 1967. (NB Covers NE Dunstable: High St. North, Old Grammar School, Grove House Gardens, Court Drive, Queensway Hall, part of Quadrant, etc.)
**(MAP) O.S. 1970 TL 0121 NW** Scale: 1:1250 (apprx 50″ = 1 mile) Surveyed 1963. Revised 1969. (NB Covers West Dunstable: West Street, Chiltern Rd., Kirby Rd., Old Mill, etc.)
**(MAP) O.S. 1968 TL 0121 NE** Scale: 1:1250 (apprx 50″ = 1 mile) Surveyed 1962. Revised 1967. (NB Covers Central Dunstable: West Street, St. Mary's R.C. Church, Princes St., Victoria St., Matthew St., Burr St., Icknield St., St. Mary's Gate, Old Baptist Church, Cross Roads, part of High St. North (to Albion St.), part of High St. South (to Priory House), site of Friary.)
**(MAP) O.S. 1974 TL 0221 NW** Scale: 1:1250 (apprx 50″ = 1 mile) Surveyed 1963. Revised 1973. (NB Covers SE Dunstable: High St. South, Viceroy Court, Church St. (to First & Last P.H.), Priory Church and Meadow, Priory Rd., Britain St., Richard St., King St.)
**(MAP) 'Dunstable Shop Plan 1974'.** Chas. E. Goad Ltd 56 Crouch Hill, London N4. 1970. (Based on O.S.)
**(MAP) O.S. 1980 Scale 1:10 000** (10 cm = 1000 m) (apprx 6″ = 1 mile) Surveyed 1962-67. Revised 1978. Sheet TL 02 SW (NB This sheet includes the whole of Dunstable.)

**(VCH) Augustinian Priory of St. Peter.** VCH. 1:371-7, 1904.
**(VCH) House of Dominican (Black) Friars,** Dunstable. VCH. 1:395-6, 1904.
**(VCH) Hospital of St. Mary Magdalene,** Dunstable. VCH. 1:400-01, 1904. (Hospital for the sick and lepers.)

**(VCH) The straw plait, hat and bonnet industry.** VCH. 2:118-22, (A. RANSOM). 1908.
**(VCH) Dunstable schools** VCH. 2: 178-9, 1908.
**(VCH) 3:349-68,** 1912. (Muriel R. Manfield.)
**(VCH) The Priory Church.** VCH. 3:364-7, 1912.
**(VCH) Dunstable Charities.** VCH. 3:367-8, 1912
**(VCH) VCH. 3: 3:389-94,** 1912. Entry on Houghton Regis (by H.S.F. Lea)

### AUTHORS

**BAGSHAWE,** Richard W. A search for the site of Durocobrivae, pt.1. B. Archaeol. 2:21-5, 1959.
**BAGSHAWE,** Thomas W. The Itinerants. III — The Migratory Labourers. B.Mag. 8: 8:206-209, 1963.
**BAGSHAWE,** Thomas W. The Passing of the Country Baker. Part One. B. Mag. 9: 9:166-170, 1964.
**BAGSHAWE,** Thomas W. The Passing of the Country Baker. Part Two. B.Mag. 9: 9:209-213, 1964.
**BAGSHAWE,** Thomas W. Dunstable Flints for the Potteries. B.Mag. 9: 9:221-222, 1964.
**BAGSHAWE,** Thomas W. Mr Beeton Visits Dunstable. 9:309-310, (no. 72) 1965. (NB St. Mary's Street businesses: Gard & Co. polishing cloth makers; Smith and Dolman 'Self-cleaning Chemical Plate Cloths')
**BAGSHAWE,** Thomas W. Memories of Three Dunstable Houses. I. The Grove House (part 1) B. Mag. 10: 91-8, (no. 75) 1965-66.
**BAGSHAWE,** Thomas W. Memories of Three Dunstable Houses. I. The Grove House (part 2) B.Mag. 10:133-7, (no. 76) 1966.
**BAGSHAWE,** Thomas W. Memories of Three Dunstable Houses. I. The Grove House (part 3) B.Mag. 10: 200-207, (no. 77) 1967.
**BAGSHAWE,** Thomas W. Memories of Three Dunstable Houses. I. The Grove House (part 4) B. Mag. 10: 221-228, (no.78) 1967. (NB Gary Cooper p 222.)
**BAGSHAWE,** Thomas W. Memories of Three Dunstable Houses. II. The Grey House. (part 1) B.Mag. 11: 9-14, (no. 81) 1967.
**BAGSHAWE,** Thomas W. 'W.G.S.' A Man to Remember. B.Mag. 11: 73-79. (no. 82) 1967.
**BAGSHAWE,** Thomas W. Memories of Three Dunstable Houses. II. The Grey House. (part 2) B.Mag. 11: 167-172, (no. 84) 1968.
**BAGSHAWE,** Thomas W. Memories of Three Dunstable Houses. III. Kingsbury (part 1) B.Mag 11: 212-216, (no. 85) 1968.

**BAGSHAWE,** Thomas W. Memories of Three Dunstable Houses. III. Kingsbury (part 2) B.Mag. 11: 237-243, (no. 86) 1968. (NB Kingsbury part 3 was written by Jessie ROBERTS – see separate entry.

**BAGSHAWE,** Thomas W. Memories of Three Dunstable Houses. III. Kingsbury (part 4) B.Mag. 11: 353-358, (no. 88) 1969.

**BAKER,** Reg. For The Generation Following. History of the Old Baptist Chapel: 1675-1975. 24pp 1975. Ill. P. Baker & J. Brandham.

**BAILEY,** John M. Timber Framed Buildings: A study of medieval timber buildings in Bedfordshire and adjoining counties. 36pp. Bedfordshire, Buckinghamshire and Cambridgeshire Historic Building Research Group. 1979. (NB includes West Street shops, nos. 7 & 9, and Middle Row shop, no. 30.)

**BAILEY,** John M. Numbers 7 and 9 West Street, Dunstable. in Beds. Archaeological Journal Volume 14 pp. 91-98. 1980.

**BANCROFT,** F.M. A Short History of Dunstable School, 1888-1963. Dunstable. 50 pp. 1963. (NB F.M. Bancroft was an English master.)

**BANKS,** A.W. A link with the past: Old Baptist church, St. Mary's Street, Dunstable. Dunstable. 1908.

**BAXTER,** A.R.W. John Dunstable. B.Mag. 10: 287-292 (no. 79), 1966. NB There is no evidence that John Dunstable was born in or lived in Dunstable: the link with this town has been assumed merely because of his name.

**BEASLEY,** Edwin R. 'Edwin Frederick Holt, Victorian Artist of Dunstable.' B.Mag. 18: 235-239 (no. 142) 1982. NB Holt lived at 78-80 Edward St., now demolished, opposite 'Holt Court' (no connection).

**BEDS C.C.** Guide to the Bedfordshire Record Office. 163 pp plus 8 pp supplement. Beds C.C. Bedford. 1957. (NB Solicitor's Deeds: Benning, Hoare and Drew p. 97; Garrard and Allen p. 98; Gutteridge p. 99)

**BEDS C.C.** Mineral Workings in Bedfordshire. (Extract from Report to the County Planning Committee dated 1st December 1954.). 32 pp.

**BEDS EDUCATION SERVICE.** Introduction to South Bedfordshire. Beds. Ed. Service. 34 pp. (No date). (c. 1980)

**BELL,** Patricia L. Early Health Care in Luton and Dunstable. B.Mag. 19: 229-236 (no. 150), 1984. (NB This covers health care before 1835; Currie's 1982 book concentrates on post-1835 health care.)

**BLAYDES,** Frederick Augustus. Genealogia Bedfordiensis. A.D. 1538-1700. London. 1890. (NB A register of Baptisms, Marriages, and Burials: pp. 92-4 Dunstable; pp. 151-2 H. Regis)

**BLUNDELL,** Joseph Hight. Bedfordshire Seventeenth Century Tokens. 1928. pp. 19-27, p. 37. (NB Includes photo of plaster cast of William Fossey's Token.)

**BODY,** Geoffrey and EASTLEIGH, Robert L. The Hatfield-Dunstable Line. B.Mag. 10: 177-182. (no. 77) 1966. (NB L. Buzzard-Dunstable, L&NWR, 1848-1962; Hertford, Luton & Dunstable Railway 1858-1965)
**BOND,** P.G. Memories of a Bedfordshire School: Ashton (Dunstable) Grammar School c. 1925-47. B.Mag. 14: 114-6, 1973.
**BROADFOOT,** R.F. Non-conformist Churches, in DBG June 1965 pp. 18-20, (Centenary Souvenir Issue).
**BROWN,** C.L.F. The Charm of Lace. B.Mag. 2:24-7, 1949.
**BROWN,** Rev. John, The Prior of Dunstable and the burgesses. (Bygone days in Bedfordshire 2.) Congr. Review, 19-28, 1887.
**BUCK,** Anne M. The Lace Schools of Bedfordshire. B.Mag. 3:3-5, 1951.
**BUCK,** Anne. The register of the Fraternity of St. John the Baptist, Dunstable, 1506-08, 1522-41. BHRS. 25:10-14, 1947.
**BUCK,** Anne. Middlemen in the Bedfordshire Lace Industry. BHRS 57:31-58, 1978. (NB p 35 lace along Watling St. to London; coaches robbed upon Dunstable hill, & lacemerchants)
**BURCHETT,** Ken. Blindness in Bedfordshire. B.Mag. 18: 255-259 (no. 142), 1982. NB Roy and Christine Gerrard, Dunstable.
**CHAMBERS,** Betty, The Fayrey Pall. B.Mag. 9: 311-5, 1965.
**CHAMBERS,** Betty. Printed Maps and Town Plans of Bedfordshire 1576-1900. Volume 62. BHRS. 250 pp. 1983. (NB cf HODSON Review.)
**CHAMBERS,** Betty. Bedfordshire Bookshelf. (Review) History All Around by Vivienne Evans. (1984). B.Mag. 19:307. (Vol. 151). 1984.
**CIRKET,** Alan F. 'Watch the Birdie' — the Photographer's Art in Dunstable and Leighton Buzzard. B.Mag. 19: 265-272 (no. 151), 1984. NB Includes: James Field, Charles Smy, Loweth Studios, Frederick S. Mills, Percy Vlado Turner.
**CLAY,** Rotha Mary. The Mediaeval hospitals of England. (The Antiquary's Books.) 1909. (Dunstable, Farley.).
**CONISBEE,** L.R. A Bedfordshire Bibliography. 333pp., BHRS. 1962.
**CONISBEE,** L.R. A Bedfordshire Bibliography 1967 Supplement. 85pp., BHRS. 1967.
**CONSIBEE,** L.R. A Bedfordshire Bibliography Second Supplement. 128pp., BHRS. 1971. (see THREADGILL for Third Supplement.)
**COOPER,** Bertram, Wesleyan Methodism in Dunstable. In Dunstable Year Book., 1910, pp. 56-63. (From the Methodist Times 2nd Dec. 1909.)
**COX,** Alan. Survey of Bedfordshire Brickmaking: A History and Gazetteer. Beds C.C. and the Royal Commission on Historical Monuments (England). 110 pp. 1979.

**COX,** Alan. Odd & Unusual Bedfordshire. Illustrations by John Johnson. Beds C.C. 26 pp. 1982

**COX,** D.C.M. Dun the robber. B.Mag. 6:126-8, 1957. (cf. Cyril Palmer. Thomas Dun — man of terror. LN 1 Nov. 1956.).

**CURRIE,** Margaret R. Hospitals in Luton and Dunstable: An Illustrated History. 162pp. 1982.

**CURTIS,** Evelyn. Crime in Bedfordshire 1660-1688. Leaflet 4 Elstow Moot Hall. 27 pp. (No date. c1956). (NB The case of Elizabeth Pratt, accused of witchcraft, in 1667 pp 9-11 cf. Beds Assize Records 1667, 1678; Highwaymen in 1671 pp 15-16; Stolen horse at Dunstable Fair 1678 pp 16-7,)

**DAY,** Vera. A Child's world of two Dunstable Schools: Ashton School . . . and Moreton House School, 1919-24. B.Mag. 14: 251-4, 1974.

**DERBYSHIRE,** George. Dunstable: a poem. Dunstable. 1833.c. With a history of Dunstable.

**DERBYSHIRE,** George. Native scenes and other poems. Dunstable. 1850 & -53. With a history of Dunstable. NB George Derbyshire (1791-1874) was a bootmaker and Parish Clerk. His son was W.H. Derbyshire. (see below)

**DERBYSHIRE,** W.H. The History of Dunstable. (A 2nd ed.) Dunstable. 1882. (1st edition was in 1872.) NB William Henry Derbyshire (1830-1905) was born in Dunstable, son of George Derbyshire. W.H.D. was an auctioneer who founded the 'Dunstable Chronicle' in 1856 and became Mayor of Dunstable in 1879. As well as sitting on Dunstable Borough Council, he was one of the first members of Beds County Council.

**DONY,** John G. A History of the Straw Hat Industry. Gibbs, Bamforth & Co. (Luton) Ltd. The Leagrave Press. Luton. 219 pp. 1942.

**DONY,** John G. Bedfordshire Bookshelf. (Review) The Book of Dunstable and Houghton Regis by Vivienne Evans. (1985). B.Mag. 20:171 (Vol. 156). 1986.

**DOROTHY,** Novitates Bedfordiensis: Here and there. B.Mag 14:172 (Vol. 108). 1974. (NB a story by Roger of Wendover refers to beer brought from Dunstable in 1178'/ excavation of bread oven & 3 malt-drying kilns.)

**DUNNO,** (=NICHOLLS, W., d. 1823) Dunno's originals . . . 1855. (ident. in DBG 10.9.24 by Bagshawe)

**DUNSTABLE TOWN COUNCIL.** Dunstable Town Guide. 52 pp. 1986. (NB Includes historical material by Mrs Vivienne Evans and description of town by Town Clerk, Richard Walden. Various small photos.)

**DYER,** J.F. The Five Knolls. B.Mag. 8:15-20. 1961.

**DYER,** James. 'W.G.S.' and the Potato Blight Mystery. B.Mag. 11: 91-96 (no. 83) 1967.

**DYER,** James. The Bedfordshire Region in the First Millennium B.C., in Beds Archaeological Journal Volume 11 pp. 7-18. 1976.

**DYER,** James, Worthington George Smith. BHRS 57:141-179, 1978. (NB The definitive work on W.G. Smith: complete life-history, bibliography, etc.)
**DYER,** James, Bedfordshire Bookshelf. (Review) Survey of Beds: The Roman Period by Angela Simco. (1984). B.Mag. 19:261-2 (vol. 150) 1984.
**EVANS,** Vivienne. A Brief History of Dunstable with the Priory 1100-1550. 42 pp. 1980.
**EVANS,** Vivienne. The Dunstable Swan Jewel. Illustrated by Omer Roucoux. Dunstable Museum Trust Publication, Dunstable, 20 pp. 1982.
**EVANS,** Vivienne. History All Around Luton and Dunstable. Maps by Lewis Evans. Photographs by Omer Roucoux. The Book Castle, Dunstable. 1984. 158 pp.
**EVANS,** Vivienne. The Book of Dunstable & Houghton Regis. Barracuda Books Ltd., Buckingham. 128pp. 1985.
**FISHER,** J.S. People of the Meeting House: Tales of a church in Luton. 98 pp. (No date). (NB Mentions 'Brother Finch', Daniel Finch, Ebenezar Baptist Chapel Dunstable 1688, p. 15.)
**FREEMAN,** Charles E. Luton and the Hat Industry. Luton Museum and Art Gallery, 1953.
**FREEMAN,** Charles E. Pillow Lace in the East Midlands. Luton Museum and Art Gallery, 1958.
**FOWLER,** F.A. Dunstable Priory, Bedfordshire. To commemorate the 750th anniversary of the Priory Church of St. Peter, Dunstable. 1213-1963. Index Publishers Ltd. Dunstable and London. (1962).
**FOWLER,** F.A. The Priory Church of Saint Peter, Dunstable: a brief history and guide. 32 pp., 7th ed. Par. Ch. Coun. 1980.
**FOWLER,** G. Herbert. A digest of the charters preserved in the cartulary of the priory of Dunstable. BHRS. 10:pts. 1&2, 1926. (NB G. Herbert Fowler, CBE 1861-1940)
**FREEMAN,** Charles. Luton and the Hat Industry. The Borough of Luton Museum and Art Gallery. 36 pp. 1953.
**FROST,** K.A. Where History was made. B.Mag. 3:96-8, 1951-2. (Dunstable Priory Church.)
**GENT,** W.L. Bedfordshire Bookshelf. (Review) Some Early Non-Conformist Church Books Edited by H.G. Tibbutt (1972). B.Mag. 13:321-2 (Vol. 103). 1972.
**GENT,** W.L. Bedforshire Bookshelf. (Review) The Old Poor Law by Peter Grey (1971). B.Mag. 13:322-3 (Vol. 103). 1972.
**GILMORE,** P.M. At the sign of the bush. B.Mag. 2:3-6, 1949.
**GODBER,** Joyce. History of Bedfordshire 1066-1888. Beds C.C. 592 pp. 1969.

**GODBER,** Joyce. Friends in Beds and West Herts. 100 pp. 1975.
**GODBER,** Joyce, Women's Institutes in Bedfordshire —I: 1919-1939. B.Mag. 20: 147-152. (no. 156), 1986. (Dunstable had first W.I. in Beds, 1917)
**GREGORY,** S.E. Dunstable's Coaching Era. B.Mag. 3:211-212, 1952.
**GURNEY,** F.G. The Church of St. Peter Dunstable. pp21-24. (No date: Extract from a Town Guide)
**HACKETT,** Frank. The Register of the Fraternity of St. John the Baptist. B.Mag. 18: 74-5. (no. 138). 1981.
**HAGEN,** Richard. A Roman Ditch in Dunstable Priory Meadow. In Bedfordshire Archaeological Journal Volume 7. pp. 35-38. 1972. (NB An excavation by Manshead Archaeological Society in Priory Meadow in 1970. Also mentions other Roman finds in Dunstable town).
**HARPER,** Charles G. The inns of old England. 2 vols. 1906.
**HARVEY,** A.D. & ASHTON, G. A design for Dunstable, prepared for the corporation. Dunstable B.C., 1944.
**HAYWARD,** M.J. (ed.) The Story of Dunstable. Dunstable Borough Council. 26 pp. 1973.
**HAYWARD,** M.J. Dunstale Manor Court. 34 pp. 1978.
**HAZELTON-SWALES,** M.J. The Growth of Dunstable 1864-1939. Dunstable Museum Trust. 32 pp. 1982.
**HENRY,** Colin. Dunstable Charity School and the impact of local and national developments. 1981. M. Phil. Thesis. (King's Coll., Cambs.) (NB Includes Chew Family Tree.)
**HICKENBOTTOM,** S. The New Dunstable. B.Mag. 14:140-4. (no. 108) 1974.
**HODDER,** M. The Mad Dog (Odell). B.Mag. 5:34-6, 1955.
**HODSON,** Donald. Bedfordshire Bookshelf. (Review) Printed Maps and Towns Plans of Bedfordshire 1576-1900 by Betty Chambers (1983). B.Mag. 19:129-130. (Vol. 147). 1983
**HORSLER,** Frank. Change on the wing. (Birds of Dunstable Downs, etc.) B.Mag. 7:144-7, 1960.
**HOSKINS,** W.G. The Making of the English Landscape. Pelican, 327 pp. 1970.
**HOWES,** Hugh. Bedfordshire Mills. Beds. C.C. (County Planning Dept.) 88 pp. 1983. (Drawing by Sarah Garner).
**KENNETT,** David H. Obituary. Thomas Wyatt Bagshawe, and Bibliography, in Beds Archaeol. Journal Volume 11 pp. 1-6. 1976.
**KENNETT,** David H. Portrait of Bedfordshire. Robert Hale. London. 208 pp. 1978.

**KUHLICKE,** F.W. (Arms of) Dunstable Priory. (A Bedfordshire Armorial 14.) B.Mag. 3:35, 1951.
**KUHLICKE,** F.W. (Arms of) Dunstable corporation. (A Bedford Armorial 15.) B.Mag. 3:35, 1951.
**KUHLICKE,** F.W. Medieval Tournaments in Bedfordshire. B.Mag. 14: 32-37 (no. 105) 1973.
**LAMBORN,** Charles. The Dunstaplelogia. James Tibbett, Albion Printing Office. Dunstable. 272 pp. 1859. NB Charles Lamborn was Headmaster of the 'British School', West St., Dunstable.
**LEAN,** V.C. Lean's Collectanea. (Collections of proverbs, folklore, etc.) 1902.
**LUTON MUSEUM.** The Romance of the Straw Hat: Being a History of the Industry and a Guide to the Collections. The Public Museum Committee. Luton. 48pp. 1933.
**LYSONS,** Daniel and Samuel. Magna Britannia Bedfordshire. Originally published 1806. Re-issued 1813 with additions and corrections. Republished by EP Pub. Ltd. 189 pp. 1978. (NB p 157-8 a 'Perfect Diurnal, June 24-July 1, 1644'... 'states'... 'that on "the last Lord's day" the King'...'sent another party to Dunstable, who plundered the town', etc. Also, 'On the 26th of August 1645, the King marched with his army' . . . 'the next day his army halted at Dunstable, and took up his quarters at the Red Lion in that town.' cf TIBBUTT)
**McGREGOR,** Margaret. Bedfordshire Wills proved in the Prerogative Court of Canterbury. 1383-1548. BHRS Volume 58. BHRS. 237 pp. 1979. (NB Dunstable Wills: pp 100-101 John Audley, 1518/19; pp 114-115 Nicholas urvey, 1521; pp 135-136 John Holdern, 1529/30; pp 138-140 William Marchall 1531; pp 150-1 Eleanor Aulaby, 1537; pp 157-9 John Fayrey, 1541; pp 164-5 John Knyghtley, 1545)
**MANDER,** R.P. Dunstable and the Drama. B.Mag. 4:81-3, 1953.
**MARTIN,** A.R. & **BAGSHAWE,** T.W. The Dominican priory of Dunstable... J. Brit. Archaeol. Assoc., Dec. 1927.
**MATTHEWS,** C.L. Ancient Dunstable: a Prehistory of the District. Manshead Archaeol. Soc. Dunstable. 96pp (plus adverts at back). 1963.
**MATTHEWS,** C.L. The Roman Cemetery at Dunstable, Durocobrivae. Beds Archaeol. Council. Luton Museum. Luton. 73pp. 1981.
**MATTHEWS,** C.L. & **HUTCHINS,** J.B. A Roman Well at Dunstable. in Beds. Archaeol. Journal. Volume 7. pp 21-34. 1972. (NB A Roman Well on the Friary Site excavated by the Manshead Archaeological Society.)
**MATTHEWS,** P.W. & **TUKE,** A.W. History of Barclays Ltd. 1926. (NB pp. 160-3 Bassett, Son and Harris).

**MEE,** Arthur. The King's England: Bedfordshire and Huntingdonshire. Revised and Edited by Joyce Godber and Philip Dickinson. Illustrated with new photographs by A.F. Kersting. Hodder and Stoughton. London. 1973. 318 pp.
**MORETONIAN (DAY,** Vera) Dunstable Days. B.Mag. 2: 157-9, 1950.
**NEWMARK,** Jim. Trade Tokens. No 79. Shire Pub. 32 pp. 1981
**PECK,** G.C. Bedfordshire Cinemas. Beds C.C. 36 pp. 1981. (NB This booklet has no page numbers.)
**PEVSNER,** Nikolaus. The Buildings of England: Bedfordshire and the County of Huntingdon and Peterborough. Penguin Books. 416 pp. 1968.
**PEYTON,** S. Ecclesiastical troubles in Dunstable, C. 1616, BHRS. 11: 109-27, 1927.
**PIKE,** W.T. (Ed.) Contemporary Biographies: Berks, Bucks & Beds. in the Twentieth Century. Pike's New Century Series No. 23. Historical Survey by J.E. Vincent. W.T. Pike & Co. Brighton. 360 pp. 1907. (NB Bassett p172; Sinkwell p212; Austin p243; Barnard p244; Benning p244; Lathom p251; Alban Neve p252; Thring p300; Garrett p336.
**RICHARDSON,** (Sir) A.E. The old inns of England. Ill. Brian Cook. Foreword by Sir Edwin Lutyens. 1934. (Beds. examples).
**ROBERTS,** Jessie. Memories of Three Dunstable Houses III. B.Mag. 11: 306-313. (no. 87) 1968. NB See Bagshawe for rest of this series.
**ROUCOUX,** Omer, The Roman Watling Street from London to High Cross. Dunstable Museum Trust Publication (no. 3). 86 pp. 1984.
**ROWE,** L.M. The Chew Family Charities of Dunstable. 1. Chew Family History. B.Mag. 13: 197-200, (no. 101) 1972.
**ROWE,** L.M. The Chew Family Charities of Dunstable. 2. Chew's School, part 1. B.Mag. 13: 270-274, (no. 102) 1972).
**ROWE,** L.M. The Chew Family Charities of Dunstable. 3. Chew's School, part 2. B.Mag. 13: 289-292, (no. 103) 1973.
**ROWE,** L.M. The Chew Family Charities of Dunstable. 4. The Charities of Jane Cart and Francis Ashton. B.Mag. 13: 355-358, (no. 104) 1973.
**ROWE,** L.M. The Chew Family Charities of Dunstable. 5. The Ashton Schools Foundation. B.Mag. 14: 9.16, (no. 105) 1973.
**SEWARD,** G.M. John Wesley in Bedfordshire, B.Mag. 3:60-4, 1951.
**SHEPHERD,** Alan M. The Bells of Dunstable Priory. B.Mag. 19: 18-94 (no. 147), 1983.
**SIMCO,** Angela. Survey of Bedfordshire: The Roman Period. Beds C.C. and the Royal Commission on Historical Monuments (England). 128pp. 1984.
**SIMCO,** Angela. Bedfordshire Bookshelf. (Review) The Roman Watling Street . . . by Omer Roucoux. (1984). B.Mag. 19:305-6. (Vol. 151). 1984.

**SMITH,** W.G. Man The Primeval Savage: His Haunts and Relics from the Hill-tops of Bedfordshire to Blackwall. Edward Stanford. London. 350 pp. 1894.

**SMITH,** W.G. A Museum For Dunstable (part of a speech accepting the title of Freeman of the Borough of Dunstable on 9th November 1903). B.Mag. 18: 51 (no. 138) 1981. ('. . . the question arises as to whether Dunstable folk have yet read themselves up to care for a collection of bones and stones or whether such a collection would not be out of place and entirely lost at Dunstable.')

**SMITH,** W.G. Dunstable: its history and surroundings . . . London and Dunstable. 1904. Re-issued, 1980.

**SMITH,** W.G. Dunstable: The Downs and District. A handbook for visitors. Homeland Handbook Series. Dunstable and London. 1904.

**SMITH,** W.G. The Dunstable Parish Register. Proc. Soc. Antiq. 21 (2nd series): 150-2 with illustrations on facing pages. 1906. (NB Ills: Title page, Shield of Arms, Legend of Dun the Robber. The full-size versions are displayed in the Priory Church N. Aisle.)

**SMITH,** W.G. Notes on mediaeval objects (from the Dunstable region). Proc. Soc. Antiq. 21:81-4, 1906.

**SMITH,** W.G. Notes on the church of St. Peter, Dunstable. Proc. Soc. Antiq. 23:154-7, 1910.(Issued separately as extract pp. 1-6.)

**SMITH,** W.G. The Sanctus Bell in Dunstable Church. B.Mag. 19: 273-275 (no. 151) 1984. NB This is an abridged version of the article in the 'Dunstable Year Book and Directory for 1910'.

**SPARKS,** H.J. A Quaker Foundry. (Brown and Green, Luton.) B.Mag. 4:99-103, 1953-4.

**STITT,** F.B. A Dunstable tournament, 1308-9. A note. Antiq. j. 32:202-3, 1952.

**STOCKDALE,** Eric. Law and Order in Georgian Bedfordshire. BHRS Volume 61. BHRS. 107 pp. 1982.

**STOREY,** Patricia M. A Way to be Special. B.Mag. 20:133-8. (Vol. 156). 1986. (NB About the 'Special' Police Force.)

**SWINSON,** Arthur. Dunstable Pageant 1963. Production by Dorian Williams. Foreword by Michael Kilby, Mayor, Dunstable (1963).

**TAYLOR,** Miles. The Dunstable Year Book and Directory. c.1910 — c. 1925

**TAYLOR,** Miles. Views of Dunstable and District. 'Gazette Office' Dunstable. (NB A collection of photographs)

**THEODORSON,** G.M. Elkanah Settle. (Bedfordshire Biographies, XI.) B.Mag. 2: 211-16, 1950.

**THREADGILL,** A.R. A Bedfordshire Bibliography Third Supplement. 1971-1975. 86pp., BHRS. 1978. (Supplement to CONISBEE.)
**TIBBETT,** James. Annual illustrated guide and directory. Dunstable Guide. 1873-c.1922.
**TIBBUTT,** H.G. Index to items of Bedfordshire interest in 'Evangelical Magazine' . . . etc. (Typed copy). (see Conisbee p.45)
**TIBBUTT,** H.G. Charles I at Dunstable. (Letter to the Editor.) B.Mag. 2:337, 1951. (NB 'Royalists raided Dunstable in June 1644, when Mr. Plott, host of the Red Lion,was reported as killed by them and they shot at the minister in his pulpit.' 'Naseby was fought in June 1645 . . .'; '. . . at 2 o'clock on Wednesday, 27th, (August) he halted at the Red Lion, Dunstable, leaving an hour or so later . . .' cf. LYSONS
**TIBBUTT,** H.G. The Quaker Folk. B.Mag. 4: 163-6, 1954.
**TIBBUTT,** H.G. (Editor) Some Early Non-Conformist Church Books. BHRS Vol. 51. 1972.
**TURVEY,** Bruce. 25 Years of Dunstable 1952-1977. A collection of 400 photographs. (Commemorating the Silver Jubilee of HM Queen Elizabeth II.) Turvey and Turvey. Dunstable. 203 pp. 1977. NB Contains a useful 'Diary' of events.
**TWADDLE,** William. Old Dunstable: A Collection of 110 Pictures. White Crescent Press Ltd. Luton. 63 pp. 1975.
**V.C.H.: Victoria History of Bedfordshire,** ed. H.A. Doubleday and W. Page, 3 vols. and index. 1904-14. NB Issued in parts in 1920 by Constable & Co. London.
Part 9 Ecclesiastical history;
Parts 13,14 & 15 Industries, Agriculture, Forestry
Part 31 Manshead Hundred (Dunstable pp 349-368)
**VIGOR,** P.C. The Weather Prophet. (Bedfordshire Biographies 26.) B.Mag. 6:132-3, 1958. (Richard Inwards, H. Regis, 1840-1937)
**WAGON,** John C. Quaker Tercentenary. B.Mag. 4: 4:267-71, 1954-55. (NB inc. Edward Chester, Dunstable Quaker Baker pp268-9)
**WEST,** Bernard & CHRYSTAL, Alexander (Jun.). Luton and Dunstable (Prospect and Retrospect VII). B.Mag. 6:140-148. 1958.
**WILDMAN,** Richard, Victorian and Edwardian Bedfordshire from old photographs. B.T. Batsford Ltd. London. 1978. (NB 130 photos; no page nos.)
**WOODCOCK,** Page. Thirst for Knowledge, 6. Victualling on the Via Vitellina. Part One. B.Mag. 2:286-293. 1950 (NB A 'pub crawl' through Dunstable by author and his companion Pryce Jones with interesting but dubious 'facts' about each pub; no indication of sources.)
**WOODCOCK,** Page. Thirst for Knowledge, 7. Victualling on the Via Vitellina. Part Two. B.Mag. 2:322-328. (NB The second and final part ending, appropriately, 'Time, gentlemen, please!')
**WOOLLARD,** Leslie S. The Brick Makers. (County Craft and Industries 3.) B.Mag. 1: 150-2. 1948.

# INDEX

## A



## B

## C

D



E

## G

## H



## I



## J

## K



## L

## M

## N



## O



## P

## Q



## R

## S

## T